MW01200145

An Interfaith Minister's Manual

by
Reverend Angela Plum
Minister of Spiritual Science

WorldComm Press

Publisher: Ralph Roberts

Executive Editor: Kathryn L. Hall

Cover Design: WorldComm®

Interior Design and Electronic Page Assembly: WorldComm®

Printed in the United States of America

First Edition

10 9 8 7 6 5 4 3 2

ISBN 1-56664-026-1

WorldComm Press—a Division of Creativity, Inc., 65 Macedonia Road, Alexander, North Carolina 28701, (704) 252-9515—is a full service publisher.

Reprinted with permission from *"Passion Oberammergau,"* published by the community of Oberammergau.

*The triumph and glorification of Christ
from the German passion play, Oberammergau.*

Contents

An Interfaith Minister's Manual

This book is gratefully

dedicated to my grandmother,

Valeria Goulden Smith, *who*

awakened me to the spiritual

life and also to all who have

found the Divine Source within.

INTRODUCTION

A large portion of this book is devoted to the ceremonies or rituals used by the various religions. This brings up several areas to be explored in the following paragraphs.

WHAT IS RITUAL?

According to Webster's unabridged dictionary, a ritual is the form of conducting a devotional service especially as established by tradition or by sacerdotal prescription; the prescribed order and words of a religious ceremony; a code or system or rites. The Random House dictionary defines ritual as any practice or pattern of behavior regularly performed in a set manner.

WHERE ARE THE ORIGINS OF RITUAL?

Most ancient or primitive societies celebrated the transition from one stage of life to another such as; birth, puberty, marriage and death. These events became religious ceremonies or rituals with set times of performance, set words and actions.

According to anthropologists, the earliest record of religious activity was found dating back to around 60,000 B.C. However, they believe that people practiced some form of ritual ever since humans appeared on the Earth about 2 million years ago. Experts think that natural events such as storms, earthquakes and the birth of babies and animals brought forth fear and wonder which led to the establishment of rituals to calm the spirit.

Several scholars have developed theories on how religion began in prehistoric times. Some of these are:

Sir Edward Burnette Taylor –   Taylor's theory was that early people believed that spirits dwelled in and controlled all things in nature. They thought spirits lived in plants, the wind, the sea, volcanoes and the sun. Because these forces were very powerful, people started to worship their spirits.

Friedrich Max Müller – Müller agreed with Taylor that religion began as spirit worship but felt that prehistoric people thought that the forces of nature themselves had human qualities such as good or bad temper. The people themselves thus transformed these fears into deities.

Wilhelm Schmidt – He believed that early people understood that life came from one Divine source and their source was the Creator of the world and everything in the world.

Ancient religions included worship of animals, fire, the wind, and the sea. It evolved through Assyria, Egypt, Persia, Greece and Rome in the Eastern Hemisphere and through the Aztecs, Incas, Mayans, American Indians and Eskimos in the Western Hemisphere.

RITUAL IN PRIMITIVE AND TRADITIONAL RELIGIONS

THE USE OF WATER

Both primitive and modern religions use water in ceremonies for cleansing or purification. Some of these are:

1. The **Zande** of Central Africa poured water over a person accused of delaying or preventing rain. This was expected to remove the curse and bring the rain.
2. The **Hebrew** "mikvah" sought purification through the use

of prescribed amounts and kinds of water.

3. The **Shinto** used a ritual bath to prepare for a visit to a shrine.

4. The **Christian** foot-washing ritual, signifying humility, traditionally took place in the early church on Holy Thursday to the accompaniment of chanted hymns.

5. The **Hindus** purify their bodies by bathing in the Ganges River, especially at the holy city of Varanasi.

THE USE OF PRAYER

1. **Ancient people** used chants, drums and dancing.

2. **Judaism** uses readings from the Torah and chanting prayers from a book called the "siddur."

3. The **Shinto** worship at small shrines in their homes but there are also many roadside and public shrines. The Shinto recite prayers and offer gifts of cakes and flowers to the "kami" or deities.

4. The **Christian** religion uses prayers from the Bible, prayer books and things like the Rosary, Stations of the Cross, hymns, and the Sacraments.

5. The **Hindus** use the Vedas, the Puranas or long epic stories, and the Bhagavad-Gita. Most homes have a shrine. They also meditate or contemplate.

6. **Buddhists** practice the Noble Eightfold Path, use mantras and meditate.

COMING OF AGE RITUALS

These are known by various names according to the tribal observance or religion practiced.

1. In **African** societies, boys who will soon be adults are separated for days or months while they learn tribal legends and technical skills. They wear special costumes, feathers, or tattoos and sometimes are circumcised.

2. In **Judaism** the ritual is known as "bar mitzvah" for a boy and "bat mitzvah" for a girl. The child must learn the appropriate Hebrew prayers and go through a ceremony.

3. The **Christian** ritual is known as "confirmation." In the Roman Catholic, Eastern Orthodox, Lutheran and Church of England it is associated with baptism. That is, it renews or affirms the promises made at baptism and confers the grace of the Holy Spirit.

THE PURPOSE OF THIS BOOK

This book is a labor of love. When I was ordained as an interfaith minister, I looked for a minister's manual which would have ceremonies and prayers appropriate for people who had been raised with a particular religious background but who now did not want to be affiliated with any religious organization. I could not find such a book. Instead, I ended up with an armful of books that had been published by the various churches. So I began gathering together the ceremonies and prayers of each major religion (those which struck strings of truth within me) and put them in my own personal Minister's Manual. Initially the only purpose for doing this was for my own ministry.

The next step in this venture occurred when I showed my Minister's Manual to Reverend Marilyn Zwaig Rossner. In 1977 she had founded the **SPIRITUAL SCIENCE FELLOWSHIP (SSF)** in Montreal, Quebec, Canada. The purpose was to provide interfaith services at which people of all traditions could share in the universal gifts of the Spirit. In addition to service, the Fellowship offered classes in personal psychic and spiritual development. Finally a need was there, so in 1984 SSF began **THE INTERNATIONAL COLLEGE OF SPIRITUAL & PSYCHIC SCIENCES** which offered comprehensive certificate and degree programs. The college has the status of a seminary, or theological college, and is empowered to award certificates and degrees for successfully completed programs. This college is also affiliated with **THE INTERNATIONAL INSTITUTE OF INTEGRAL HUMAN SCIENCES**, a non-governmental organization affiliated with the United Nations, which was founded by Dr. John Rossner, an Anglican priest and professor of comparative religions at Concordia University.

When Rev. Marilyn Zwaig Rossner saw my personal manual, she asked if I would write an interfaith minister's manual for publication. SSF is affiliated with several interfaith seminaries and there is a need for a single manual in which the major religions (Christian, Jewish, Hindu, Buddhist, Yogi, and Native Medicine people) are represented. This book is my effort to produce such a manual.

There are many other prayers and ceremonies specific to particular religions. However, the ones I have chosen are those which spoke to my soul. I hope they will speak to yours.

$$\backsim\backsim\backsim$$

ACKNOWLEDGEMENTS

I wish to thank the following persons and organizations for their permission to use copyrighted materials.

The Christward Ministry
20560 Questhaven Road
Escondido, CA 92029

Rev. Carol E. Parrish-Harra
Sparrow Hawk Press
P.O. Box 1274
Tahlaquah, OK 74465

Thames and Hudson, Inc.
500 Fifth Avenue,
New York, NY 10110

Sundial House, Nevill Court
Tunbridge Wells
Kent, England TN4 8NJ

Abingdon Press
201 Eighth Avenue, South
Nashville, TN 37202

Although there were no copyrights on some material, I appreciate the use of excerpts from the manuals of the Universal Spiritualist Church, The Liberal Catholic Church, United Research, The Report of a Commission Convened by the Bishop of Exeter, and the newsletter "The Spirit of A.I.M." from the Association of Interfaith Ministers.

An Interfaith Minister should be familiar with the logos of most of the world's major religions. In order to familiarize you with them, they are shown on the following page.

LOGOS OF THE MAJOR WORLD RELIGIONS

CHRISTIANITY Latin Cross	CHRISTIANITY Descending Dove: Holy Spirit
JUDAISM Star of David	JUDAISM Menorah
HINDUISM Aum; Brahman-Atman	HINDUISM Shiva
ISLAM Star and Crescent	ISLAM Holy Qur-ān
TAOISM Yin-Yang	ZOROASTRIANISM Sacred Fire
CONFUCIANISM Confucius	CONFUCIANISM Conjugal Bliss
TAOISM Water: Life-giving Source	JAINISM Brush and bowl

An Interfaith Minister's Manual

PART I

GENERAL
INFORMATION

CHAPTER I

REQUIREMENTS FOR A MINISTER

EDUCATION

The minister should be a person recognized by their congregation as one capable and qualified to minister to their spiritual needs. They should have completed a recognized seminary course of study or apprenticeship and be fully ordained as a Priest, Minister, Rabbi, Yogi, Sikh, Lama, or Native Medicine Man or Woman.

DEDICATION

The minister should be a person who has dedicated their life to: (1) being true to the God within; (2) to be of service to God and humanity; (3) to be in contact with his/her inner guidance; and (4) to be a blessing to everyone and everything.

ETHICS

A minister should always act with dignity, tact, good taste, and ethics. Everything told to a minister is a sacred trust and must not be disclosed to anyone else. At no time should the minister interfere in domestic problems unless counseling is requested by both husband and wife. If a minister is not trained in the specific skill needed for a situation, the minister should recommend the professional service needed.

ACT OF FAITH

We believe that God is Love, Power, Truth, and Light; that

perfect justice rules the world; that all His sons/daughters shall one day reach His feet; however far they stray. We hold the Father/Motherhood of God, the brotherhood of man, we know that we do serve Him best when best we serve our brothers/sisters. So shall His blessing rest on us and give us peace for evermore. Amen.

LEGAL ADHERENCE

Marriage is a legal contract and subject to civil law. The minister should be familiar with local civil requirements and adhere to them. Most local authorities require the marriage to be performed in the county in which the license has been issued.

Before performing any marriage, the minister must be sure that both parties are free of impediments or any illegality, especially when either is of foreign birth or under age. All legal forms must be completed promptly and returned to the civil authorities to protect the good name and legal record of the parties concerned. The minister should keep a permanent register of all marriages performed for future reference.

CHAPTER 2

FEAST DAYS OF THE MAJOR RELIGIONS

From ABINGDON DICTIONARY OF LIVING RELIGIONS, Keith Crim, General Editor. Copyright 1981 by Abingdon. Used by permission of the publisher.

JEWISH FEAST DAYS

In Judaism, years are numbered from a traditional reckoning of the year of creation; hence September 9, 1991 (on the Christian calendar) is the first day of the month of Tishri in the year 5752 anno mundo. The Jewish calendar is based on a 354-day year of twelve lunar months, each of which begins with the new moon. To bring the lunar year into harmony with the solar year of 365 days, a thirteenth month (Adar II) is inserted into seven of every nineteen

American Jewish Archives, Hebrew Union College—
Jewish Institute of Religion

years. This calendar is credited to Hillel II (mid-fourth century A.D.).

The names of the months were adopted from the Babylonians after 586 B.C., and in the Bible are found only in such late books as Nehemiah; earlier books simply number the months, sometimes adding descriptive names. The first day of a month was celebrated in accordance with Num. 28:11, with the first two days sometimes celebrated (I Sam. 20:34). The months are:

Tishri	Sept./Oct.
Heshvan	Oct./Nov.
Kislev	Nov./Dec.
Tevet	Dec./Jan.
Shevat	Jan./Feb.
Adar	Feb./Mar.
Adar II	Added every 3rd, 6th, 8th, 11th, 14th, 17th, and 19th year of a 19-year cycle.
Nisan	Mar./Apr.
Iyyar	Apr./May
Sivan	May/June
Tammuz	June/July
Av	July/Aug.
Elul	Aug./Sept.

The feast days are:

Rosh Ha-Shanah	Tishri I (The year begins) This is also called the "Day of Remembrance" on which the ram's horn (Shofar) is sounded. Ten days of penitence (the Days of Awe) follow, leading up to:
Yom Kippur	Tishri 10 (The Day of Atonement) is the holiest day in the Jewish calendar. During the first 10 days of the New Year, God reviews His book of life, recording everyone's deeds during the past year. On Yom Kippur, God decides how each person will live in the year to come. Many Jews spend the day fasting and praying.
Suckot	Tishri 15 (Feast of Tabernacles)
Simhat Torah	Tishri 22 (Joy in the Torah) on which the annual reading of the Torah is joyfully completed.

Hanukkah	Kislev 24 (Dedication) Celebrated for 8 days with the lighting of lamps.
Purim	Adar 14 (Commemorates events described in the Book of Esther.)
Passover	Nisan 15 (Lasts 7 days, also called the Festival of Matzah, it is explained during the Seder meals from Haggadah booklets, with accounts of the exodus from Egypt.)
Shavuot	Sivan 6 (Anniversary of giving of the Ten Commandments.)
Fast day	Tammuz 17 begins a 3-week mourning period climaxed by the fast Tishah Be'Av which memorializes the burning of the Temples.
Sabbath	Occurs every 7 days, and supersedes all calendar holidays when in conflict. Each day begins at nightfall, but holidays and most calendar events begin as soon as the sun has passed the horizon.

ABRIDGED HEBREW CALENDAR
5753 (1992)

1 Rosh Hashonah	Mon.	Sep 28
2 Rosh Hashonah	Tue.	Sep 29
Fast of Gedalia	Wed.	Sep 30
Kol Nidre	Tue.	Oct 6
Yom Kippur	Wed.	Oct 7
Erev Succoth	Sun.	Oct 11
1 Succoth	Mon.	Oct 12
2 Succoth	Tue.	Oct 13
1 Chol Hamoed	Wed.	Oct 14
2 Chol Hamoed	Thur.	Oct 15
3 Chol Hamoed	Fri.	Oct 16
4 Chol Hamoed	Sat.	Oct 17

Hashanah Rabbath	Sun.	Oct 18
Shemini Azereth	Mon.	Oct 19
Simchath Torah	Tue.	Oct 20
1 Chanukah	Sun.	Dec 20
2 Chanukah	Mon.	Dec 21
3 Chanukah	Tue.	Dec 22
4 Chanukah	Wed.	Dec 23
5 Chanukah	Thur.	Dec 24
6 Chanukah	Fri.	Dec 25
7 Chanukah	Sat.	Dec 26
8 Chanukah	Sun.	Dec 27

5753 (1993)

Arbor Day - 15 Shevat	Sat.	Feb 6
Purim	Sun.	Mar 7
Shushan Purim	Mon.	Mar 8
1 Seder Eve	Mon.	Apr 5
Pesach - 1	Tue.	Apr 6
Pesach - 2	Wed.	Apr 7
1 Chol Hamoed	Thur.	Apr 8
2 Chol Hamoed	Fri.	Apr 9
3 Chol Hamoed	Sat.	Apr 10
4 Chol Hamoed	Sun.	Apr 11
Pesach - 7	Mon.	Apr 12
Pesach - 8	Tue.	Apr 13
Lag B'Omer	Sun.	May 9
Erev Shevuoth	Tue.	May 25
1 Shevuoth	Wed.	May 26
2 Shevuoth	Thur.	May 27
Fast of Tamuz	Tue.	Jul 6
Fast of Ab.	Tue.	Jul 27
Erev Rosh Hashona	Wed.	Sep 15

BUDDHIST RITUALS & CEREMONIES

In all Buddhist ceremonies there are certain basic ritual actions that are performed by the worshipper. First, there are the offerings, usually in the form of flowers, food, water, or candles. Second, there is what is commonly called motor behavior, such as bowing before the image of the Buddha, an act of reverence that consists of the worshipper touching the ground three times with his forehead. Another is removing one's shoes when entering the place of worship. Finally, there is the verbal behavior, such as the uttering of devotions, charms, or spells.

James Ware

Bowing and making offerings before the Buddha image are usually performed as part of larger ceremonies, the most common of which are the calendrical rites, so called because they may be divided into a daily, monthly, or annual cycle.

The **daily cycle** consists mainly of the private devotions performed morning and evening by the faithful worshipper before the family shrine, which invariably consists of an image of Buddha and a vase to hold floral offerings. The ceremonies include the offering of flowers, the lighting of candles, and the recitation of such expressions as the formula of the Triratna and the five cardinal precepts (not to kill, steal, tell lies, commit adultery, or drink intoxicating liquor). The devotee also asks for certain boons, e.g., rebirth in a good state of existence, avoidance of misfortunes, and freedom from personal defects. Public devotions are also performed daily in the village chapel.

Monthly ceremonies

The most important is the observance of the **uposatha**, held on the days of the new and full moon.

Annual ceremonies

Buddha Day The first festival in the annual cycle occurring at the full moon in May and commemorating the birth, attainment of enlightenment, and death of the Buddha.

Rainy Season From July to October. At the end of this season in October, the kathina ceremony, the offering of robes to the monks, is observed by the royalty, nobility, and commoner alike.

Ullambana All Soul's Feast celebrated on the 15th day of the seventh lunar month.

Tooth Festival In August in Kandy, Sri Lanka, lasts for ten days.

∽∽∽∽

ISLAMIC FESTIVALS

The major "festival" of the year is the fast month (Ramadan) which is observed faithfully by the devout. During this period many men worship in evenings in the mosque with special prayers known as terarih. At the end of the fast, the day is spent in visiting with parents and others to ask their forgiveness for wrongs of the past year.

Other festivals include a day to celebrate the embarkation of pilgrims to Mecca, a day to give food to the poor, and celebrations of the birth of Muhhammad. Traditionalists practice a more elaborate set of rituals than do reformists, and in syncretic settings localized festivals have cropped up also. An example is the Sekaten fair in Jogjakarta, where syncretists march in a parade from mosque to palace to symbolize their unity.

∽∽∽∽

CHRISTIAN FEASTS

The following is taken from THE LITURGY OF THE LIB-ERAL CATHOLIC CHURCH.

Fixed Feasts

Jan 1 - **Circumcision of Our Lord**

Jan 6 - **Epiphany** (Visit of the Wise Men to the infant Jesus)

Feb 2 - **Candlemas Day** (Blessing of throats)

Mar 25 - **The Annunciation of Our Lady** (The Archangel, Gabriel, announces to Mary that she is to be the Mother of Jesus)

Aug 15 - **Assumption of Our Lady** (Rising of her body into heaven)

Sep 8 - **Birthday of Our Lady**

Nov 1 - **All Saints' Day**

Nov 2 - **All Souls' Day**

Dec 8 - **The Immaculate Conception** (When Mary's mother conceived her)

Dec 25 - **Christmas** (The birth of Jesus)

(CHRISTIAN) TABLE OF MOVEABLE FEASTS FOR 1992-2008

Year	Lent Begins	Easter	Ascension	Pentecost	Advent Begins
1992	MAR 4	APR 19	MAY 28	JUN 7	NOV 29
1993	FEB 24	APR 11	MAY 20	MAY 30	NOV 28
1994	FEB 16	APR 3	MAY 12	MAY 22	NOV 27
1995	MAR 1	APR 16	MAY 25	JUN 4	DEC 3
1996	FEB 21	APR 7	MAY 16	MAY 26	DEC 1
1997	FEB 12	MAR 30	MAY 8	MAY 18	NOV 30
1998	FEB 25	APR 12	MAY 21	MAY 31	NOV 29
1999	FEB 17	APR 4	MAY 13	MAY 23	NOV 28
2000	MAR 8	APR 23	JUNE 1	JUN 11	DEC 3
2001	FEB 28	APR 15	MAY 24	JUN 3	DEC 2
2002	FEB 13	MAR 31	MAY 9	MAY 19	DEC 1
2003	MAR 5	APR 20	MAY 29	JUN 8	NOV 30
2004	FEB 25	APR 11	MAY 20	MAY 30	NOV 28
2005	FEB 9	MAR 27	MAY 5	MAY 15	NOV 24
2006	MAR 1	APR 16	MAY 25	JUN 4	DEC 3
2007	FEB 21	APR 8	MAY 17	MAY 27	DEC 2
2008	FEB 6	MAR 23	MAY 1	MAY 11	NOV 30

CHAPTER 3

THE MEANING OF SYMBOLS

𝕴n all religions, objects are used to represent otherworldly concepts or as a means to further spiritual growth or to honor the Divine Presence. Most of us are familiar with some of these such as; water used in Baptism, oil to anoint the sick, bells and candles used in ceremonies, but few of us realize the true significance behind these symbols. Therefore, I have decided to put a chapter in this Minister's Manual listing some of the most used symbols and their meaning. By understanding the true meaning of these things, you will have a much greater appreciation of the power and far-reaching effects of ceremonies you may use in your ministry. I would even suggest that, after you understand the symbology of the different objects, you may want to invent your own ceremonies to fit various circumstances.

The following information is taken from "<u>An Illustrated Encyclopaedia of Traditional Symbols</u>" by J.C. Cooper, Copyright 1978 by Thames and Hudson Ltd., 500 Fifth Avenue, New York, New York 10110. Reprinted by permission of the publisher. This is <u>NOT</u> for reproduction.

<u>Alb</u> (Christian) A sacrificial vestment; the white garment in which Christ was clothed by Herod; its white linen represents purity and chastity, as the celebrant says "make me white."

<u>Altar</u> The Divine Presence, reunion with the deity by means of sacrifice, integration, thanksgiving. In the various religions:

   <u>Aztec:</u> The cylindrical solar stone was used for both sacrificial and astronomical purposes.

Buddhist: The center of devotion is a shrine rather than an altar, although the latter may be applied where it serves to carry images, books, sacred objects and offerings to the Buddha, but the idea of an instituted rite as sacrifice is absent.

Christian: The altar represents both the tomb and the resurrection, death transformed into life, the sacrifice of Christ in the Eucharist and Christ as the Sun of Righteousness.

Hebrew: The Altar of Perfumes is "the operation of grace for the elements."

Hindu: The Vedic Fire Altar takes on the vertical symbolism of a world center, it is an "imago mundi" and the creation of the world and also represents Agni, Vaya and Aditya, the lights of the world.

Angels Messengers of God; intermediaries between God and man, heaven and this world: powers of the invisible world; enlightenment.

Ankh An Egyptian symbol of life; the universe; all life both human and divine; the key of knowledge of the mysteries and hidden wisdom; power; authority; covenant.

Anointing Consecration; that which is made sacred or set apart; prosperity; joy; an infusion of divine grace.

Ascension Transcendence; the breakthrough to a new ontological plane and transcending the merely human state; the way to Reality and the Absolute; reintegration; the soul's union with the divinity; uplifting the soul; the passage from earth to heaven, from darkness to light; freedom.

Baptism Initiation; death and rebirth; regeneration; renewal; dying to the titanic nature of man and being born again of water, fire, or wind, into the divine. Baptism represents regression into the undifferentiated; the dissolution of form and reintegration with the pre-formal; crossing the sea of life; reemergence from the water is rebirth and resurrection. By fire it symbolizes the purging and burning away of dross. By wind, winnowing away the chaff. It is a rite of passage, emerging from the darkness of the womb to the outer light, hence the passage of the soul from matter to spirit.

Bell Consecration; the motion of the elements; a charm against the powers of destruction. In the various religions:

Buddhist: The pure sound of the doctrine of perfect wisdom.

Chinese: Respect; veneration; obedience; faithful ministers, meritorious warriors, it averts the evil eye and wards off evil spirits. The ritual bell symbolizes harmony between man and heaven.

Christian: The sanctus bell announces the presence of Christ at the mass. Church bells call and encourage the faithful, put evil spirits to flight and quell storms.

Hebrew: Vestments; bells with pomegranates are the Quintessence, with the pomegranates as the four elements, on the Ephod. They are also suggested as symbolizing thunder and lightning. Bells also signified virginity as they were worn until marriage.

Hindu: Rank, dignity. The Bull of Nandi is always depicted with a bell round his neck, or a chain.

Blood The life principle; the soul; strength; the rejuvenating force, hence blood sacrifice. Blood and wine are interchangeable symbols. Blood and water are the life of the body and life of the spirit in Christianity.

Book The open book depicts the book of life, learning and the spirit of wisdom, revelation and wisdom of the scriptures. In the various religions:

Buddhist: Perfection of wisdom, language and expression.

Chinese: Scholarship. The leaves of the book are the leaves of the Cosmic Tree, symbolizing all beings in the universe. The book is one of the Eight Precious Things of Chinese Buddhism.

Christian: Books are the Apostles teaching the nations. Christ is often portrayed holding a book.

Islamic: The universe is a vast book. The book, with the pen, is creative substance, static being, while the pen is the creative principle. The Sacred Book is the Name of God; truth; mercy.

Bread Life; the food of the body and the soul; the visible and manifest life. In Christianity it is the "body of Christ." Bread and wine denote the two natures of Christ, the body and blood of Christ in the eucharistic meal.

15

Breath Life; the soul; life-giving power; the power of the spirit. The intaking and outgoing of the breath symbolize the alternating rhythm of life and death, manifestation and reabsorption in the universe. In Christianity, the breathing or blowing upon a person or thing, signified the influence of the Holy Spirit and the expelling of evil spirits.

Candle Light in the darkness of life; illumination; the vitalizing power of the sun. Candle lit at death illuminates the darkness and represents the light in the world to come; they are a feature of Catholic and Oriental funeral rites. In religions:

> **Christian:** Christ is the light of the world; Christ risen from the dead in the light of transfiguration; the pious lit with love. Candles on either side of the cross on the altar are the dual nature of Christ, human and divine. In Eastern orthodox Christianity three joined candles depict the Holy Trinity and two joined candles the dual nature of Christ.

> **Hebrew:** The Mosaic seven-branched candlestick, the Menorah, indicates the divine presence; the stem of the candlestick is suggested as the Cosmic Tree and an "axis mundi." Josephus says that the seven branches are the sun, moon, and planets, also the seven days of the week, the seven stars of Ursa Major and the seven cycles or forces in the world. According to Philo, the Menorah represents the operation of grace for all things celestial. In Qabalism the three candles, or candlesticks, are wisdom, strength and beauty.

Chalice The source of inexhaustible sustenance; abundance. It is associated with the symbolism of the heart, containing the blood which, in the chalice, is represented by wine -- wine and blood having the same portent; it is also connected with the GRAIL.

Chasuble (Christian) Christ's seamless robe, representing charity. The cross on the back is the cross carried to Calvary and Y of Christ's arms on the cross; the stripe on the front is the pillar of scourging; covering other vestments portrays the protection of charity; it is also the purple robe of royalty put on the "King of the Jews."

Christmas Tree The evergreen tree is the Winter Solstice; the New Year and a fresh beginning. It is the tree of rebirth and immortality, the Tree of Paradise of lights and gifts, shining by night. Each light is a soul and the lights also represent the sun, moon, and stars shining in the branches of the Cosmic Tree.

Circle A universal symbol; wholeness, the self-contained, eternity, celestial unity; God. "God is a circle whose centre is everywhere and circumference is nowhere." (Hermes Trismegistus) In the religions:

American Indian: The circle radiating outward and inward, as the Feathered Sun is a symbol of the universe. Camp circles and the circular tepee are a pattern of the cosmos with the North side as the heavens and the South side as the earth.

The four directions of space in the celestial circle are the totality comprising the Great Spirit. The North American Indian lodge cross inscribed in the circle symbolizes sacred space and is a Cosmic Centre.

Buddhist: The circle is the Round of Existence enclosing all in the phenomenal world. Three circles in triangular form are the Three Jewels. In Zen the empty circle is enlightenment.

Chinese: The circle is the heavens with the square as the earth, as in the old cash; the circle with the square at the centre depicts the union of heaven and earth, yin and yang and, by analogy, the perfect man. The circle is also the moving heavens which revolve round the unmoving square of the earth.

Christian: The Church Universal; three concentric or interlocking circles depict the Trinity. Two concentric circles signify intellect and will, according to Dante. Twin circles, as love and knowledge, represent Christ, also his dual nature. A Christian church frequently forms a cross inside the circle of the churchyard.

Egyptian: The winged circle is the rising sun, Ra, and the resurrection.

Greek: The circle of Ouroboros round the Cosmic Egg was called Cronos and was defined by Pythagoras as the psyche of the universe. Cronos was mated to Necessity, also circling the universe, hence Time and Fate were both circles.

Hindu: The Round of Existence in the phenomenal world. The flaming circle is a symbol of Prakriti, "that which evolves, produces, brings forth."

Islamic: The dome; the vault of heaven; divine light.

Semitic: The winged circle is an aniconic symbol of solar gods; divinity; solar power.

Taoist: A circle with a point at the centre represents the supreme power, the Tao; the circle is also the Precious Pearl.

Circumcision Initiation; dedication; purity; a rite of religious or tribal membership.

Corn Ears or sheaves of corn or wheat are attributes of all corn deities, especially the Greek mysteries, and symbolize the fertility of the earth, awakening life, life springing from death; germination and growth through solar power; abundance. In religions:

American Indian: The ear of corn (maize) with all its seeds represents the people and all things in the universe.

Christian: Ears of wheat are the bread of the Eucharist, the body of Christ; bounty; the righteous; the godly. Corn and the vine together also represent the Eucharist.

Egyptian: The ear of corn is an attribute of Isis and a corn measure is an emblem of Serapis.

Graeco-Roman: Fertility; abundance; life springing from death; creation; emblem of Demeter/Ceres, Gaia and Virgo. Corn was offered to Artemis. The ear of corn was the central symbol of the Eleusinian Mysteries: "There was exhibited as the great, the admirable, the most perfect object of mystic contemplation, an ear of corn that had been reaped in silence" (Philosophoumena). In the cult of Cybele, Attis is "the reaped yellow ear of corn." The Roman planting of corn on graves secured the power of the dead for the living.

Mexican: The maize plant with a humming bird indicated the Sun Hero; awakening vegetation.

Sumero-Semitic: Corn was sacred to Cybele and bread was eaten sacramentally at her feast; it was also an attribute of Tammun/Dumuzi. Dagon, the pre-eminent deity of Philistia, was a corn and earth god at Ascalon and Gaza.

Crescent The crescent moon is the symbol of the Great Mother, the lunar Queen of Heaven, and is the attribute of all moon goddesses; it is the passive, feminine principle and is both the Mother and Celestial Virgin. In religions:

Celtic: The crescent moon and two crescents back to back symbolize immortality.

Christian: The Virgin Mary, Queen of Heaven.

Egyptian: Isis, Queen of Heaven, and Hathor as the cow with the solar disk between her horns.

Hindu: The crescent moon of the newborn; quick and eager growth, the cup of the elixir or immortality.

Islamic: The crescent with the star depicts divinity, sovereignty. The emblem of Byzantium, Islam and the Turks.

Cross A universal symbol from the most remote times, it is the cosmic symbol par excellence. It is a world center and a point of communication between heaven and earth. The cross is the figure of man at full stretch, also the descent of spirit into matter. It is formed by the four rivers of Paradise flowing from the root of the Tree of Life. It comprises the cardinal axes, the four elements of the world united at the fifth point, the Centre. In religions:

African: (Bushmen and Hottentot) The divinity; protection in childbirth.

American Indian: The human form; rain; stars; wood-fire; maidenhood; the four cardinal directions and the four winds. The north arm of the cross is the north wind, the most powerful, cold, the all-conquering giant, the head and intelligence. The east is the east wind, the heart, the source of life and love. The west is the gentle wind from the spirit land, the last breath and going out into the unknown. The south wind is the seat of fire and passion, melting and burning. The centre of the cross is earth and man, moved by conflicting forces of gods and winds. The lodge cross, inscribed in the circle, is sacred space, a cosmic Centre.

Buddhist: The axis of the Wheel of the Law and of the Round of Existence.

Chinese: The cross in the square is the earth symbol with the circle as the heavens.

Christian: Salvation through Christ's sacrifice; redemption; atonement; suffering; faith; the acceptance of death or suffering and sacrifice. St. Andrew's cross depicts martyr-dom. Ecclesiastical crosses with two crossbars denote arch-bishops and patriarchs and with three crossbars, the Pope.

19

The pectoral cross is jurisdiction.

Egyptian: The "crux ansata" or Egyptian ankh is the union of heaven and earth; life; immortality; the key to the mysteries of life and knowledge; the union of the male and female symbols.

Hebrew: The six-rayed cross signifies the six days of creation and the six phases of time and world duration.

Hindu: The rajas, the expansion of being, the vertical represents the sattvas or higher, celestial states of being, while the horizontal is the tamas or lower earthly states. The cross is also associated with the sacred Ganges and with the crossed fire sticks of Agni.

Islamic: Perfect communion of all states of being, both in amplitude and exaltation, the Supreme Identity.

Maya: The tau cross is the Tree of Life of nourishment.

Dove The life spirit; the soul; the passing from one state or world to another; the spirit of light; peace. In religions:

Chinese: Longevity, faithfulness, orderliness, filial piety, Spring, also associated with the Earth Mother.

Christian: The Holy Spirit; purity; inspired thought, peace; baptism; the Annunciation, the waters of creation. Seven doves denote the seven gifts of the spirit; a flock of doves is the faithful; a dove with an olive branch is peace, forgiveness, and deliverance. The dove  with the palm branch is victory over death. A white dove is the saved soul. Doves in a vine are the faithful seeking refuge in Christ.

Egyptian: Innocence, the dove sits in the branches of the Tree of Life and appears with the fruit of the tree and vases of the waters of life.

Hebrew: White doves, as purity, were offerings at the Temple for purification; a symbol of Israel. In the Old Testament the dove represents simplicity, harmlessness, innocence, meekness, guilelessness, incubation. Embodies the soul of the dead.

Hindu: Yama, god of the dead, has owls and doves or pigeons as messengers.

Islamic: The three Holy Virgins are represented by stones, or pillars, surmounted by doves.

Japanese: Longevity; deference, sacred to Hachiman, god of war, but a dove, bearing a sword, announces the end of a war.

Parsee: The Supreme Being.

Drum Sound; the primordial sound; speech; divine truth; revelation, tradition; the rhythm of the universe. The drum, cymbals and tambourine were all used in ecstatic dancing.

African: The heart; magic power.

American Indian: Indian rituals and celebrations were often accompanied by dancing, drumming, and singing. Many drums could be heard for long distances and were used to transmit signals or messages.

Buddhist: The voice of the Law; gauze tidings; the drum of the immortal in the darkness of the world. The beating of the drum of the Dharma wakens the ignorant and slothful.

Chinese: The voice of heaven. An emblem of the Taoist genii, or immortal.

Hindu: Attribute of Siva and Kali as destroyers; also of Durga. Sarasvati, goddess of music and arts, has the drum as an emblem. Siva's drum gives the primordial sound of creation.

Japanese: The drum calls to prayer.

Shamanistic: Magic power summoning spirits, the drum is symbolically made from the Cosmic Tree.

Fire/Flame Transformation; purification, the lifegiving and generative power of the sun; renewal of life, impregnation; power, strength; protection; passing from one state to another. Fire manifested as flame symbolizes spiritual power and forces, transcendence and illumination and is a manifestation of divinity or of the soul, the breath of life. It is also inspiration and enlightenment. A flame resting on the head, or surrounding it, like the Nimbus, represents divine power, potency of soul or genius, the head being regarded as the seat of the life-soul. A flame leaves the body at death. In religions:

American Indian: In the Medicine Lodge fire is the sacred, central dwelling place of the Great Spirit; it is also an intermediary between God and man.

Aztec: Ritual death, redemption; penitence.

Buddhist: Wisdom, which burns all ignorance. A fiery pillar is an aniconic symbol of Buddha. Fire is consuming and water purifying.

Chinese: Flame signifies the presence of divinity. Fire is danger; anger; ferocity; speed; but as a spiritual power it is solar, yang, combined with the yin of water; it is symbolized by the trigram which has yang lines without and a yin line within.

Christian: Religious fervor; martyrdom. "Tongues of fire" are the advent of the Holy Spirit; the voice of God; divine revelation; the emblem of St. Anthony of Padua.

Egyptian: Associated with Thoth as inspiration.

Hebrew: Divine revelation; the voice of God. "The Lord thy God is a consuming fire" (Deut. 4:24).

Hindu: Transcendental light and knowledge; the vital energy of wisdom. Fire is also identified with the forces of destruction, release and recreation wielded by Siva. The column of flame and mounting smoke of the Vedic fire god, Agni, represents the world axis. Three fires are lit on the Vedic fire altars at the South, East and West, representing the sun and sky, ether and winds, and the earth. Kali is destructive fire and the ring of flame around Siva depicts the cosmic cycle of creation and destruction. Fire, as the vital flame, is also Krishna: "I am the fire residing in the bodies of all things which have life." (Bhagavad Gita)

Iranian: The Parsee temple has the fire as the Sacred Centre, the place of divinity and the divine light in the soul of man. It is also associated with law and order. In Zoroastrianism "the seeds of men and bulls have their origin in fire, not in water."

Islamic: Fire and flame are light and heat, divinity and hell.

Initiation The archetypal pattern of death and rebirth; transition from one state to another, from one ontological plane to another; death before rebirth and victory over death; return to the darkness before the rebirth of light; death of the old man and rebirth of the new; acceptance, either spiritual or physical, into adult society. Initiation usually requires a "descent into hell" to overcome the dark side of nature before resurrection and illumination and the ascent into heaven, thus initiation ceremonies are usually held in caves, or some underworld place, or a labyrinth from which the reborn man emerges into light.

Key The key denotes liberation; knowledge, the mysteries; initiation. In religions:

Christian: Emblem of St. Peter as guardian of the gate of heaven, also an attribute of the Pope. St. Martha has a bunch of keys.

Hebrew: The keys of God are the raising of the dead; birth, fertilizing rain.

Japanese: The three keys of the granary are love, wealth and happiness.

Ladder Communication between heaven and earth with a two-way traffic of the ascent of man and the descent of the divinity. In religions:

American Indian: The rainbow is the ladder of access to the other world.

Buddhist: The ladder of Sakya-muni is often depicted with the footprint of Buddha on the bottom and top rungs.

Christian: An emblem of Christ's passion, also of Jacob and St. Benedict.

Egyptian: A symbol of Horus surmounting the material world and connecting it with heaven. "I set up a ladder to Heaven among the gods" (Book of the Dead).

Hebrew: The means of communication through angels, between God and man.

Islamic: The ladder seen by Mohammed leads the faithful to God.

Japanese: The ladder is an attribute of the thunder god and represents traffic between heaven and earth.

Mithraic: The initiate ascends the stages of the seven-runged planetary ladder, which is the passage of the soul through the seven heavens.

Shamanistic: The Shaman ascends the ladder, or seven-notched pole, to communicate with spirits and the spirit world.

Man Cosmic man is the microcosm, a reflection of the macrocosm and the elements, with the body representing the earth; the heat of the body, fire; the blood, water; the breath, the air. The masculine principle is symbolized by the sun and the heavens in most traditions, with Teutonic and Oceanic exceptions, and by all that is phallic, piercing, penetrating, upright and associated with heat. In **American Indian** symbolism the male principle is represented by the white eagle feather. In **Taoism** man is the central and mediating power of the Great Triad of Heaven-Man-Earth. In **Islam** he signifies universal existence, "the link between God and Nature." The **Sufis** define man as "the symbol of universal existence."

Music Sacred music is symbolic of nature in her transitory and ever-changing aspect; it is the relative, but contains an underlying reality, the Absolute. The music of the spheres signifies the harmony of the spheres and of life. Musical instruments denote felicity.

Oil Consecration; dedication; spiritual illumination; mercy; fertility. Anointing with oil is infusing new divine life; consecration; bestowing the grace of God or conferring wisdom.

OM (AUM) The sacred sound; the primordial AUM, the totality of all sounds and that which penetrates and sustains the whole cosmos; the Self; the light of the supernal sun. It is also a Trinity as it has the three factors A.U.M., the three-fold Brahman. "All the universe is but the result of sound." (Vakya Padiya).

Ouroboros Depicted as a serpent or dragon biting its own tail. "My end is my beginning." It symbolizes the undifferentiated; the Totality; primordial unity; self-sufficiency. It begets, weds, impregnates, and slays itself. It is the cycle of disintegration and reintegration, power 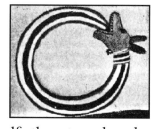 that eternally consumes and renews itself; the eternal cycle, cyclic time; spatial infinity; truth and cognition in one; the united primordial parents; the Androgyne; the primeval water; darkness before creation; the restriction of the universe in the chaos of the waters before the coming of light; the potential before actualization. In many myths it encircles the world and is the circular course of the waters surrounding the earth. It can both support and maintain the world and injects death into life and life unto death. Apparently immobile, it is yet perpetual motion, forever recoiling upon itself. In Orphic cosmology it encircles the Cosmic Egg. It is also called "heracles" which identifies it with the solar passage; Macrobius associates it with the movement of the sun. The Alpha and Omega are often depicted with the Ouroboros. In various religions:

Alchemic: The unredeemed power of nature; latent power; the unformed materia; the opus circulare of chemical substances in the hermetic vessel.

Buddhist: The wheel of samsara.

Egyptian: The circle of the universe; the path of the sun god.

Greek: "All is one." The All was from the beginning like an egg, with the serpent as the tight band or circle round it." (Epicurus). In Orphic symbolism it is the circle round the Cosmic Egg and is Aeon, the life-span of the universe.

Hindu: The wheel of samsara. As latent energy, Ouroboros shares the symbolism of Kundalini.

Sumero-Semitic: The All One.

Palm Solar; exultation; righteousness; fame, as always growing erect; blessings; triumph; victory - "The Palm, never shedding in foliage, is continually adorned with the same green. This power of the tree men think agreeable and fit for representing victory." (Plutarch). It is a Tree of Life and, as self-creative, it is equated with the Androgyne. In the various religions:

Arabian: The Tree of Life.

Chinese: Retirement; dignity; fecundity.

Christian: The righteous who "shall flourish like a palm tree"; immortality and, as such, is sometimes depicted with the phoenix; divine blessing; Christ's triumphal entry into Jerusalem; the martyr's triumph over death; Paradise. Palm branches signify glory; triumph; resurrection; victory over death and sin; it was a funerary emblem among the early Roman Christians, an attribute of one who had made the pilgrimage to the Holy Land, hence "Palmer." Emblem of St. Paul the Hermit, who holds a palm in his hand, and numerous martyrs. Palm Sunday commemorates Christ's entry into Jerusalem.

Egyptian: The tree of the calendar, producing a branch for each month.

Greek: Emblem of Apollo at Delphi and Delos.

Hebrew: The righteous man; emblem of Judea after the Exodus.

Sumero-Semitic: A Tree of Life; emblem of the Phoenician Baal-Tamar, the Lord of the Palm, and of Astarte and the Assyro-Babylonian Ishtar.

Pearl Lunar; the power of the waters; the essence of the moon and controller of tides; the embryo; cosmic life; the divine essence; the life-giving power of the Great Mother; the feminine principle of the ocean; the self-luminous; initiation; law in cosmic life; justice. The pearl was thought to be the result of lightning penetrating the oyster, hence it was regarded as the union of fire and water, both fecundating forces, and so denotes birth and rebirth; fertility. It also symbolizes innocence, purity, virginity, perfection, humility and a retiring nature. In the religions:

Buddhist: One of the Eight Treasures; the heart of Buddha, pure intentions; the Third Eye of Buddha, the "flaming pearl" is the crystallization of light; transcendent wisdom; spiritual consciousness; the spiritual essence of the universe.

Chinese: The yin, feminine principle; immortality; potentiality; good augury; genius in obscurity.

Christian: Salvation; Christ the Saviour; the Word of God; baptism; the hidden gnosis necessary for salvation, the "pearl of great price" for which man must dive into the waters of baptism and encounter dangers. It is also virgin birth; purity; spiritual grace.

Gnostic: The Fall and subsequent salvation.

Graeco-Roman: Love and marriage, emblem of Aphrodite/Venus, the "Lady of the Pearls" who rose from the waters.

Hindu: The urna, the shining spot, the "flaming pearl" on the forehead of Siva; the Third Eye/transcendent wisdom; the crystallization of light; spiritual consciousness; enlightenment.

Iranian: The Saviour, giver of life, birth and death; longevity.

Islamic: The Divine Word; heaven.

Sumero-Semitic: The generative power of the waters.

Taoist: "The pearl of effulgence," the "pearl of potentiality" and the "night-shining Pearl" are yin powers of the waters and the lunar control of the waters with all the potentialities. The "flaming pearl" symbolizes man's search for reality; spiritual unfolding; the experience of Light.

Rainbow Transfiguration; heavenly glory; different states of consciousness; the meeting of Heaven and Earth; the bridge or boundary between this world and Paradise; the throne of the Sky God. The celestial serpent is also associated with the rainbow in that it, too, can be a bridge between one world and another. In French, African, Indian and American Indian symbolism the rainbow is also a serpent which quenches its thirst in the sea. In religions:

African: In some regions of Africa the celestial serpent is equated with the rainbow and is a guardian of treasures; or it encircles the earth.

American Indian: A ladder of access to the other world.

Buddhist: The highest state attainable in the realm of samsara before the "clear light" of Nirvana.

Chinese: The sky dragon; the union of heaven and earth.

Christian: Pardon; reconciliation between God and man; the throne of the Last Judgment. Christ, "by whom we are protected from spiritual flood" (Dante).

Graeco-Roman: The memorable sign to humans which Zeus printed on the clouds. The rainbow is sometimes depicted on the breastplate of Agamemnon as three serpents. It is the personification of Iris, winged messenger of the gods and especially of Zeus and Hera, or Jupiter and Juno.

Hindu: The "rainbow body" is the highest yogic state attainable in the realm of samsara; the rainbow is also the bow of Indra.

Islamic: The rainbow has four colors, red, yellow, green, blue, corresponding to the four elements.

Scandinavian: The bridge, Bifrost, the Tremulous Way, over to Asgard.

Rice Shares the symbolism of corn in the West and, as an essential food, has a divine origin. It can be magic and provide supernatural nourishment, like manna, and can also replenish granaries miraculously. It is a symbol of abundance and divine provision and only had to be cultivated after the loss of Paradise and the separation of Heaven and Earth. Rice represents immortality; spiritual nourishment; primordial purity; glory; solar power; knowledge; abundance; happiness and fecundity which is its significance when thrown over brides at weddings. In Chinese Alchemy red rice is associated with cinnabar; with red sulphur in esoteric Islam and with sulphur in the Work in Hermeticism.

Ring The ring is equated with the personality, and to bestow a ring is to transfer power, to plight a troth, to join the personalities. It is also a binding symbol: the wedding ring binds to a new state of union, completeness, fulfillment. In religions:

Chinese: Eternity; the origin of all creation; authority; dignity. A complete ring is acceptance, favor; a broken ring is ambivalent as either rejection, disfavor, or as the two halves being kept as a contract or renewal of friendship. A ring being sent by the Emperor was a summons to court; a half ring was a banishment, exile.

Christian: Eternity; union; spiritual marriage to the Church. Various rings denote the office of the wearer: the sapphire for cardinals and the bishop's ring signifying a bridegroom of the Church. A new Pope wears the Fisherman's Ring as an emblem of St. Peter. The British Coronation Ring is "the ensign of Kingly Dignity and Defence of the Catholic Faith."

Egyptian: The origin of the symbol of the ring and the rod is unknown, but is suggested as an axis mundi or the revolving universe; the All; eternity.

Hindu: The flame ring round Siva represents the cosmic cycle of creation and destruction.

Sumero-Semitic: The ring, often a triple ring, is a divine attribute and worn by all gods; with the crown, scepter and sickle it is a symbol of royalty.

Rosary The circle of wholeness and of time; perpetuity; endless duration; asceticism. In religions:

Buddhist: The 108 beads represent the 108 Brahmins present at the birth of Buddha; the circle is the Wheel of the Law, also the Round of Existence with the individual beads of manifestation strung upon it.

Christian: The mystic rose garden of the Virgin Mary; the 165 beads are divided into five decades; each set of five decades has its own "mysteries" of the joys, sorrows and glories of the Virgin Mary. The large beads represent the Our Father, and a Gloria, the small beads the Hail Mary. Attribute of St. Dominic.

Hindu: The thread is the nonmanifest, the beads are the multiplicity of the manifestation and the circle is Time. The rosary is an attribute of Brahma, Siva and Ganesha. The rosary of Siva has 32 or 64 berries of the Rudraksha tree, and usually accompanies the figure of a Shaivite saint. Other rosaries have 108 beads of Tulasi wood.

Islamic: The 99 beads are the "circular" number and correspond to the Divine Names; the 100th bead, which is the Name of the Essence, can be found only in Paradise.

Scroll Learning; knowledge; the unfolding of life and knowledge; the passing of time; the extent of a life; the scroll of the Law; destiny. The scrolls are the first five books of the old testament called the "Pentateuch." They are sacred to both Christians and Jews. In religions:

Picture taken in Dothan, Israel by author in 1975.

Buddhist: The unfolding of the Law; the scroll of the tests or sutras.

Chinese: Longevity; scholarship.

Christian: The Book of Life. The seven-sealed scroll which none can read shares the symbolism of the tablets of destiny. The scroll is an attribute of St. James the Great, also associated with Isaiah, Jeremiah and the prophets.

Greek: Attribute of Aesculapius as medical learning.

Egyptian: Knowledge; associated with the papyrus as the emblem of Lower Egypt.

Shepherd Leader and protector of any flock; a saviour. The Good Shepherd occurs in Sumerian, Iranian, Hebrew, Orphic, Hermetic, Pythagorean, Tibetan and Christian traditions. In religions:

Buddhist: (Tibetan) Chenrezig, "the All-merciful Good Shepherd" is incarnated in the Dalai Lama.

Christian: Christ, the Good Shepherd, symbolizes His humanity and compassion, also the redemption of those gone astray.

Egyptian: Ra is "the Shepherd of all men." Egyptian kings were shepherds of their flocks.

Greek: Orpheus Boukolos, the Herdsman, is the Good Shepherd, his attribute being a ram, or kid, on the shoulder. Hermes Kriophorus, the ram-bearer, is a Good Shepherd. Pan is a herdsman and Hermes, or Mercury, is a shepherd of souls.

Hindu: Siva is a herdsman and Krishna is associated with herdsmen and the young women who tended the cows.

Iranian: Yima, the Good Shepherd, possessing the solar eye, holds the secret of immortality.

Islamic: "The divine glory is among the shepherds."

Sumero-Semitic: Tammuz, a lunar god and a shepherd, is the protector of flocks. The Phoenician Amynos and Magos taught herding to the people.

Solstice At the Winter Solstice the Great Mother, Queen of Heaven, gives birth to the Son of Light. "The Virgin has given birth, the light grows" (Death and Resurrection of Osiris). The full moon is seen at its nadir and Virgo rises in the East. The Junua coeli, the Winter Solstice, in Capricorn, is the "door of the gods" and symbolizes the ascent and the growing power of the sun. The Summer Solstice in Cancer, the Junua inferni, is the "door of men" and its descent and the waning power of the sun.

Staff Masculine power; authority; dignity; magic power; journeying; pilgrimage; it is also a solar and axial symbol. The staff, or crook, is an attribute of all Good Shepherd. In religions:

Buddhist: Law and order; a symbol of Buddha's mace, i.e. his teaching.

Christian: Christ as the Good Shepherd; pilgrimage. The staff with rings denotes episcopal power and authority; the staff borne before high dignitaries depicts the dignity of office; in the left hand the staff signifies cardinals, archbishops, bishops, abbots and abbesses. The staff of pilgrimage is an emblem of St. James the Great, St. John the Baptist, St. Jerome, St. Christopher, St. Philip the Apostle, and St. Ursula. The budding staff is an emblem of St. Ethelreda and Joseph of Arimathaea.

Egyptian: The staff and the flail are the chief attributes of

Osiris as judge of the dead; the staff with the pen depicts the soul awakening and is an attribute of Theut or Logios.

Graeco-Roman: The herald's staff, as the caduceus, is the chief attribute of Hermes/Mercury.

Hindu: The three combined sticks of the staff of Vaishnava tradition symbolize the phenomenal world, or the control of thought, word, and deed of the saint or sage.

Caduceus

Steps Ascension; the steps up to an altar or throne symbolize the priest, king, or ruler, having the authority or mandate of heaven to ascend the steps leading to heaven. In religions:

American Indian: The months are the "steps of the year."

Buddhist: The seven steps of Buddha represent the mounting of the seven cosmic stages, the seven planetary heavens, which is to transcend time and space, also to attain the center in the seventh heaven, the highest state.

Egyptian: Osiris is "god of the stairs" leading to heaven; the nine steps up to his throne are the days of the ancient Egyptian week and the fourteen steps represent the days of the full growth of the moon.

Hindu: The three steps, or strides, of Vishnu denote the three manifestations of light; the sun, lightning, fire; also the rising zenith and setting sun; the earth, air and heaven; the three steps which gained control of the universe.

Mithraic: The seven steps of different metals, corresponding to the major planets, are the seven grades of ascension of the initiate.

Parsee: The three steps at an altar denote the three degrees of initiation.

Sumerian: The steps up the Ziggurat, or Sacred Mountain, represent the seven heavens and were of different symbolic colors.

Stole A narrow vestment made of the same material as the casuble and worn around the neck. As a Mass vestment it is crossed over the breast, after having been put around the neck. As he vests with this, the priest says: "Restore to me, O Lord, the garment of immortality which I lost

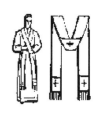

31

through the sin of my first parents and, although unworthy to approach Thy sacred mysteries, may I deserve, nevertheless, eternal joy."

The origin of the stole is obscure, but it seems to have developed from an ornamented border on a larger scarf or shawl.

Worn on the neck, the stole suggests a yoke, the yoke of the Lord, which is sweet and light.

Trinity A unity, three-in-one and one-in-three, symbolizing unity in diversity; the third uniting the opposites; the catalyst; "The mean, acting as mediator, links the other two into a single complete order" (Proclus). In religions:

Buddhist: The Triratna: the Buddha, Dharma, Sangha; also the Buddhas, the Sons of the Buddhas and the Dharmakaya.

Celtic: There are numerous trinities, the three Bridgits are three-in-one as the lunar Great Mother, and the family is three-in-one.

Christian: Father, Son, Holy Spirit, or Mary, Joseph, Jesus. Symbols of the Trinity are the hand as the Father, the lamb the Son, and the dove the Holy Spirit; in colors these are represented by yellow, red and green and in qualities by Charity, Faith and Hope; triangles or circles and the trefoil.

Egyptian: Father, Mother, Son; Osiris, Isis, Horus.

Graeco-Roman: Zeus, Poseidon, Hades; Jupiter, Neptune, Pluto; Sky, Ocean, Underworld.

Hebrew: (Qabalism) The original Trinity of male-female and uniting intelligence.

Hindu: The Trimurti, also the three-fold Brahman, the AUM, the imperishable Word.

Scandinavian and Teutonic: Odin, Thor, Frigg; Woden, Donar, Frija.

Sumero-Semitic: Anu, Ea, Bel; Sin, Shamash, Ishtar; Asshur, Anu, Hoa. In a trinity "two-thirds of him is God and one third of him is man" (Gilgamesh).

Veil Hidden or esoteric; knowledge, secrecy; the illusion of the manifest world; ignorance; concealment; the darkness of mourning. But that which conceals can also reveal; direct and naked truth can be dangerous; thus the veil is also protective, both of the truth and the inquirer. The veil divides the Holy of Holies, the Highest Heaven, from the Holy Place, the temple or church on earth. The veil represents submission to authority, hence the nun's and bride's veil, which also symbolizes sacrifice and death to the old life since the heads of sacrificial victims were often veiled and garlanded. Like hats and caps, the veil protects the inner life of the head where the life-power resides. It also obscures the personality and allows integration with others as in ancient priesthood, where the deity worshipped was often veiled. Passing the veil denotes degrees of initiation and gaining esoteric knowledge. Blue veils indicate sky gods or goddesses. In religions:

Buddhist and Hindu: The veil of illusion, maya, is the fabric from which the phenomenal world is woven; the obscuring of reality.

Christian: Modesty; chastity; renunciation of the world; the division between Jews and Gentiles which was removed by Christ when the Veil of the Temple was rent in twain. The rood screen is the veil of the Ark of the Covenant separating the Holy of Holies from the earthly body of the church. The cross on the altar is symbolically veiled during the period when Christ was in the tomb.

Egyptian: The veil of Isis, the mysteries of the universe and creation, "I am all that has been, and is, and shall be, and my veil no mortal man has yet lifted. The veil is the universe which the goddess weaves" (Proclus). It is revelation, illumination and concealment.

Graeco-Roman: An attribute of Hera/Juno.

Hebrew: The Veil of the Temple and the Ark of the Covenant is the dividing place of the Holy of Holies, the Highest Heaven, from the Holy Place, the earth. In four colors are the elements: bysus, the earth; purple, the sea; red, fire; blue, the air. Moses veiled his face and its radiance when he spoke to the people of Israel.

Islamic: The veil is of particular significance in Islamic spiritual symbolism; it represents veiled knowledge and revelation; revelation in the parting of the veil. The veil both reveals the Divine Nature and veils the Essence, and the Face of God is hidden by veils of light and darkness. Al Hallaj says that the veil is a curtain interposed between the seeker and his object. A veil separates the elite from the damned, believers from infidels. God speaks in revelation behind a veil, and the Veil of the Name preserves the seeker from direct vision which would be too much for him to endure. The passional nature of man is "veiled" nature since it does not see the light, but it is man, not God, who is veiled in this case. Mohammed, when portrayed, is often veiled. It is also shame and guilt. The Sufis say that seventy thousand veils separate Allah, the One Reality, from the world of matter and sense.

Sumero-Semitic: The world of manifestation woven by the Great Goddess. The veil of Tamit at her temple was the palladium of Carthage. The shrine of Nabu, at Babylon, was veiled during the time of the descent of the Dying God into the underworld.

Vestments According to Josephus the Hebrew, vestments represented: the linen, the earth; the cap of blue, the heavens and the sky; pomegranates, lightning; bells, thunder; the ephod, the universe made of the four elements; gold, the splendor of enlightenment; the breastplate, the world center; the girdle, the ocean; the two sardonyxes on the shoulders, the sun and moon; the twelve stones, the twelve months and signs of the Zodiac; the crown of gold, the splendor which pleases God; the emerald, Spring; the ruby, Summer; the sapphire, Autumn, truth, sincerity, constancy and chastity; the diamond, Winter, the sun, light; the topaz, true love and friendship.

Water Signifies a releasing or purification. The alchemists described it as a natural medium containing the substance of Sol (sun) and Luna (moon) which comes to moisten the earth that it may spring forth and in due season bring forth much fruit. "It is vegetable, mineral, and animal fire, which conserves the fixed spirits of Sol and Luna, but destroys and conquers their bodies; for it annihilates, overturns and changes bodies and metallic forms, making them to be no bodies, but a fixed spirit" (Dr. Herbert Silberer of Vienna). Water is used for purification and transformation. In the religions:

American Indian: The flowing power of the Great Spirit.

Aztec and Inca: The waters are primeval chaos.

Buddhist: Ablutions at the initiation of a monk represent the washing away of the past as a layman. Out of the primordial waters rose the stem of the great lotus, the world axis.

Celtic: The waters, lakes, sacred well, etc. have magical properties and are the dwelling place of supernatural beings, such as the Lady of the Lake; they also give access to the other world.

Chinese: The yin, lunar principle, symbolized by the trigram K'an with fire as the yang and solar power. Water denotes purity, the North region, and its symbol is the Black Tortoise, black being the color of primordial chaos.

Christian: The waters of regeneration; renewal; cleansing; sanctification; refreshment; baptism. A spring of water depicts Christ as the fountain of life; the living spring also represents the Virgin Mary, who is also the waters as the womb of creation; water mixed with wines the passive acted upon by the Spirit, "born of water and of the Spirit." The mingling of the human and divine at the Incarnation.

Egyptian: Birth; regeneration; growth; the fecundation of the waters of the Nile, symbolized by the God Hapi who pours water from two pots.

Graeco-Roman: Aphrodite/Venus arose from the waters; Poseidon/Neptune controls the power of the waters. The river Lethe is oblivion and the river Styx is crossed at death.

Hebrew: The water of the Torah is the life-giving waters of the sacred law. The spring of water constantly available to the Israelites is wisdom, the Logos, according to Philo. At the creation "the Spirit of God moved on the face of the waters."

Hindu: Agni is born of the waters and the earth and is the pillar supporting all existence. Varuna is controller of the waters. Vishnu sleeps on the waters, on the serpent, and from his navel grows a lotus enthroning Brahma, "He who walks on the waters."

Iranian: Apo, the water, is both solar and lunar power and the primordial ocean.

Islamic: Water signifies mercy; gnosis; purification; life. As rain, or a spring, water is divine revelation of reality. It is also creation; "From the water We made every living thing. His Throne was upon the waters" (Qoran).

Sumero-Semitic: Apsu, the primordial waters, existed in the beginning, with Tiamat as the sea and chaos. The serpents Lakhmu and Lakhamu were born of the waters. Marduk, as light, created the earth by overcoming Tiamat as chaos and the unmanifest.

Taoist: The strength of weakness; the power of adaptation and persistence; the fluidity of life as opposed to the rigidity of death. Water is the expression of the doctrine of wu-wei—giving at the point of resistance. It envelops and passes beyond it, ultimately wearing down even the hardest rock.

Wings Wings are almost entirely exclusive to Western and Middle East representations of divinities and supernatural beings. Wings are solar and depict divinity; spiritual nature; the moving, protecting and all-pervading power of the deity; the power to transcend the mundane world; the flight of time; the flight of thought; mind; freedom; victory, swiftness. Wings are attributes of swift messenger gods and denote the power of communication between gods and men. Outspread wings are divine protection. In religions:

Buddhist: Two wings represent wisdom and method.

Chinese: The winged dragon is the celestial power, vital spirit. The Cosmic Horse is winged and yang. Two birds together with only one wing each depict indissoluble unity, fidelity and a pair of lovers.

Christian: Angels are winged as divine messengers or as having divine qualities. The Devil is often portrayed as having bat's wings.

Egyptian: Neith is sometimes winged, but wings are rare in Egyptian iconography. However, in the occult mysteries, there is the winged Pharaoh depicted as one who is initiated.

Graeco-Roman: The four wings of Cronos, as the flight of time, are depicted as two spread and two resting, symbolizing perpetual movement and vigilance. Wings are also an attribute of Hypnos who fanned people to sleep with his dark wings. Hermes/Mercury has the winged cap, sandals and caduceus of the messenger of the gods. Iris has wings as a messenger of Hera/Juno. The Roman Victory is winged.

Hebrew: Archangels and angels, seraphim and cherubim are winged.

Hindu: The Garuda is winged.

Iranian: The winged disk is a symbol of Ahura Mazda or Ormuzd as light.

Islamic: Eight angels support the throne which encompasses the world.

Mithraic: The four winds and four seasons are represented by wings.

Shamanistic: The winged horse, birds, or feathered robes symbolize communion between this world and the spirit world.

Sumero-Semitic: The winged disk is a symbol, or direct representation, of the solar gods Shamash and Asshur. Four wings denote the four winds and seasons. The Semitic El has six wings or four wings, two at rest and two flying, having the same symbolism of vigilance and "flying while resting while flying" as Cronos.

Woman The Great Mother, the Great Goddess, the feminine principle symbolized by the moon, the earth and the waters; the instinctual powers as opposed to the masculine rational order. It is a highly complex symbolism as the Great Mother can be either beneficent and protective or malefic and destructive; she is both the pure spiritual guide and the siren and seducer, the virgin Queen of Heaven and the harpy and harlot, supreme wisdom and abysmal folly; the total complexity of nature. In religions:

Buddhist and Hindu: She is the shakti or Prakriti. In Indian art a beautiful woman depicts the beneficent aspect of Maya, the Great Mother, while the Black Kali, or Durga, represents the reverse.

Chinese: She is the yin, the feminine principle.

Christian: The Virgin Mary, Queen of Heaven. In art the Church "the bride of Christ" is depicted as a woman holding a cross or chalice or wearing a crown.

Hebrew: A woman with veiled, or bandaged eyes denoted the Jewish Synagogue. Figures of women were used to symbolize the virtues and vices and the seasons.

~~~~~

PART II

CEREMONIES
OR
RITUALS

INTRODUCTION

Ceremony or ritual has always been used by humankind to express strong emotions. From **"THE BOOK OF RITUALS"** by Reverend Carol E. Parrish-Harra, (published by IBS Press, Inc., available through Sparrow Hawk Press, Sparrow Hawk Village, 11 Summit Ridge Drive, Tahlequah, Oklahoma 74464), I have taken the following explanation of the power of these ceremonies.

"Ritual is a mode of action purposefully used to contact other planes. The acts can be simple or complex, but conscious intent and sincere desire are of absolute necessity. The clearer the ability to focus, to create thought-forms and to command, the more effective the energy transference will be.

The body is the real instrument in any ritual. Tipping one's head in respect or shaking hands are rites of our society, as genuflecting is a ritual of religious worship. Lighting a candle and placing it in front of a picture can be a ritual of great love or a simple act without much thought.

The intent, and both the concentration and consecration we bring to a ritual, affects the psychological world and the mental world. Any act creates a reaction on the other planes; therefore, a ritualist with conscious attention to details magnifies every opportunity to create an even greater effect on the planes involved. He or she enlists aids on the physical plane that will amplify the impact of his or her effort, i.e., candles, incense, music - a conscious effort to invoke the high and the holy into the physical world."

There are many ceremonies being used today in all religions. The Interfaith Minister needs to be knowledgeable about the most prominate ones. Part II of this book includes ceremonies that you may need to do at some stage in your ministry.

CHAPTER 4
THE SACRAMENTS

CHRISTENING AND BAPTISM

An explanation of the spiritual significance of Baptism from "THE MEANING AND VALUE OF THE SACRAMENTS" by Rev. Flower Newhouse:

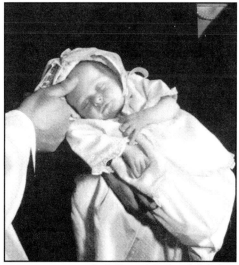

Used with permission from Catholic Press

"Baptism has a most stimulative effect upon those who are mature enough to be aware of its value. In itself, baptism is a coronation, a step deliberately taken in the purification of self. Every individual should be baptized, not that it is a spiritual duty, but because it signifies man's willingness to be more integrated to God's Presence.

Before baptism is taken we should ponder upon the value of this step toward the magnification of our spiritual lives. Only when we believe we are capable of living devotedly as a conscious son (or daughter) of God should we apply for the ministration of this rite.

During the ceremony, the great Angel of His Presence

43

transmits to the Soul body the rapturous benediction of the Divine Host. After the acceptance of the candidate into the ranks of conscious God-worshippers, the radiations from the recipient are noticeably extended. Thereafter the consecration and regeneration of the self must be dedicated to the Christ Cause through self-forgetting service."

There are immensities of power generated by the simple acts of the sacraments. Two ceremonies which are quite similar are those of Christening and Baptism. Jesus implied the importance of these rites in His statement, "Verily, verily, I say unto thee, except a man be born of water and of the Spirit, he cannot enter into the kingdom of God." (John 3:5). Both christening and baptism signify the initiation of the soul into the kingdom of God. On the day of Pentecost, Peter exhorted his listeners, "Repent and be baptized every one of you in the name of Jesus Christ for the remission of sins, and ye shall receive the gift of the Holy Ghost." (Acts 2:38).

In christening a baby, two specific acts are commemorated - the naming of the child, and his consecration to the Spirit of God. The choice of a name requires research and inspiration so that its intoning will emanate a generic quality.

The dedication of the infant to the love and protection of God links the child in every body to the Imminent Source. The rite itself has a spiritual effect in stabilizing the Soul's control of its newly created physical form. A permanent magnetic beam is produced (by the will of the Angel of the Christ Presence who invisibly officiates at such a service) which unites the Soul and all its faculties with the ever-present Spirit of God.

Following are ceremonies from various backgrounds:

Aztec
(From the Aztec ceremony of bathing the newborn)

Merciful Eternal Parent (**SAY CHILD'S NAME HERE**), thy servant here present is come into the world. Wash him/her and deliver him/her from imperfections. Cleanse him/her of the contamination he/she hath received from before the foundation of the world.

(SPRINKLE AND LIPS AND BOSOM OF THE CHILD WITH WATER WHILE SAYING THE FOLLOWING PRAYER) "Let the holy drops (water) take away the soil and the stain and let him/her be freed from all taint and be born anew. May it please thee, O beings, that his/her heart and life be purified, that he/she may dwell in this world in peace and wisdom. May this water take away all ills. Wash from him/her the errors which he/she beareth from before the beginning of the world."

Roman Catholic - The Rite of Baptism

The child presented here for baptism has begun a long life of receiving invitations. First of all, the parents have generously invited the child into this world by giving a share in the life of their own bodies. This invitation will be prolonged with every mouthful of food, every drop of medicine and every inch of shelter they provide. As religious people, the parents are aware of the thrilling fact that it is not only themselves who have extended and must make ever more enticing this invitation to life, but, even more important, that it is God, His creative power working through them, who has summoned this special little person into existence. The fact that this child has been conceived means that God himself has spoken. The living of this life is, indeed, a command performance before the Lord of Life.

By bringing this child to the waters of Baptism, an invitation to another Life has been extended to this child. This is a Life far above our earthly life and, yet, a Life which will carry and continue for eternity all that is wonderful and lastingly important in this life of the human race. This new Life is Life in Christ. Indeed, we have been invited into this life in humanity for the sole purpose that we might be invited into Life in Christ. As with human life, so with Life in Christ, it is not only we who bring this child to the new birth of Baptism but, far more important, it is Jesus Christ who is sending His Holy Spirit into His Church, into us, to give a life which is more than human. In giving this Life through us, then, Jesus Christ Himself summons this child with an invitation which admits of no rejection.

This moment of Baptism, then, is a moment of generous invitation to Life, to be accepted freely, written indelibly into a Christian's very being, and extended by God, Father, Son and Holy Spirit, through us, now in the waters of Baptism and again and again through our word and example as parents, godparents and pastors in the Church, all the days of the human life of this very special little person. This new rite of Baptism is the Church's way of alerting you to the irrevocable results of what we do here today, both for this child, and for us who will put this child on the path of life. Jesus Christ is saying to us, "Let the little children come to Me for such is the Kingdom of Heaven."

Reverend Edward J. Bayer
Archdiocese of Baltimore

The Rite of Baptism

The following is an accepted version of the rite of Baptism.

RECEPTION OF THE CHILD

Celebrant: What name do you give your child?
Parents: (....Name....)

Celebrant: What do you ask of God's Church for (..name..)?
Parents: Baptism (faith, the grace of Christ, entrance into the Church, eternal life, etc. may be substituted).

Celebrant to parents: You have asked to have your child baptized. In doing so you are accepting the responsibility of training him (her) in the practice of the faith. It will be your duty to bring him (her) up to keep God's command-

46

ments as Christ taught us, by loving God and our neighbor. Do you clearly understand what you are undertaking:
Parents: We do.

Celebrant to godparents: Are you ready to help the parents of this child in their duty as Christian parents?
Godparents: We are.

Celebrant: (Name), the Christian community welcomes you with great joy. In its name I claim you for Christ our Savior by the sign of His cross. I now trace the cross on your forehead, and invite your parents (and godparents) to do the same.

CELEBRATION OF GOD'S WORD

Scriptural Readings and Homily

Intercessions (Prayer of the Faithful)

Celebrant: My dear brothers and sisters, let us ask our Lord Jesus Christ to look lovingly on this child who is to be baptized, on his (her) parents and godparents, and on all the baptized.

Leader: By the mystery of your death and resurrection, bathe this child in light, give him (her) the new life of Baptism and welcome him (her) into your holy Church.
All: Lord, hear our prayer.

Leader: Through Baptism and confirmation, make him (her) your faithful follower and a witness to your gospel.
All: Lord, hear our prayer.

Leader: Lead him (her) by a holy life to the joys of God's kingdom.
All: Lord, hear our prayer.

Leader: Make the lives of his (her) parents and godparents examples of faith to inspire this child.
All: Lord, hear our prayer.

Leader: Keep his (her) family always in your love.
All: Lord, hear our prayer.

Leader: Renew the grace of our Baptism in each one of us.
All: Lord, hear our prayer.

INVOCATION OF THE SAINTS

Leader: Holy Mary, Mother of God
All: Pray for us.

Leader: Saint John the Baptist
All: Pray for us.

Leader: Saint Joseph
All: Pray for us.

Leader: Saint Peter and Saint Paul **(other saints may be added)**
All: Pray for us.

Leader: All holy men and women
All: Pray for us.

PRAYER OF EXORCISM AND ANOINTING BEFORE BAPTISM

Celebrant: Almighty and ever-living God, you sent your only Son into the world, to cast out the power of Satan, spirit of evil, to rescue your people from the kingdom of darkness, and bring them into the splendor of your kingdom of light. We pray for this child: set him (her) free from original sin, make him (her) a temple of your glory, and send your Holy Spirit to dwell with him (her). We ask this through Christ our Lord.
All: Amen.

Celebrant: We anoint you with the oil of salvation in the name of Christ our Savior; may He strengthen you with His power, who lives and reigns for ever and ever.
All: Amen.

Celebrant: May you have strength in the power of Christ our Savior, who lives and reigns for ever and ever.
All: Amen.

CELEBRATION OF THE SACRAMENT

Celebrant: My dear brothers and sisters, we now ask God to give this child new life in abundance through water and the Holy Spirit.

Blessing and Invocation of God
over Baptismal Water

Celebrant: Father, God of mercy, through these waters of baptism you have filled us with new life as your very own children.
All: Blessed be God.

Celebrant: From all who are baptized in water and the Holy Spirit, you have formed one people, united in your Son Jesus Christ.
All: Blessed be God.

Celebrant: You have set us free and filled our hearts with the Spirit of your love, that we may live in your peace.
All: Blessed be God.

Celebrant: You call those who have been baptized to announce the Good News of Jesus Christ to people everywhere.
All: Blessed be God.

Celebrant: You have called your child, (name), to this cleansing water that he (she) may share in the faith of your Church and have eternal life. By the mystery of this consecrated water lead him (her) to a new and spiritual birth. We ask this through Christ our Lord.
All: Amen.

Renunciation of Sin and Profession of Faith

Celebrant: Dear parents and godparents: You have come here to present this child for baptism. By water and the Holy Spirit he (she) is to receive the gift of new life from God, who is love.

On your part, you must make it your constant care to bring him (her) up in the practice of faith. See that the divine life which God gives him (her) is kept safe from the poison of sin, to grow always stronger in his (her) heart. If your faith makes you ready to accept this responsibility, renew now the vows of your own baptism. Reject sin; profess your faith in Christ Jesus. This is the faith of the

Church. This is the faith in which this child is about to be baptized.

Celebrant to parents and godparents: Do you reject Satan?
Parents and godparents: I do.

Celebrant: And all his works:
Parents and godparents: I do.

Celebrant: And all his empty promises?
Parents and godparents: I do.

Celebrant: Do you believe in God, the Father almighty, creator of heaven and earth?
Parents and godparents: I do.

Celebrant: Do you believe in Jesus Christ, His only Son, our Lord, who was born of the Virgin Mary, was crucified, died, and was buried, rose from the dead, and is now seated at the right hand of the Father?
Parents and godparents: I do.

Celebrant: Do you believe in the Holy Spirit, the holy catholic Church, the communion of saints, the forgiveness of sins, the resurrection of the body, and life everlasting?
Parents and godparents: I do.

Celebrant: This is our faith. This is the faith of the Church. We are proud to profess it, in Christ Jesus our Lord.
All: Amen.

Baptism

Celebrant: Is it your will that (name) should be baptized in the faith of the Church, which we have all professed with you?
Parents and godparents: It is.

Celebrant: The celebrant sprinkles water from the baptismal font on the forehead of the one being baptized while saying: (Name), I baptize you in the name of the Father, and of the Son, and of the Holy Spirit.
All: Blessed be God who chose you in Christ.

Anointing with Chrism

The celebrant dips his thumb in the oil of the catechumens and anoints the one being baptized on the breast, between the shoulders, and on top of the head in the form of the cross and says:

Celebrant: God the Father of our Lord Jesus Christ has freed you from sin, given you a new birth by water and the Holy Spirit, and welcomed you into his holy people. He now anoints you with the chrism of salvation. As Christ was anointed Priest, Prophet, and King, so may you live always as a member of His body, sharing everlasting life.
All: Amen.

Clothing with the White Garment:

The celebrant places a white linen cloth on the head or shoulder of the person being baptized and says:

Celebrant: (Name), you have become a new creation, and have clothed yourself in Christ. See in this white garment the outward sign of your Christian dignity. With your family and friends to help you by word and example, bring that dignity unstained into the everlasting life of heaven.
All: Amen.

Lighted Candle

The sponsor or baptized person (if older) is given a candle. A member of the family lights the candle from the Easter candle on the altar.

Celebrant: Receive the light of Christ. Then to the parents and godparents, he says: This light is entrusted to you to be kept burning brightly. This child of yours has been enlightened by Christ. He (she) is to walk always as a child of the light. May he (she) keep the flame of faith alive in his (her) heart. When the Lord comes, may he (she) go out to meet Him with all the saints in the heavenly kingdom.

51

Prayer over Ears and Mouth

Celebrant: The Lord Jesus made the deaf hear and dumb speak. May He soon touch your ears to receive His word, and your mouth to proclaim His faith, to the praise and glory of God the Father.

All: Amen.

CONCLUSION OF THE RITE

Baptismal song: You have put on Christ, in Him you have been baptized. Alleluia, alleluia.

Celebrant: Dearly beloved, this child has been reborn in baptism. He (she) is now called the child of God, for so indeed he (she) is. In confirmation he (she) will receive the fullness of God's Spirit. In holy communion he (she) will share the banquet of Christ's sacrifice, calling God his (her) Father in the midst of the Church. In the name of this child, in the Spirit of our common sonship, let us pray together in the words our Lord has given us:

All: Our Father who art in heaven, hallowed be thy name. Thy kingdom come, Thy will be done on earth, as it is in heaven. Give us this day our daily bread. And forgive us our trespasses as we forgive those who trespass against us. And lead us not into temptation, but deliver us from evil.

Blessing

Celebrant: God the Father, through His Son, the Virgin Mary's child, has brought joy to all Christian mothers, as they see the hope of eternal life shine on their children. May He bless the mother of this child. She now thanks God for the gift of her child. May she be one with him (her) in thanking Him for ever in heaven, in Christ Jesus our Lord.

All: Amen.

Celebrant: God is the giver of all life, human and divine. May He bless the father of this child. He and his wife will be the first teachers of their child in the ways of faith. May they be also the best of teachers, bearing witness to the faith by what they say and do, in Christ Jesus our Lord.

All: Amen.

Celebrant: By God's gift, through water and the Holy Spirit, we are reborn to everlasting life. In His goodness, may He continue to pour out His blessings upon these sons and daughters of His. May He make them always, wherever they may be, faithful members of His holy people. May He send His peace upon all who are gathered here, in Christ Jesus our Lord.

All: Amen.

Celebrant: May almighty God, the Father, and the Son, and the Holy Spirit, bless you.

All: Amen.

(Closing hymn)

Universal Spiritualist Baptism

For each child to be baptized there should be a godfather and godmother. Parents shall be admitted as sponsors, if it be desired.

The Minister, having come to the Baptismal font, which is to be filled with pure water, shall say as follows, the people all standing:

"Holy Baptism is a Sacrament by which the recipient is solemnly admitted to membership of Christ's holy Church and grafted into His mystical body. Has this child been already baptized, or no?"

If the godparents answer, No, then shall the Minister proceed as follows:

"Let us pray. Almighty God, we call upon Thee for this child coming to Thy holy baptism. Receive him/her into the arms of Your love and keep him/her ever in Your watchful care. Give us grace to help him/her grow in grace, both by our own good example and by instruction the teachings of the Church, and may he/she remain a faithful servant of our Lord Jesus Christ, to his/her life's end."

HERE READ THE GOSPEL OF ST. MARK 10:13 - (THE MINISTER OR A PARENT OR GRANDPARENT CAN READ THIS.)

"They brought young children to Christ, that He should touch them; and His disciples rebuked those that brought them. But when Jesus saw it, He was much displeased and said unto them: Suffer the little children to come unto Me, and forbid them not; for of such is the kingdom of God. Verily I say unto you, whosoever shall not receive the kingdom of God as a little child, he shall not enter therein. And He took them up in His arms, put His hands upon them and blessed them."

Prayer from the Spiritualist Manual (can be omitted)

"O Christ, our Lord, we humbly ask Thee to enfold in Thy protection this little one. Surround him/her with Thy spiritual strength and be very near to him/her so that he/she may hear Thy voice and follow Thy call. Open his/her eyes to the beauty of Spirit, and help him/her as he/she grows to see that beauty of Spirit, and the beauty in all creation. We pray Thee to inspire his/her spirit guides and helpers so that they may hold his/her safety and well-being in truth and under Thy guidance. O Thou who was a little child, be Thou this child's companion in play, in sleep, in wakefulness, and in all his/her growing days; be his/her friend most dear, to understand, to console, and to bless. Amen."

Then the Minister says to the godparents or sponsors:

"You have brought this child here to be baptized and thus received into the fellowship of the Christian Faith. Give now your pledge to endeavor, earnestly and in truth, to teach and inspire this little one in the way of life as taught by the master Jesus Christ; to let your example and influence guide him/her to be upright and honorable before all men; to train him/her in prayer, in worship, in reverence, and in the knowledge and love of God, through Christ our Lord, and through His ministering angels."

The godparents or sponsors answer: "We will, by God's help."

The Minister then asks the godparents: "Do you renounce Satan and all the spiritual forces of wickedness that rebel against God?"

The godparents together say: "I renounce them."

The Minister then asks the godparents: "Do you renounce the evil powers of this world which corrupt and destroy the creatures of God?"

The godparents together say: "I renounce them."

The Minister then asks the godparents: "Do you believe in Jesus Christ and put your trust in His grace and love?"

The godparents together say: "I do believe."

The Minister then asks all present: Will you who witness these vows do all in your power to support this child in his/her life in Christ?"

People: "We will."

Minister asks people: "Do you believe in God the Father?"

People: "I believe in God, the Father almighty, creator of heaven and earth."

Minister asks people: "Do you believe in Jesus Christ, the Son of God?"

People: "I believe in Jesus Christ, His only Son, our Lord. He was conceived by the Holy Spirit and born of the Virgin Mary. He suffered under Pontius Pilate, was crucified, died, and was buried. He descended to the dead. On the third day He rose again, He ascended into heaven, and is seated at the right hand of the Father. He will come again to judge the living and the dead."

Minister: "Do you believe in God the Holy Spirit?"

People: "I believe in the Holy Spirit, the holy Catholic Church, the communion of saints, the forgiveness of sins, resurrection of the body, and the life everlasting."

Minister: "Will you continue in the apostles' teaching and fellowship, in the breaking of bread, and in prayers?"

People: "I will, with God's help."

Then the Minister, placing his/her hand over the water in the font, says:

"May the waters of the Spirit mingle with this water, to consecrate this child of God and keep him/her pure and holy. Amen. O Holy Spirit, come now with Thy gifts to endow this child, to strengthen and prepare him/her for the way ahead, so that he/she may be strong in faith, courageous in spirit, and valiant for right; that at the last he/she may hear the loving words, 'Well done, thou good and faithful servant.' Amen."

The Minister then takes the child and says: "Name this child."

The godparent of the same sex as the child then names the child. Only Christian names are given (the first and middle names, not the last name).

The Minister then sprinkles water over the head and forehead of the child three times, saying:

"(NAME OF CHILD) I baptize thee in the Name of the Father, and of the Son, and of the Holy Ghost. Amen."

With his/her thumb, the Minister then makes the Sign of the Cross upon the child's forehead, saying:

"I receive this child into the fellowship of Christ's holy Church and do sign him/her with the Sign of the Cross in token that hereafter he/she shall not be ashamed to confess the faith of Christ our Lord, and that he/she shall continue Christ's faithful servant throughout the ages of ages. Amen."

The Minister gives the child back to the godmother and says:

"Seeing now that this child is grafted into the mystical body of Christ, let us give thanks unto Almighty God and with one accord pray that this child may continue his/her life according to this beginning."

Minister: "Now let us all say the Lord's Prayer."

ALL SAY IT TOGETHER.

The Minister places his/her hand on the head of the child saying:

"(NAME OF CHILD) go in peace and may the Lord be with you. Amen."

For Adults

All gather around the baptismal font and the Minister says to those who came to be baptized:

"Holy Baptism is a Sacrament by which the recipient is solemnly admitted to membership in Christ's holy Church. It is to be only once in a person's physical life. Have you been already baptized, or no?"

If they say, No, the Minister continues:

"For as much as Christ our Lord said that none can enter into the kingdom of God, except he be regenerated and born again of Water and of the Holy Ghost; I beseech you to call upon God the Father that of His bounteous mercy He will grant that you may be baptized with Water and the Holy Spirit, and be received into Christ's holy Church. Let us pray. Almighty God, we call up Thee for (this Thy servant/these Thy servants) coming to Thy holy baptism. Receive him/her/them, O Father, as Thou has promised by Thy well beloved Son Who said: 'Ask, and ye shall have; seek, and ye shall find; knock, and it shall be opened unto you.' So give now unto us who ask; let us who seek, find; open the gate unto us who knock; that (this Thy servant/these Thy servants) may enjoy the everlasting benediction of Thy heavenly washing, and may come to the eternal kingdom which Thou has promised by Christ our Lord. Amen."

Hear the words of the Gospel written by St. Matthew in the twenty-eighth chapter, beginning at the eighteenth verse:

"Jesus came and spake unto them, saying: All power is given unto Me in heaven and in earth. Go ye therefore, and make disciples of all nations, baptizing them in the name of the Father, and of the Son, and of the Holy Ghost; teaching them to observe all things whatsoever I have commanded you; and lo, I am with you always, even unto the end of the world."

"Let us pray."

"O Christ our Lord, we humbly ask Thee to enfold in Thy protection (this Thy servant/these Thy servants). Surround (him/her/them) with Thy spiritual strength and be very near so that (he/she/they) hear Thy voice and follow Thy call. Open (his/her/their) eyes to the beauty of the Spirit and aid in seeing that beauty everywhere in all creation. Be Thou that friend most dear, to understand, to console, and to bless. Amen."

The Minister then asks the petitioners: "You have come here desiring to receive holy Baptism and thus the fellowship of the Christian faith. Do you affirm your promise to God to strive to fulfill His will, as laid down by Christ our Lord?"

Petitioners answer: "I do."

The Minister places his/her hand over the water in the font and says:

"May the waters of the Spirit mingle with this water,

consecrating all that is touched by it, making pure and holy. Amen. O Holy Spirit, come now with Thy gifts, strengthening and preparing for the way ahead; making strong in faith, courageous in spirit, and valiant for right; so that at the last the loving words may be heard, 'Well done, thou good and faithful servant.' Amen."

The Minister then asks the petitioner: "What is your full name?"

The petitioner gives their whole name. The Minister repeats only the first and middle names as he/she sprinkles water over the head of the person three times saying:

"(NAME) I baptize you in the Name of the Father, and of the Son, and of the Holy Ghost. Amen."

After all have been baptized, the Minister asks all present to say the Lord's Prayer.

The Minister then gives a blessing to all, putting his/her hand on the head of each person who has been baptized and making the Sign of the Cross over others present.

CONFIRMATION

This ceremony is taken from "The Liturgy of the Liberal Catholic Church".

Used with permission from Catholic Press

Confirmation is, literally, the making of the person firm or strong in the life in Christ begun at baptism. It has the two-fold effect of strengthening the soul and giving it greater power to express itself through the body.

The candidate pledges himself to endeavor to set aside the smaller life of personal interests and to work for the common good. Having offered himself thereunto as a knight in Christ's service, the sacramental act of confirmation follows and he is sealed once again with the sign of the holy cross, the emblem of the life of sacrifice and service.

The candidates for confirmation are seated in due order before the bishop outside the chancel - their sponsors also, if still alive and able to attend, being near at hand. All stand.

THE INVOCATION

Bishop: "In the name of the Father + and of the Son, and of the Holy Ghost. Amen."

The people are seated. The bishop is seated before the altar. If desired, an address may here be delivered to the candidates, explaining to them the nature of the sacrament of confirmation and of the responsibilities they take upon themselves. The bishop delivers the following charge:

THE CHARGE

"(My Beloved Children:) On your entry into this mortal life you were brought into the house of God and our holy mother the church met you with such help as then you could receive. Now she offers you a further help - the gift of God's most holy Spirit. This world in which we live is God's world and it is growing better and better day by day and year by year; but it is still far from perfect. There is still much of sin and selfishness; there are still many who know not God, neither understand His laws. So there is a constant struggle between good and evil and, since you are members of Christ's church, you will be eager to take your stand upon God's side and serve under the banner of our Lord.

But if you enter His most holy service take heed that you are such servants as He would have you be. Strong must you be, yet gentle, ready ever to protect the weak, watchful ever to help where help is needed, to give reverence to those to whom it is due and to show knightly courtesy to all. Never forgetting that God is love, make it your constant care to shed love around you wherever you may go; so will you fan into living flame the smouldering fires of love in the hearts of those in whom as yet the spark burns low. Remember that the servant of the cross must utterly uproot from his heart the giant weed of selfishness and must live not for himself but for the service of the world; for this commandment have we from Him, that he who loveth God love his brother also. Remember that the power of God, which you are now about to receive from my hand, will ever work within you for righteousness, inclining you unto a noble and upright life. Strive therefore earnestly that your thoughts, your words and your works shall be such as befit a child of Christ and a knight dedicated to His service. All this shall you zealously try to do for Christ's sweet sake and in His most Holy Name."

THE INTERROGATIONS

All rise and the bishop addresses the candidates as follows:

Bishop: Will you then strive to live in the spirit of love with all mankind and earnestly to fight against sin and selfishness?

Candidates: I will.

Bishop: Will you strive to show forth in your thoughts, your words and your works the power of God which shall be given to you?

Candidates: I will.

The candidates kneel; and the bishop blesses them as follows:

Bishop: May the + blessing of the Holy Ghost come down upon you and may the power of the Most High preserve you in all your ways. Amen.

The following hymn is sung, all kneeling.

VENI CREATOR

Come, Thou Creator Spirit blest
And in our soul take up Thy rest;
Come with Thy grace and heavenly aid,
To fill the hearts which Thou hast made.

Great Paraclete, to Thee we cry,
O highest gift of God most high;
O living fount, O fire, O love
And sweet anointing from above.

Thou in Thy sevenfold gifts are known;
Thee, finger of God's hand, we own,
The promise of the Father, Thou
Who dost the tongue with power endow.

Kindle our senses from above
And make our hearts o'erflow with love;
With patience firm and virtue high
The weakness of our flesh supply.

Far let us drive our tempting foe
And Thine abiding peace bestow;
So shall we not, with Thee for guide,
Turn from the path of life aside.

O may Thy grace on us bestow
Thy Father and the Son to know

And Thee, through endless times confessed,
Of both eternal Spirit blest.

All glory while the ages run
Be to the Father and the Son,
Who gave us life; the same to Thee,
O Holy Ghost, eternally. (Amen.)

The people are seated.

THE CONFIRMATION

Each candidate is severally led up to the bishop and instructed to kneel upon the cushion and to place his hands together, palm to palm, resting them upon the gremail which covers the bishop's knees. The candidate (prompted if necessary) says:

"Right Reverend Father, I offer myself to be a knight in Christ's service."

The bishop, taking the candidate's hands between his own and pressing them lightly, answers:

"In Christ's most holy name do I accept thee."

The bishop takes some chrism upon his right thumb and, placing his right hand upon the head of the candidate, says:

"Receive the Holy Ghost for the sweet savor of a godly life; whereunto I do + sign thee with the sign of the cross and I confirm thee with the chrism of salvation. In the name of the + Father and of the + Son and of the Holy + Ghost. Amen."

At the words, "I do sign thee", the bishop makes the sign of the cross with the chrism upon the forehead of the neophyte. He makes the sign of the cross three times over the head of the neophyte as he recites the names of the Holy Trinity. After a momentary pause, the bishop again lays his hand upon the head of the neophyte, saying:

"Therefore go thou forth, my brother, in the name of the Lord, for in His strength thou canst do all things."

The bishop touches the neophyte lightly on the left cheek, saying:

"Peace be with thee."

The neophyte rises, bows reverently to the bishop and is led back to his seat. When all have been confirmed, the following hymn may be sung:

HYMN

O Master, I have promised
    To serve Thee to the end;
Be Thou for ever near me,
    My helper and my friend;
I shall not fear the battle
    If Thou art by my side,
Nor wander from the pathway,
    If Thou wilt be my guide.

The people are seated. The bishop, seating himself, addresses the newly-confirmed as follows:

"My brothers, now have you received the gift of the Holy Ghost; see to it that your bodies are ever pure and clean, as befits the temple of the most high God and the channel of so great a power; and understand that as you keep that channel open by a useful life spent in the service of others, so will His life that is within you shine forth with ever greater and greater glory."

The people rise. The bishop rises and faces towards the altar; the newly-confirmed kneel.

Bishop: + Our help in the name of the Lord.
Congregation: Who hath made heaven and earth.

Bishop: Blessed are the pure in heart.
Congregation: For they shall see God.

Bishop: Trust ye in the Lord for ever.

Congregation: For He is our Rock of Ages.

Bishop: The Lord be with you.
Congregation: And with thy spirit.

Bishop: Let us pray.

The people kneel. The bishop extends his hands towards the newly-confirmed and says:

"O Lord Christ, who didst give the Holy Spirit to Thine apostles and didst ordain that by them and their successors He should be given to the rest of the faithful, we render Thee heartfelt thanks for this Thine inestimable benefit now bestowed upon us.

We offer unto Thee the lives which Thou today has blessed, that they, whom Thou hast thus accepted as servants in Thy church on earth, may so bear themselves as true and faithful knights in Thy service, that they may be found worthy hereafter to stand before Thee in the ranks of Thy holy church eternal, O Thou great King of Glory, to whom be praise and adoration from men and from the angel host. Amen."

THE BENEDICTION

The bishop blesses the persons confirmed as follows:

"God the + Father, God the + Son, God the Holy + Ghost, bless, preserve and sanctify you; the Lord in His loving kindness look down upon you and be gracious unto you; the Lord lift up the light of His countenance upon you and give you His peace, now and for evermore. Amen."

The following Benediction may be used where authorized.

"May the Holy Ones, whose pupils you aspire to become, show you the light you seek, give you the strong aid of their compassion and their wisdom. There is a peace that passeth understanding; it abides in the hearts of those who live in the eternal; there is a power that maketh all things new; it lives and moves in those who know the self as one. May that peace brood over you, that power uplift you, till you stand where the One Initiator is invoked, till you see His + star shine forth. Amen."

EUCHARISTIC FEAST OR HOLY COMMUNION

Following is an explanation of Communion from "THE MEANING AND VALUE OF THE SACRAMENTS" by Rev. Flower Newhouse of The Christward Ministry.

Used with permission from *Passion Oberammergau*

"Holy Communion contains a high Mystery. Communion relates us mystically to the Christ Presence. It infuses us with Christ energies which are present in the blessed bread and juice. In these symbols are impregnated Light particles which benefit and enlighten those who receive them. We should realize something of that adoration which the Knights of the Grail felt when the Holy Cup was revealed to them.

The influence of this sacrament will persist according to the degree of one's sensitivity to spiritual realities. For those who look upon this ceremony superficially it will hold but little value. Others who are spiritually consecrated recognize the threefold effect of Communion. First, it is an ennobling ceremony to observe and reflect upon. Second, the symbology suggests high at-one-ment with God. Third, its innermost benediction has a vital effect upon the higher dimensional faculties of man.

Consecrated bread signifies God's life-giving force and His constant provision. When the bread is given, realize this thought: 'This symbol of the living Lord Christ heals my body, cleanses my emotions and mind, and activates my soul.' As the bread slowly melts on our tongue we should all reflect on this thought directed to the Christ: 'Thee I receive in new life and unfoldment.' The juice symbolizes the flowing of Christ's life-giving forces through our bodies. As we accept it we say: 'This symbol of the regenerating influence of the Lord Christ, renews His Living Presence within me.' As you drink the juice, realize this thought: 'Thy life currents now infuse and strengthen me.'

The more reverent and developed we are, the better will we sense the influences from the foods we have received. With every communion we celebrate we should be awakened to greater awareness and accomplishment. We cannot force unfoldment by intense longing without this forcing being harmful. **Communion bestows power.** Whatever spiritualizing effects we perceive should be realized with appreciation and trustful usefulness.

When we call upon the vibrant name of our Unseen Host, we invite His Christly power. The Angelic Presences who help to usher in the active forces of the Lord Christ mantle the entire service and They assist us to become more conscious receivers and dispensers of the Christ Spirit.

The more we understand and cherish the symbolical sacrament of Communion, the more of His power we receive and use. With purified intention we accept the high benefits and endeavor to turn them into daily acts of achievement."

The Minister or Priest can use prepared hosts from a religious store, or unleavened bread, or home baked bread for the Eucharistic feast. It depends on the circumstances of the occasion.

~

Roman Catholic Communion Service:

The Communion Service is part of the Canon or unchangeable part of the Mass and is the same every day of the year. It starts after the Epistle, Gospel, sermon and creed. The priest says prayers for (1) the Church; (2) the living, and (3) an invocation of the saints. Then he says two prayers of offering:

Extending his hands over the bread and wine, the priest says the following prayer. The server rings the bell to remind the congregation that the moment of the Consecration is near.

"Graciously accept, we beseech Thee, O Lord, this service of our worship and that of all Thy household. Provide that our days be spent in Thy peace, save us from everlasting damnation, and cause us to be numbered in the flock Thou hast chosen. Through Christ our Lord. Amen."

Making five Signs of the Cross over the bread and wine (one at each of the small crosses in the prayer) the priest says:

"Do thou, O God, deign to + bless what we offer, and make it + approved, + effective, right and wholly pleasing in every way, that it may be for our good, the Body + and the Blood + of Thy dearly beloved Son, Jesus Christ Our Lord."

Consecration

Taking the bread into his hands, raising his eyes to heaven, blessing the bread and bowing down over, the priest says:

"Who, the day before He suffered, took bread into His holy and venerable hands, and having raised His eyes to heaven, unto Thee, O God, His Father almighty, giving thanks to Thee, + blessed, broke it, and gave it to His disciples, saying: Take, all of you, and eat of this. FOR THIS IS MY BODY."

The priest genuflects, elevates the Host above his head for all to see, and genuflects again, as the server rings the bell. Then taking into his hands the chalice, the priest says:

"In like manner, when the supper was done, taking also this goodly chalice into His holy and venerable hands, again giving thanks to Thee, He + blessed it and gave it to His disciples, saying: Take, all of you, and drink of this. FOR THIS IS THE CHALICE OF MY BLOOD OF THE

69

NEW AND ETERNAL COVENANT, THE MYSTERY OF FAITH, WHICH SHALL BE SHED FOR YOU AND FOR MANY UNTO THE FORGIVENESS OF SINS. As often as you shall do these things, in memory of Me shall you do them."

The priest genuflects, elevates the chalice above his head for all to see, and genuflects again, as the server rings the bell.

After the Consecration a three-part prayer again makes our offering to God, asks Him to accept it, and begs His blessings.

"Mindful, therefore, O Lord, not only of the blessed passion of the same Christ, Thy Son, our Lord, but also of His resurrection from the dead, and finally His glorious ascension into heaven, we, Thy ministers, as also Thy holy people, offer unto Thy supreme majesty, of Thy gifts bestowed upon us, the pure + Victim; the holy Bread + of life eternal and the Chalice + of unending salvation."

The priest then offers prayers for the souls in Purgatory and for sinners. This ends the Canon and then begins the communion part of the Mass with The Lord's Prayer.

Holding the paten in his hand, the priest develops in the following prayer the final thought expressed in the Our Father.

"Deliver us, O Lord, we beseech Thee, from all evils, past, present, and to come; and through the intercession of the glorious and blessed Mary, ever virgin, mother of God, together with Thy blessed apostles, Peter and Paul and Andrew, and all the saints (the priest blesses himself with the paten and kisses it), grant, of Thy goodness, peace in our days, that aided by the riches of Thy mercy we may be always free from sin and safe from all disquiet."

Breaking the Host in two equal pieces, the priest continues:

"Through the same Jesus Christ, Thy Son, our Lord."

The priest breaks off a small particle of the Host and says:

"Who liveth and reigneth with Thee in the unity of the Holy Ghost, God, world without end. Amen."

The priest drops the small particle into the chalice and says:

"May this mingling and hallowing of the Body and Blood of our Lord Jesus Christ help us who receive it unto life everlasting. Amen."

Having genuflected, the priest bows at the center and says:

"Lamb of God, who takest away the sins of the world, have mercy on us. Lamb of God, who takest away the sins of the world, have mercy on us. Lamb of God, who takest away the sins of the world, grant us peace."

<u>Communion of the Priest</u>

The priest genuflects, takes the Host in his hands, and says:

"I will take the Bread of Heaven, and call upon the name of the Lord."

At the following words the server rings the bell three times, reminding the faithful that the priest is about to receive.

"Lord, I am not worthy that Thou shouldest come under my roof; but only say the word and my soul will be healed. (3 X)"

Making the Sign of the Cross with the Host, the priest says:

"May the Body of our Lord Jesus Christ keep my soul unto life everlasting."

The priest reverently receives the Host. He then pauses for a short time in meditation. Then, he uncovers the chalice,

genuflects, purifies the paten over the chalice, and says:

"What return shall I make to the Lord for all He hath given me: I will take the chalice of salvation, and I will call upon the name of the Lord. Praising I will call upon the Lord, and I shall be saved from my enemies."

Making the Sign of the Cross with the chalice, he says:

"May the Blood of our Lord Jesus Christ keep my soul unto life everlasting. Amen."

The priest then receives the Precious Blood from the chalice.

<u>Communion of the People</u>

The people say the Confiteor, then the priest turns to the people and asks God to forgive them.

"May almighty God have mercy upon you, forgive you your sins, and bring you to life everlasting. Amen."

Making the Sign of the Cross over the people, he continues.

"May the almighty and merciful God grant you pardon, + absolution, and full remission of your sins. Amen."

Having turned back to the altar, the priest takes the ciborium, turns again and faces the people, holding one of the hosts a little above the ciborium so that all may see it, and says:

"Behold the Lamb of God, behold Him who taketh away the sins of the world. (All the people say 3 times) Lord I am not worthy that Thou shouldest come under my roof; but only say the word and my soul will be healed."

As he places the Host on the tongue or in the hand of each person, the priest says:

"Receive the Body of Christ."

<u>Ablutions</u>

The priest purifies the chalice with a little wine, which

is poured into the chalice by the server while the priest says:

"What has passed our lips as food, O Lord, may we possess in purity of heart, that what is given us in time may become our healing for eternity."

At the Epistle side the server pours a little wine and water over the priest's fingers into the chalice, as the priest says:

"May Thy Body, O Lord, which I have eaten, and Thy Blood, which I have drunk, cleave unto my very soul, and grant that no trace of sin be found in me, whom these pure and holy mysteries have renewed. Who livest and reignest world without end. Amen."

The priest drinks from and dries the chalice. He then covers it with the veil, goes to the book on the altar, and reads the Communion Antiphon from the missal.

"The Lord will give goodness, and our earth shall yield her fruit."

The priest turns to the people and says:

"The Lord be with you. (People reply) And with they spirit."

The priest then reads post-communion prayers and gives the last blessing:

"May God almighty bless you: the Father, the Son, + and the Holy Ghost. Amen."

Communion Service from the Universal Spiritualist's Manual

The table is set with a white cloth. Wafers of unleavened bread and red wine or grape juice shall be provided. One wafer is to be placed on a small paten, the rest, sufficient to

serve all who are to partake, is on a large plate or tray. A tray with a sufficient number of small individual cups filled with the wine or juice is on the table along with an empty chalice and two small pitchers (one of the pitchers contains wine or juice, the other a small amount of water). A cover-cloth of gauze or bridal veiling may cover the table and its contents and is to be removed at the time of the offertory.

THE ORDER OF WORSHIP

The parts in parentheses may be omitted.

(MUSICAL PRELUDE)
(PROCESSIONAL)
CALL TO WORSHIP

"Blessed are they that hunger and thirst after righteousness, for they shall be filled. I am the bread of life, saith the Lord. He that cometh to Me shall not hunger, and he that believeth on Me shall never thirst."

HYMN (congregation standing)
INVOCATION
CONFESSION OF FAITH
THE GLORIA
SCRIPTURE
OFFERTORY

OFFERTORY SENTENCE

"The Holy Supper is kept, indeed, in what we share with another's needs; not what we give, but what we share, for the gift without the giver is bare. Who gives himself with his alms feeds three - himself, his hungering neighbor, and Me.

The ushers will wait upon you for your love offering.

THE INGATHERING OF GIFTS

The ushers approach the table, remove the veiling, take the collection plates or baskets and begin passing them. The minister goes to stand behind the table, facing the

74

congregation. **While the offering is being collected by the ushers, a hymn or anthem may be sung by choir or people, or special music may be provided.**

OFFERTORY ACTS AND PRAYERS

The ushers shall come before the communion table with the gifts of the people. The minister shall stretch forth his/her hands in blessing toward the gifts and say:

> "All things come of Thee, O Lord, and of Thine own have we given them."

The minister receives the plates from the ushers, places them upon the table and says:

> "With these gifts we bring Thee, O Lord, our grateful hearts for all Thy goodness to us."

The minister takes the paten containing a wafer of bread, offers it by lifting it chin high with both hands, and says:

> "We offer unto Thee this token of Thine own life-giving gifts bestowed upon us."

He/she replaces the paten, then pours wine and a little water into the chalice, saying:

> "According to immemorial custom, we now mix water with this wine, praying Thee, O Lord, that we may evermore abide in Thee and Thou in us."

The minister then offers the chalice by lifting it chin high with both hands, saying:

> "We offer unto Thee, O Lord, this chalice with joy and gladness. May the worship which we offer ascend before Thy divine majesty as a sacrifice, pure and acceptable in Thy sight. Amen."

The minister returns to the pulpit and the ushers return to the back of the church, taking with them the plates of gifts.

(ANNOUNCEMENTS)
(HYMN OR SPECIAL MUSIC)
(THE MESSAGE SERVICE)

The minister now says:

"After this next hymn we shall observe the ordinance of the Lord's Supper. Whosoever his spirit inviteth, we beseech to tarry with us, in remembrance of Christ's sacrifice for us. However, those who so wish may leave while the hymn is being sung."

HYMN OF INVITATION (congregation standing)

INVOCATION OF ANGELS

"Guide us, O Almighty Father, in all our doings, and from Thy heavenly throne send down Thy holy angels to be with us, Thy people, who are met together to serve and worship Thee. Metatron, Angel of the Presence; Raphael, Divine Physician; Michael, Like Unto God; Gabriel, Potent of God; Auriel, Light of God; Sandalphon, Angel of the Gate; be with us or send thy ministers to be with us as we celebrate the last supper of Him who is Lord of angels and of men. Amen."

THE INVITATION, to be said by the minister before coming to the table, in these or other suitable words:

"We are now about to observe Holy Communion. This table of the Lord is open to all fellow Christians; and although none should partake of these sacred elements impenitent or without faith in Christ, we cordially invite all who are sincerely seeking Him to come to His table in the assurance that He Who came into the world to be the saviour of all will in no wise cast them out.

Come to this sacred table, not because you must, but because you may; come to testify not that you are righteous, but that you sincerely love our Lord Christ and desire to be His true disciple. Come, not because you are strong, but because you are weak; not because you have any claim on heaven's rewards, but because in your frailty you stand in constant need of heaven's mercy and help. Come not to express an opinion, but to seek a presence."

COMMUNION HYMN

The minister shall say, with the people joining in, the Confiteor:

"O Lord, Thou hast created man to be immortal and made him to be an image of Thine own eternity; yet often we forget the glory of our heritage and wander from the path which leads to righteousness. But Thou, O Lord, has made us for Thyself and our hearts are ever restless till they find their rest in Thee. Look with the eyes of Thy love upon our manifold imperfections and pardon all our shortcomings, that we may be filled with the brightness of the everlasting light and become the unspotted mirror of Thy power and the image of goodness; through Christ our Lord. Amen."

Then the minister, making the gesture of the Benediction, shall say:

THE ABSOLUTION

"God the Father, God the Son, God the Holy Ghost, bless, preserve and sanctify you; the Lord in His loving kindness look down upon you and be gracious unto you; the Lord absolve you from all your sins and grant you the grace and comfort of the Holy Spirit. Amen."

The minister now goes to stand behind the communion table facing the congregation, saying or singing, with the people joining in:

THE INTROIT

"Blessed be the Holy Trinity, the undivided Unity, eternal, immortal, invisible, to whom be honor and glory for ever and ever. Amen. O Lord our God, how excellent is Thy name in all the world. Glory be to the Father and to the Son and to the Holy Ghost. As it was in the beginning, is now, and ever shall be, world without end. Amen. Blessed be the Holy Trinity, the undivided Unity, eternal, immortal, invisible, to whom be honor and glory for ever and ever. Amen."

WORDS OF INSTITUTION, to be said by the minister standing at the table:

"Our Lord Jesus Christ, on the day before He suffered, took bread **(here the minister takes the paten containing the single wafer into his hands)** and when He had given thanks **(minister places paten on the table)** He brake it **(the minister breaks the wafer on the paten)** and gave it to His disciples **(here the minister lays his/her hand upon all the bread) saying:** Take and eat ye all of this, for THIS IS MY BODY **(here he/she lifts with both hands the paten high then returns it to the table).** In like manner, after supper, He took the Cup **(minister takes chalice into hands, pauses, then returns it to the table)** and when He had given thanks, He gave it to His disciples **(here minister lays hands on tray of individual glasses)** saying: Take and drink ye all of this, for THIS IS MY BLOOD **(here lifts with both hands the chalice high then returns it to the table).** As oft as ye shall do these things, ye shall do them in remembrance of Me. Let us pray."

THE PRAYER OF CONSECRATION

"Wherefore, O most loving Father, we Thy servants do pray Thee, through Christ our Lord, to receive (Sign of Cross), to purify (Sign of Cross), and to hallow (Sign of Cross), this oblation which we make unto Thee. We desire to offer this holy sacrifice first for Thy holy universal Church; likewise that it may please Thee to bless and keep all Thy people, to give them increase of grace to bring forth the fruits of the Spirit. We do also call to mind all who in this transitory life are in trouble, sorrow, need, sickness, or other adversity, (especially........................). Likewise do we offer it for all those Thy children whom it hath pleased Thee to deliver from the burden of the flesh (especially for ....), that, freed from earthly toil and care, they may enjoy the felicity of heaven. Amen."

THE LORD'S PRAYER, to be said by all.

THE COMMUNION

"Let us eat of this bread in remembrance of Christ; and may the life which was in Him be in us also." **(The minister partakes of the bread.)** "Let us drink of this Cup in remembrance of Christ; and may the spirit in which He died be our spirit." **(The minister partakes of the wine.)**

The minister thus first receives Holy Communion himself, then proceeds to deliver the same to any clergy present. Then he says to the people:

"Ye that desire to partake, draw nigh and receive this most holy sacrament."

The people come forward and receive into their hands, first the bread, then the wine. As he administers the Holy Communion, the minister says:

"Take and eat this in remembrance that Christ died for you, and feed on Him in thy heart by faith with thanksgiving.

Drink this in remembrance that Christ's blood was shed for you, and be thankful."

BENEDICTION

"Now the God of peace, who brought again from the dead our Lord Jesus, that great Shepherd of the sheep, through the blood of the everlasting covenant, make you perfect in every good work to do His will, working in you that which is well-pleasing in His sight; through Christ our Lord, to whom be glory for ever and ever. Amen."

DOXOLOGY
(RECESSIONAL)
(POSTLUDE)

From the Liturgy of the Liberal Catholic Church

This is usually done in conjunction with a mass.

THE PRAYER OF CONSECRATION

The priest continues, using either of the following alternative wordings:

"O Lord, these our ablations have served as tokens and channels of our love and devotion towards Thee; but now we + break the link with us and with all lower things and we pray Thee to + purify and to + hallow them as earthly channels of Thy wondrous power."

OR

"O Lord, these our oblations have served as tokens and channels of our love and devotion towards Thee; but now we pray Thee to + receive, to + purify and to + hallow them as earthly channels of Thy wondrous power."

*****

"We desire to offer this holy sacrifice especially for Thy holy catholic church, for (Name of head of state), our Bishop, for all our bishops, clergy and faithful, for those here present and for all who in this transitory life are in trouble, sorrow, need, sickness, or any other adversity (especially ....) and for those who are about to enter this earthly life through the portal of birth; and likewise for their mothers-to-be. Likewise do we offer it for all those Thy children whom it hath pleased Thee to deliver from the burden of the flesh (especially for ....) that, freed from earthly toil and care, they may enjoy the felicity of the presence, evermore praising Thee in word and deed, O God everlasting, living and true."

With his/her hands spread over the offerings, the minister continues:

"Wherefore, O holy Lord, Father almighty, we pray

80

Thee to look down on and accept as a channel these offerings and with Thy Holy Spirit and Word to + bless, + approve and + ratify them that they may become for us the most precious + Body and + Blood of Thy Son.

Who the day before He suffered took bread into His holy and venerable hands and, with His eyes lifted up to heaven unto Thee, God, His almighty Father, giving thanks to Thee, He + blessed, brake and gave it to His disciples, saying: Take and eat ye all of this, for

THIS IS MY BODY

In like manner, after He had supped, taking also this noble chalice into His holy and venerable hands, again giving thanks to Thee, He + blessed it and gave it to His disciples, saying: Take and drink ye all of this, for

THIS IS MY BLOOD

As oft as ye shall do these things, ye shall do them in remembrance of Me."

After some moments of silent adoration, the following verse shall be sung very softly, all devoutly kneeling:

Thee we adore, O hidden splendor, Thee,
Who in Thy sacrament dost deign to be;
we worship Thee beneath this earthly veil
and here Thy presence we devoutly hail.

After a short pause, sing another hymn then the people kneel.

"Wherefore, O Lord and heavenly Father, we Thy humble servants do offer unto Thee this, the most precious gift which Thou has bestowed upon us, in token of our + love and of the perfect + devotion and + sacrifice of our + minds and + hearts to Thee; and we pray that Thou wouldst command Thy holy angel to bear our oblation to Thine altar on high, there to be offered by Him Who, as the eternal High Priest, for ever offers Himself as the eternal sacrifice."

The people may be seated.

"And we do pray for Thy servant who ministers at this altar, that meetly celebrating the mysteries of the most holy + Body and + Blood of Thy Son, he/she may be + filled with Thy mighty power and blessing."

The priest makes this last cross upon himself.

"Likewise we pray Thee to sanctify Thy people here present with these Thy heavenly gifts and through these mysteries do Thou + hallow, + quicken and + bless them, that both in their hearts and in their lives they may show forth Thy praise and glorify Thy holy name."

The priest makes with the host the sign of the cross three times over the chalice.

"All these things do we ask, O Father, in the name and through the mediation of Thy most blessed Son, for we acknowledge and confess with our hearts and lips that + by Him were all things made, yea, all things both in heaven and earth, + with Him as the indwelling life do all things exist and + in Him as the transcendent glory all things live and move and have their being."

Then horizontally twice between the chalice and his breast:

"To whom with Thee, O mighty + Father, in the unity of the Holy + Spirit, be ascribed all honor and glory, throughout the ages of ages." (Congregation replies....Amen.)

The priest here holds the host directly over the chalice and raises both to the level of his eyes.

THE COMMUNION

Priest says: "Let us pray. Instructed by the words of sacred scripture and following the tradition of the holy church from old, we now say the Our Father."

ALL NOW SAY THE OUR FATHER.

THE COMMEMORATION OF THE SAINTS

Priest: Here do we give unto Thee, O Lord, most high praise and heartfelt thanks for the wonderful grace and virtue declared in the holy Lady Mary, our heavenly Mother, and in all Thy glorious saints from the beginning of the world who have been the choice vessels of Thy grace and a shining light unto many generations.

Here the priest crosses himself with the paten.

"And we + join with them in worship before Thy great white throne, whence flow all love and light and blessing through all the worlds which Thou has made.

O Son of God, who showest Thyself this day upon a thousand altars and yet art one and indivisible, in token of Thy great sacrifice we break this Thy Body."

Here he breaks the host in half over the chalice and with a small particle thereof makes the sign of the cross thrice over the chalice and finally at the words 'one in Thee' drops the particle into the chalice.

"We pray that by this action, ordained from of old, Thy + strength, Thy + peace and Thy + blessing, which Thou dost give us in this holy sacrament, may be spread abroad upon Thy world; and as Thou, O Lord Christ, wast made known to Thy disciples in the breaking of bread, so may Thy many children know themselves to be one in Thee, even as Thou are one with the Father." (Congregation replies ......Amen.)

THE SALUTATION OF PEACE

The priest faces the people and, with outstretched arms, says or sings:

Priest: The peace of the Lord be always with you.
Congregation: And with thy spirit.

Priest: "O Thou Who in this adorable sacrament has left us a living memorial and pledge of Thy marvelous love for mankind and dost therein graciously draw us into wondrous and mystic communion with Thee, grant us so to receive the sacred mysteries of Thy Body and Blood that our souls may be lifted into the immensity of Thy love and that, being filled with a high endeavor, we may ever be mindful of Thine indwelling Presence and breathe forth the fragrance of a holy life. Amen."

The priest communicates in both kinds, then administers to the clergy and servers. The people meanwhile may say privately the following prayer:

"Unto Thee, O Perfect One, the Lord and love of men, do we commend our life and hope. For Thou art the heavenly bread, the life of the whole world; Thou art in all places and endurest all things, the treasury of endless good and the well of infinite compassion."

After the priest and those in the sanctuary have received holy communion, the priest, with a particle, blesses the people, as he says:

"+ Ye that desire to partake of the body of the Lord, draw nigh and receive this most holy sacrament."

The people should come forward to the communion rail and kneel. As he administers the holy communion to each, the priest says:

"The Body + of our Lord Christ keep thee unto life eternal."

The communion being ended, the priest says:

"Under the veil of earthly things now have we communion with our Lord Jesus Christ; soon with open face shall we behold Him and, rejoicing in His glory, be made like unto Him. Then shall His true disciples be brought by Him with exceeding joy before the presence of His Father's glory."

All stand and sing:

"Amen. Blessing and glory and wisdom and thanksgiving and honor and power and might be unto our God for ever and ever. Amen."

POSTCOMMUNION

Priest: Let us pray. **(The people kneel.)** We who have been refreshed with Thy heavenly gifts do pray Thee, O Lord, that Thy grace may be so grafted inwardly in our hearts that it may continually be made manifest in our lives; through Christ our Lord.
Congregation: Amen.

Priest: The Lord be with you.
Congregation: And with thy spirit.

Priest: The mass is over.
Congregation: Thank God.

THE BENEDICTION

Priest: The peace of God, which passeth all understanding, keep your hearts and minds in the knowledge and love of God and of His Son, Christ our Lord; and the blessing of God almighty, the Father, + the Son and the Holy Ghost, be amongst you and remain with you always.
Congregation: Amen.

MARRIAGE

In Christian marriage the union of husband and wife is a beautiful symbol of the union of Christ and His Church. The mutual exchange of consent, by which the two spouses enter into the married state, is also a sacrament, that is, a vehicle for Christ's grace. This sacrament is administered by the two parties themselves; the priest, who asks for their expression of consent, is merely an official witness. The grace of the sacrament in the souls

Used with permission from Catholic Press

of the husband and wife will enable them to fulfill the duties of married life.

From **"The Meaning and Value of the Sacraments"** by Rev. Flower Newhouse of **THE CHRISTWARD MINISTRY** is taken the **"Symbolic Meaning of Marriage."**

"Most beloved of the sacraments is the one of marriage. It symbolizes the fulfillment of earth's sweetest dream. We should be trained for marriage from childhood, so that the noblest and finest traits are developed to care for and companion one's helpmate. Individuals about to be wedded should consider how they can purify and discipline themselves before and after marriage, and their personal preferences and traits that may need understanding on the part of the other partner. These topics should be condensed and put into a notebook which will be reviewed each anniversary or whenever an occasion warrants.

Almost any sensitive person can testify to the emergence of power that is broadcast during a marriage ceremony. This force is created by the beauty and intent of the rite itself. The spiritual fusion of two individualities into a duad of love generates an energy and luminosity that reaches even the most impersonal onlooker. As in other sacraments, the Host is represented by the Angel of the Christ Presence. It is this Being who seals the pledges of the couple and who sends forth the flashing beam when the celebrant utters words of this kind. 'I join you together in marriage in the name of the Father, and of the Son, and of the Holy Ghost.'"

Roman Catholic - The Sacrament of Matrimony

Those to be married, accompanied by at least two witnesses, come before the officiating priest, and clearly answer his inquiries as to their consent. (Before asking and receiving their consent, the priest usually gives a short exhortation to the two parties on the dignity and duties of the married state.) The priest first inquires of the bridegroom, then of the bride.

Priest: (Name of groom), wilt thou take (Name of bride) here present, for thy lawful wife, according to the rite of our Holy Mother, the Church?

Groom: I will.

He then asks about the bride's consent with the same question.

Priest: (Name of bride), wilt thou take (Name of groom) here present, for thy lawful husband, according to the rite of our Holy Mother, the Church?

Bride: I will.

After they have expressed their consent, the priest bids them join their right hands. Then, according to a common custom in many places, he asks them to pledge faith to each other in the following form, which is repeated by both husband and wife:

"I, (Name) take thee, (Name) for my lawful wife (husband), to have and to hold from this day forward, for better, for worse, for richer, for poorer, in sickness and in health, till death do us part."

While their hands are joined, the priest says these words:

"I unite you in marriage, in the name of the Father, and of the Son, and of the Holy Ghost. Amen."

He sprinkles them with holy water. Then he blesses the ring.

Priest: Our help is in the name of the Lord.
Response: Who made heaven and earth.

Priest: Lord, hear my prayer.
Response: And let my cry come unto Thee.

Priest: The Lord be with you.
Response: And with your spirit.

Priest: Let us pray. Bless, + O Lord, this ring, upon which we invoke a blessing + in Thy name; that she who is to wear it, being true to her husband in all things, may abide in peace according to Thy will, and live with him always in well-requited affection. Through Christ, our Lord.
Response: Amen. **(If it is a double ring ceremony, use the plural noun in the above prayer.)**

The priest sprinkles the ring(s) with holy water and gives it to the bridegroom, who places it on the bride's finger, saying.

"With this ring I thee wed, and promise thee my fidelity."

(Repeat for bride to give groom a ring.)

Priest: In the name of the Father, and of the Son + and of the Holy Ghost. Amen. **The priest continues:**

Priest: Preserve, O Lord, what Thou has wrought in us.
Response: From out Thy holy Temple, which is in Jerusalem.

Priest: Lord, have mercy on us.
Response: Christ have mercy on us.

Priest: Lord have mercy on us. Our Father, etc.
Response: Amen.

Priest: Save Thy servants.
Response: Who hope in Thee, my God.

Priest: Send them help from Thy holy place, O Lord.
Response: And out of Sion defend them.

Priest: Be unto them, O Lord, a tower of strength.
Response: From the face of the enemy.

Priest: Lord, hear my prayer.
Response: And let my cry come unto Thee.

Priest: The Lord be with you.
Response: And with your spirit.

Priest: Let us pray. Look with favor, we beseech Thee, O Lord, upon these Thy servants, and deign in Thy goodness to protect the institution which Thou hast established for the increase of the human race, that those who are now made one according to Thy will, may be safeguarded by Thy protection. Through Christ our Lord.
Response: Amen.

This ends the marriage ceremony but is usually followed by a mass.

⤳

Marriage of Best Friends

The minister begins with the following poetry:

"When the evening sky is painted crimson by the
    setting sun,
The birds all cease to twitter, knowing the day is
    done.
It is then we like to ponder, and forgetting worldly
strife,

Realize that love and friendship are the greatest things
    in life."

"It is indeed wonderful that two **BEST FRIENDS** have come together before their families and friends to declare their love and friendship and sanctify it with marriage. Marriage is the union of two divinities......... It is the union of two souls in a strong love for the <u>abolishment of separateness</u>. It is the higher unity which fuses the separate unities within the two spirits. It is the golden ring in a chain whose beginning is a glance, and whose ending is E T E R N I T Y......"

And the Prophet said: (poem from Kahlil Gabran)

"You were born together, and together you shall be forever more.
You shall be together when the white wings of death scatter your days.
Aye, you shall be together even in the silent memory of THE GREAT CONSCIOUSNESS.
But let there be spaces in your togetherness,
And let the winds of the heavens dance between you.
Love one another, but make not a bond of love;
Let it rather be a moving sea between the shores of your souls.
Fill each other's cup but drink not from one cup.
Give one another of your bread but eat not from the same loaf.
Sing and dance together and be joyous, but let each one of you   be alone,
Even as the strings of a lute are alone though they quiver with the same music.

Give your hearts, but not into each other's keeping.
For only the hand of Life can contain your hearts.
And stand together yet not too near together;
For the pillars of the temple stand apart,
And the oak tree and the cypress grow not in each other's shadow."

MUSICAL INTERLUDE

(Lights & candles) **Have at least two lighted candles and one unlighted candle on the altar or if the wedding is in a**

garden or home, then have the candles on a small table.

Minister: We stand here surrounded by lighted candles which are symbolic of the cosmic creation and of the light and truth in the human mind and soul. You are about to make your pledges to one another.

The Minister hands a lighted candle first to the bride and then one to the groom.

Minister: Take into your beings the warmth, radiance and light that each flame represents. Let them light your way on the journey of life you will now travel together.

The bride and groom together light the unlighted candle with their candles and then place their candles back on the altar or table.

Minister picks up the wine cup and holds it up while saying:

"Wine is the symbol of the spiritual nature of love and wisdom. It is the fruit of the vine and "the tree of life". Together, partake of the juice of the tree of life and gladden your hearts and souls as you journey upon your paths. Enjoy the fruits of life for LIFE IS THE COSMIC GIFT."

The Minister now offers the cup to the bride, who drinks, and then to the groom who drinks from the cup and replaces it on the tray.

"As you have shared the wine from this cup, so may you draw contentment, comfort and felicity from the cup of life. May you find life's joys heightened. Its bitterness sweetened, and all things hallowed by true companionship and love."

The Minister blesses the rings.

"May the blessing of God, the Father almighty, the Son and the Holy Ghost be upon these rings. The ring is a circle and is the symbol of the UNIVERSE - THE ALL -INFINITY. It is also the symbol of completeness, peace, unbroken harmony and endless friendship. These two rings are the symbol of the unity in which your two lives have been joined in one unbroken circle."

The Minister hands the bride's ring to the groom and says: "Your pledges, please."

Groom, as he puts the ring on the bride: I give you this ring to wear upon your hand as a symbol of our unity. You are my beloved and my friend. I take you to be my wife, together to love, to work, to share, and to discover a deeper, fuller and richer life.

The Minister hands the groom's ring to the bride and she says: I give you this ring to wear upon your hand as a symbol of our unity. You are my beloved and my friend. I take you to be my husband, together to love, to work, to share, and to discover a deeper, fuller and richer life.

Minister continues: Your rings always represent the unbroken circle of love given and received in freedom. Now let each person assembled here offer in his or her own way a silent prayer that the merged spirit of this gathering engulf and bless the union of (Name of bride) and (Name of groom).

In as much as _____ and _____ have grown in knowledge, respect, and love of one another; because they have agreed in their desire to travel forward in life together seeking an ever richer, deepening relationship and because they pledged themselves to meet all of life's experiences together, we their families and friends, rejoice. May all that is noble, true, enriching, creative and beautiful be with you both, always.

In the presence of this company as witness, you have spoken the words and performed the rites which unite your lives. I therefore, declare you _____ and _____ husband and wife, married in accordance with the laws of the State of _____.

As kisses are messengers of love, KISS NOW! And let soul meet soul on your lover's lips.

92

Minister says to those gathered: You may now congratulate the happy couple.

BEST MAN MAKE TOAST
MUSIC BEGINS AND SO DOES THE JOURNEY.

Holy Matrimony
(From the Liberal Catholic Church)

Christ did not institute marriage, but the sacrament blessing such marriage. This is intended to help the parties to live together in a state of love and mutual aid. When they have pledged their love and fidelity to each other in the presence of Christ, the priest blesses them in His name. The ring, which is the symbol of their spiritual union, is also blessed.

Invocation

"Dearly beloved, we are gathered together here in the sight of God, and in the face of this congregation, to join this man and this woman in holy matrimony, which is an honorable estate, not by any to be entered into unadvisedly, lightly, or wantonly, but reverently, discreetly, advisedly, and soberly, in the sight of God. Into which estate these two persons now come to be joined. Therefore, if any man can show any just cause why they may not lawfully be joined together, let him now speak or else hereafter forever hold his peace."

No impediment being alleged, the celebrant questions the man and woman separately concerning their consent to marry.

Celebrant: (To the man) Wilt thou, (name) take (name) here present for thy lawful wife according to the rite of our holy mother the church?

Groom answers: I will.

Celebrant: (To the woman) Wilt thou, (name) take (name) here present for thy lawful husband according to the rite of our holy mother the church?

Bride answers: I will.

The rings are placed on a tray, the celebrant sprinkles them with holy water in the form of the cross and then blesses them, saying:

"Bless + O Lord and + hallow these rings, that they who shall wear them may ever keep true faith unto one another, and so, abiding in Thy peace and in conformity to Thy holy will, may ever live in love unchanging; through Christ our Lord. Amen."

Celebrant: Who giveth this woman to be married to this man?

The bride is then given away by her father or friend, who places her right hand in that of the priest, who in turn bestows her upon the bridegroom with the words:

"Receive the precious gift of God."

(If there is no one to give the bride away, the bride herself may place her right hand in that of the priest.)

The bridegroom, taking her right hand in his, receives her, to keep her in God's faith and his own. Then shall the bridegroom give the bride his promise in these words, repeated by him after the celebrant:

"I (name) take thee, (name) to be my wedded wife (husband), to have and to hold, from this day forward, for better, for worse, for richer, for poorer, in sickness and in health, to love, to cherish and to honor; and thereunto, in the presence of God and in the power and love of Christ our Lord and Master, I plight thee my troth. Amen."

The bride repeats the above pledge.

The celebrant then hands the bride's ring to the groom who places it on her finger, repeating after the celebrant:

"In the name of the Father, and the Son, and the Holy Ghost with this ring I thee wed; my truest love I thee pledge; with my body I give thee reverence, and with all my heart I thee enfold. Amen."

The bride repeats the above, putting the ring on the groom.

The celebrant joins their right hands and, after touching the forehead of the man and woman with holy water, says:

"I join you together in marriage in the name of the Father + and of the Son and of the Holy Ghost. Amen."

Covering their joined hands with the end of his stole, he adds:

"Those whom God hath joined together, let no man seek to put asunder."

Then the celebrant speaks to the people:

"For as much as (name of bride) and (name of groom) have consented together in holy wedlock and have witnessed the same before God and this company and thereto have given and pledged their troth each to the other and have declared the same by giving and receiving rings and by joining of hands; I declare to you that they be husband and wife together, in the name of the Father, and of the Son and of the Holy Ghost. Amen."

The newly married pair kneel.

Celebrant: O Lord, bless Thy servant and Thy handmaid.
Congregation: Who put their trust in Thee.

Celebrant: Pour forth upon them of the fullness of Thy love.
Congregation: And lighten them with Thy heavenly grace.

Celebrant: Send them wisdom from Thy sanctuary.
Congregation: And do Thou dwell in their understanding.

Celebrant: Be unto them, O Lord, a tower of strength.
Congregation: And evermore defend them.

Celebrant: The Lord be with you.
Congregation: And with thy spirit.

Celebrant: Let us pray.

"O eternal God, creator and preserver of all mankind, giver of all spiritual grace, the author of everlasting life, send Thy blessing upon these Thy servants, this man and this woman, whom we + bless in Thy name; that these persons may surely perform and keep the vow and covenant betwixt them made and may so hold their lives in the knowledge and love of Thee that they may dwell together in holy love and peace; through Christ our Lord. Amen.

Almighty God pour upon you the riches of His grace, sanctify and + bless you, that you may serve Him both in body and soul and live together in holy love unto your lives' end. Amen."

The couple rise and greet the congregation.

ANOINTING THE SICK

In all societies there have been practices of praying for the sick and an anointing of the bodies of the sick to aid in their state of mind (peacefulness).

Liberal Catholic Church

This Form of Healing Service is intended to be used ministering to the sick in their homes, in hospitals or privately in the

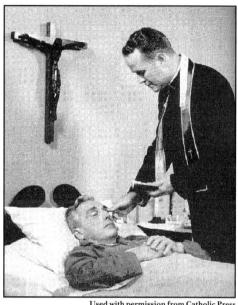

Used with permission from Catholic Press

church at times when the public is not attending. The priest wears a green stole.

THE INVOCATION

Priest: In the name of the Father + and of the Son and of the Holy Ghost. Amen.

The priest now touches the forehead of the patient with holy water and sprinkles his surroundings.

Priest: I pray our heavenly Father that He will send His healing angel to minister unto this His servant that he/she may be restored to health of mind and body; through Christ our Lord. Amen.

CONFITEOR

The sick person should now recite the confiteor, or, if he feels his conscience troubled with any weighty matter, make a special confession (but without the usual form and preliminaries). If the patient be very weak, the confiteor may be said on his behalf by the priest or another, or it suffices

that he make a mental act of aspiration.

"O Lord, Thou hast created man to be immortal and made him to be an image of Thine own eternity; yet often we forget the glory of our heritage and wander from the path which leads to righteousness. But Thou, O Lord, hast made us for Thyself and our hearts are ever restless till they find their rest in Thee. Look with the eyes of Thy love upon my manifold imperfections and pardon all my shortcomings, that I may be filled with the brightness of the everlasting light and become the unspotted mirror of Thy power and the image of Thy goodness, through Christ our Lord. Amen."

THE ABSOLUTION

Priest: Our Lord Christ, Who hath left power on earth to His church to absolve all those that with hearty repentance and true faith turn unto Him, of His tender compassion forgive thee thine offences; and by His authority committed unto me I + absolve thee from all thy transgressions. In the name of the Father + and of the Son and of the Holy Ghost. Amen. The King of love and fountain of all goodness restore unto thee the fellowship of the Holy Spirit and give thee grace to continue in the same, that thou mayest inherit the kingdom of heaven and be made like unto His own pure and glorious image. Amen.

THE UNCTION

Priest: O Lord, Who hast given unto man bodily health and vigor to serve Thee, we pray Thee to free Thy servant from his/her sickness so far as may be expedient for him/her and by the might of Thy + blessing to restore unto him/her full health, both outwardly in body and inwardly in soul; through Christ our Lord. Amen.

The priest now says over the person:

"In the Name which is above every name, in the power of the + Father and of the + Son and of the Holy + Ghost, I exorcise all influences of evil, that thou mayest be rightly purified to receive this sacrament of holy unction."

Taking upon his thumb some of the oil for the sick, the priest anoints the person in the form of a cross upon the forehead, saying:

"In the Name of our Lord Christ and invoking the help of the holy Archangel Raphael, I + anoint thee with oil, that thou mayest gain refreshment both of soul and body."

The priest now proceeds to anoint, in the same manner as before but in silence, the centers at the top of the head, the front of the throat and the nape of the neck. He then places both hands upon the head of the person with the definite intent to heal, saying:

"Christ the Son of God pour down His healing power upon thee and enfold thee in the light of His love."

The priest administers holy communion to the patient saying:

"The Body of our Lord Christ keep thee unto life eternal. We who have been refreshed with Thy heavenly gifts do pray Thee, O Lord, that Thy grace may be so grafted inwardly in our hearts, that it may continually be made manifest in our lives; through Christ our Lord. Amen."

THE BENEDICTION

Priest: Unto God's gracious love and protection we commit you; the Lord + bless and keep you; the Lord make His face to shine upon you and be gracious to you; the Lord lift up the light of His countenance upon you and give you His peace, now and for evermore. Amen.

EXTREME UNCTION
(from Liturgy of the Liberal Catholic Church)

The purposes of the Sacrament of Holy Unction are: (a) to aid in the restoration of bodily health, (b) to prepare a person for death, (c) to which may be added remission of sin, since it also involves a form of absolution.

Extreme Unction is a form of unction which with the giving of holy communion, is used in the case of a person who appears to be about to die. The name is sometimes said to originate from the idea that it is the last of the unctions given to the ordinary Christian, those of Baptism and Confirmation preceding it.

If convenient, a table should be provided, covered with a linen cloth and bearing upon it a cross and two lighted candles. The priest wears a violet stole.

THE INVOCATION

Priest: In the name of the Father + and of the Son and of the Holy Ghost. Amen.

CONFITEOR

The priest should exhort the dying person to make a momentary act of contrition and then to turn with love and devotion to his Master. If the person be very weak, the Confiteor may be said on his behalf by the priest.

"O Lord, Thou has created man to be immortal and made him to be an image of Thine own eternity; yet often we forget the glory of our heritage and wander from the path which leads to righteousness. But Thou, Lord, has made us for Thyself and our hearts are ever restless till they find their rest in Thee. Look with the eyes of Thy love upon our manifold imperfections and pardon all our shortcomings, that we may be filled with the brightness of the everlasting light and become the unspotted mirror of Thy power and the image of Thy goodness; through Christ our Lord. Amen."

THE ABSOLUTION

Priest: Our Lord Christ, Who hath left power on earth to His church to absolve all those that with hearty repentance and true faith turn unto Him, of His tender compassion forgive thee thine offences; and by His authority committed unto me I + absolve thee from all thy sins. In the Name of the Father, + and of the Son, and of the Holy Ghost. Amen.

If the person is very weak or about to die, the priest pronounces the absolution using, if necessary, the following shortened form:

Priest: I + absolve thee from all thy transgressions, in the name of the Father + and of the Son and of the Holy Ghost. Amen.

THE UNCTION

Taking upon his thumb some of the holy oil for the sick, the priest anoints in the form of a cross the organs of sense, using the following words:

Priest: (Upon the closed eyelids) By this holy + unction and of His most tender love, the Lord pardon thee whatever faults thou has committed through seeing. Amen. **(Upon the ears)** By this holy + unction and of His most tender love, the Lord pardon thee whatever faults thou has committed through hearing. Amen. **(Upon the nostrils)** By this holy + unction and of His most tender love, the Lord pardon thee whatever faults thou has committed through smelling. Amen. **(upon the closed lips)** By this holy + unction and of His most tender love, the Lord pardon thee whatever faults thou has committed through tasting. Amen.

(Upon the inside of the palms of the hands but outside in the case of priests.) The feet and small of the back may also at this time be anointed but this is optional.

By this holy + unction and of His most tender love, the Lord pardon thee whatever faults thou has committed through touch. Amen.

(In cases of extremity, or at the option of the priest, the

forehead only need be anointed, with these words:)

By this holy + unction and of His most tender love, the Lord pardon thee whatever faults thou has committed through thy thoughts and desires and the senses of thy body. Amen.

The priest may now proceed to anoint the sacral plexus (at base of the spine), the spleen, the solar plexus, the heart, the front of throat and the center at the top of the head, in that order. Of these it is sufficient to anoint the last four or five, more especially if the person's infirmity be great.

If impracticable to reach any center the sign of the cross is made with the thumb (moist with oil) in the air as close as possible to the center with the intent to affect the center. The nape of the neck may be anointed in place of the sacral plexus.

VIATICUM

The viaticum is then given, unless there be danger of the body's rejecting or being unable to swallow, the sacred Host. The Host may be placed in a spoon and given with a little wine or water.

Priest: Brother (or sister), receive the viaticum of the most holy Body of our Lord Jesus Christ and may the peace of the Lord go with thee. Amen.

THE BENEDICTION

Priest: Unto God's gracious love and protection we commit you; the Lord + bless you and keep you; the Lord makes His face to shine upon you and be gracious to you; the Lord lift up the light of His countenance upon you and give you His peace, now and for evermore. Amen.

If death takes place, the priest may at once proceed to the absolution, as set forth in the order of the burial of the dead. In the absence of a priest, a deacon may administer

Extreme Unction. He uses the following form for the absolution:

Deacon: May the Lord + bless us and absolve us from all our transgressions; in the name of the Father + and of the Son and of the Holy Ghost. Amen. The grace of our Lord Jesus Christ and the love of God and the fellowship of the Holy Ghost, be with us all evermore. Amen.

ORDINATION

From the Universal Spiritualist Manual

THE ORDINATION OF MINISTERS

The sponsor, a minister of the Universal Spiritualist Association, escorts the ordinand to the chancel where the officiating minister stands. The sponsor shall say:

"Reverend _____, I present unto you this person, Deacon _____, to be admitted into the ministry of the Universal Spiritual Church."

The officiant says:

"Take heed that the person whom you present unto us be apt and meet, for his/her learning and godly conduct, to exercise his/her ministry duty, to the honor of God, and the edifying of the church."

The sponsor replies:

"We have inquired concerning him/her, and also examined him/her and believe him/her so to be."

The minister then charges the ordinand:

"Dearly beloved, it is now my part solemnly and for the last time, before the irrevocable act shall be accomplished which shall lay upon you the sweet but heavy burden of the ministry, to charge you how great is the dignity and responsibility of this office and how weighty are the duties to be performed by those ordained thereto. It appertains to the minister to offer sacrifice, to bless, to preside, to loose, and to bind, to anoint, to preach, and to baptize. Wherefore, dearly beloved, strive without ceasing to increase within yourself the perfection of heavenly love, that having your heart filled with love of God and man, you may be an almoner of God's blessing and a bearer of His love to the hearts of mankind. You whose

104

duty it is to offer unto God the sweet incense of prayer and adoration, let your teaching be a spiritual remedy unto God's people, let your words of blessing and consolation be their help and strength, let the sweet savor of your life be a fragrance in the church."

(Pause)

"Will you strive to use worthily the powers entrusted to you?"

Ordinand answers: "I will, so help me God."

The minister prays:

"Almighty, everlasting God, by Whose spirit the whole body of the church is made holy and governed, do Thou pour forth (makes Sign of Cross) Thy sanctifying grace into the heart of this Thy servant, that with pure heart, clean hands, and open mind, he/she may faithfully receive and transmit Thy blessing from on high. Amen."

The officiating minister lays aside this book and places both of his hands upon the head of the ordinand. At the same time the sponsor lays his or her right hand upon the head of the ordinand. The minister says:

"I ordain you a minister of the Universal Spiritual Church."

The minister and sponsor remove their hands. The minister takes back the Ritual book. The minister and sponsor then say together:

"You are ordained a priest after the Order of Melchizedek."

The minister hands the ordinand a Certificate of Ordination and says:

"Take thou the authority to exercise the functions and the duties of a minister. Dedicate yourself now as your first action as a minister."

The newly ordained minister then says a prayer of self-

dedication. Afterward the officiant says:

"Go forth, Reverend, to your work as a laborer for the Lord, for the fields are white for the harvest and few there be to labor therein."

(He raises his hand in benediction.)

"The Lord bless you and keep you, the Lord make His face to shine upon you, and be gracious unto you, the Lord lift up His countenance upon you, and give you peace. Amen."

From the Liturgy of the Liberal Catholic Church

The Ordination of Priests

The bishop celebrates the Holy Eucharist, at which the following special collect and epistle are used:

THE COLLECT

"Almighty, everlasting God, by Whose Spirit the whole body of the church is made holy and governed, do Thou pour forth Thy sanctifying grace into the hearts of these Thy servants, who are about to be numbered among the priests of Thy church, that with pure heart and open mind they may faithfully receive Thy blessing from on high; through Christ our Lord. Amen."

The collect of the day and such other collects as are usual follow here.

THE EPISTLE

The epistle is taken from the fifth chapter of the First Epistle General of St. Peter, beginning at the first verse.

"The elders which are among you I exhort, who am also an elder and a witness of the sufferings of Christ and also a partaker of the glory that shall be revealed: Feed the flock of God which is among you, taking the oversight thereof not by constraint, but willingly; not for filthy lucre, but of a ready mind; neither as being lords over God's heritage, but being examples to the flock. And when the Chief Shepherd shall appear, ye shall receive a crown of glory that fadeth not away. The God of all grace, Who hath called us unto His eternal glory by Christ Jesus, after that ye have suffered a while, make you perfect, establish, strengthen, settle you. To Him be glory and dominion for ever and ever. Amen."

The epistle and gradual being ended, the bishop takes his seat upon a footstool before the altar. All are seated, the ordinands come forward bearing lighted candles, and a priest appointed for the purpose presents them to the bishop, saying:

"Right Reverend Father, our holy mother the church catholic prays that you would ordain these deacons here present to the charge of the priesthood."

Bishop: Knowest thou them to be worthy?

Priest: As far as human frailty allows me to judge, I do both know and attest that they are worthy of the charge of this office.

Bishop: Thanks be to God.

The ordinands are then seated and the bishop charges the clergy and people as follows:

Bishop: "Dearly beloved brethren, as both the captain of a ship and the passengers it carries have equal cause for security or for fear, it behooves them whose interests are common to be of one mind. Nor was it without purpose that the Fathers decreed that the people also should be consulted touching the election of those who are to be employed in the service of the altar, for what is unknown of the many concerning the life and conversation of those who are presented, may oft-times be known to a few and all will necessarily yield a more ready obedience to one when ordained, to whose ordination they have signified their assent. If, then, any one has aught to the prejudice of these men, in the name of God and for the benefit of His church, let him boldly come forward and speak, however, let him be mindful of his own estate."

After a pause, the bishop, addressing himself to the ordinands, charges them as follows:

Bishop: "Dearly beloved sons, it is now our part solemnly and for the last time, before the irrevocable act shall be accomplished which shall lay upon you the sweet but heavy burden of the priesthood, to charge you how great is the dignity and responsibility of this office and how weighty are the duties to be performed by those ordained thereto. It appertains to the priest to offer sacrifice, to bless, to preside, to loose and to bind, to anoint, to preach, and to baptize.

Wherefore, dearly beloved sons, whom the award of our brethren has chosen that you may be consecrated to this office as our helpers, after solemn premeditation only and with great awe is so sublime an office to be approached and great indeed must be the care with which we determine that they who are chosen to represent our blessed Lord and to preside in His church commend themselves by great wisdom, by worthiness of life and the persevering practice of justice and truth. Do you, then, dearly beloved sons, keep these things in remembrance and let the fruit thereof be seen in your walk and conversation, in chaste and holy integrity of life, in continually abounding in all manner of good works. Strive without ceasing to increase within yourselves the perfection of heavenly love that, having your hearts filled with the love of God and of man, you may be almoners of Christ's blessing and bearers of His love to the hearts of mankind. Forget never how great a privilege is yours to bring the little ones to Him through the gateway of baptism and to lift the heavy burden of the sorrow and sin of the world by the grace of absolution. Consider attentively what you do; imitate those things which in the church of God it is your duty to handle and to transact. And forasmuch as you will now be called upon to offer the holy sacrifice before the throne of God and to celebrate the sacred mysteries of the Lord's love, be earnest in ridding your members of all imperfections. Ye whose duty it is to offer unto God the sweet incense of prayer and adoration, let your teaching be a spiritual remedy unto God's people; let your words of blessing and consolation be their help and strength; let the sweet savor of your life be a fragrance in the church of God.

Thus both by what word and deed may you fashion the temple of God, so that neither shall we appear blameworthy before the Lord, who in His name shall thus advance you, nor ye who shall be advanced; but rather may we all find acceptance and abundant recompense for this day's act, which of His infinite goodness and loving kindness may He deign to grant."

The ordinands rise.

Bishop: Will you thus strive to use worthily the powers entrusted to you?

Ordinands: I will.

Bishop: The Lord keep you in all these things, well beloved sons, and strengthen you in all goodness. Amen.

The bishop rises and addresses the people as follows:

Bishop: Let us pray, dearest brethren, that almighty God, in His great loving kindness and watchful care over His church, may bestow a plentiful grace on these deacons, now about to be raised to the order of the priesthood.

THE LITANY

All kneel and sing the following litany, during which the ordinands lie prostrate.

God the Father, seen of none.
God the co-eternal Son,
God the Spirit, with them one;
    Hear us, Holy Trinity.

God eternal, mighty King,
Unto Thee our love we bring,
Through the world Thy praises ring;
    We are Thine, O Trinity.

Christ, the Lord of life and light,
Ruler of the starry height,
Fount of glory infinite;
    Thee we worship, Master.

Mighty Lord, we hail Thee here,
Recognize Thy presence dear,
Feel and know that Thou are near,
    Keeping thus Thy promise.

Though Thy face we cannot see
As of old in Galilee,
Strong in faith we worship Thee,
    Ever present Master.

From our fathers we have heard
Of the gift Thy hand conferred;
We have proved Thy holy word;
    Be that gift outpoured.

Though Thy form from earth hath gone,
Thine apostles handed on
Sacramental blessing;
    Be that blessing with us.

We this power would now convey,
Strengthen Thou our hands, we pray,
Pour Thy might through us today;
    Hear us, Holy Master.

Monarch, at Thy feet we kneel,
For Thy servants we appeal,
Fill their hearts with holy zeal;
    In Thy service, Master.

Thou of holy church the head,
Mystic power upon them shed,
By Thy love may they be led;
    Hear us, Holy Master.

Link in mystic bond with Thee
These Thy priests that they may be
From the world and self set free,
    By Thy power, O Master.

May they stand before Thy face
Filled with love and heavenly grace;
Grant them with Thy saints a place
    Near Thee, Lord and Master.

The three verses which follow are sung by the bishop alone:

We beseech Thee, hear our prayer;
Bless + Thy servants prostrate there;
Hold them in Thy loving care;
    Hear us, Holy Trinity.

Hear Thy servants as they pray;
Help Thy chosen priests today,
Bless + and + hallow them for aye;
    Hear us, Holy Trinity.

Pour Thy loving kindness great
On each chosen candidate;
Bless + them, + hallow, + consecrate;
    Hear us, Holy Trinity.

The following verse is sung by all:

God the Father, seen of none,
God the co-eternal Son,
God the Spirit, with them one;
    We are Thine, O Trinity.

The people are seated. The bishop rises and, with hands extended towards the ordinands who kneel before him, says the following prayer:

Bishop: "O Lord Christ, the fountain of all goodness, Who by the operation of the Holy Spirit hast appointed divers orders in Thy church and for its greater enrichment and perfecting dost shed Thy gifts abundantly upon men, do Thou pour forth Thy sanctifying grace upon these Thy servants, who are about to be numbered among the priests of Thy church. May their hands be strong to achieve, may wisdom guide them and shed a spiritual fragrance about their path, so that in all their works begun, continued and ended in Thee, they may show the abundance of Thy power and glorify Thy holy name, O Thou great King of love, to Whom be praise and adoration from men and from the angel host. Amen."

In silence the bishop lays both hands on the head of each ordinand. The same is done after him successively by all the priests present. When this is over, both the bishop and the priests, having their right hands extended towards the ordinands, the bishop says the following:

Bishop: O Lord Christ, whose strength is in the silence, grant that these Thy servants whom now Thou dost join unto Thyself in the holy bond of the priesthood may henceforth minister faithfully of the priestly power to those who ask in Thy name. Amen. Let us pray, dearest brethren, that almighty God may multiply the gifts of the Spirit in these His servants for the work of the priesthood.

They lower their hands and all kneel while the Veni Creator is sung.

VENI CREATOR

Come, Thou Creator Spirit blest,
And in our souls take up Thy rest;
Come with Thy grace and heavenly aid,
To fill the hearts which Thou hast made.

Great paraclete, to Thee we cry,
O highest gift of God most high;
O living font, O fire, O love,
And sweet anointing from above.

Thou in Thy sevenfold gift are known;
Thee, finger of God's hand, we own;
The promise of the Father, Thou
Who dost the tongue with power endow.

Kindle our senses from above
And make our hearts o'erflow with love;
With patience firm and virtue high
The weakness of our flesh supply.

Far let us drive our tempting foe
And Thine abiding peace bestow;
So shall we not, with Thee for guide,
Turn from the path of life aside.

O may Thy grace on us bestow
The Father and the Son to know
And Thee, through endless time confessed,
O both eternal Spirit blest.

All glory while the ages run
Be to the Father and the Son,
Who gave us life; the same to Thee,
O Holy Ghost, eternally. Amen.

The bishop rises and again imposes his hands upon the head of each ordinand, saying to each:

"Receive the Holy Ghost for the office and work of a priest in the church of God; whose sins thou dost forgive, they are forgiven; and whose sins thou dost retain, they are retained."

The bishop, with his hands extended towards the ordinands, continues:

"O God, the source of all holiness, of whom are true consecration and the fullness of spiritual benediction, we pray Thee, O Lord, to + open to Thy heavenly grace the hearts and minds of these Thy servants, who have been raised to the priesthood, that through them Thy power may abundantly flow for the service of Thy people. May they be earnest and zealous as fellow workers in our order

113

and thus prove themselves worthy of the sacred charge committed unto them. And, as by a spotless blessing they now shall change for the service of Thy people bread and wine into the most holy Body and Blood of Thy Son, may they be ever watchful that they keep the vessel of their ministry pure and undefiled. May every kind of righteousness spring forth within them and may their hearts be so filled with compassion for the multitude that they may forget themselves in the love of others. May the radiance of Thy love and Thy glory shine ever more brightly in their hearts till, steadfast in Thy most joyous service, they rise unto mature spiritual manhood, unto the measure of the stature of the fullness of Christ, when their lives shall be hid with Christ in God. Amen."

The people are seated. The bishop is seated and, taking the stole that hangs after the manner of a deacon, he places it on the right shoulder and crosses it over the breast of each new priest, saying:

"Take thou this stole, for a symbol of the power of the priestly office and as a channel of the everflowing stream of Christ's love."

The bishop vests each new priest with the chasuble, saying:

"Take thou the priestly vestment, that in it thou mayest offer with our Lord Christ the most holy sacrifice of His sacred Body and Blood."

The bishop anoints the hands of each new priest with the holy oil of the catechumens, saying:

"Be pleased, O Lord, to consecrate and hallow these hands by this anointing and our + blessing; that whatsoever they + bless may be blessed and whatsoever they consecrate may be consecrated and hallowed, in the name of our Lord Christ. Amen."

The bishop closes the hands together, palm to palm, and they are bound together with a white linen strip. The

bishop delivers to each new priest a chalice containing wine and water, with a paten and a host upon it, saying:

"Take thou authority to offer sacrifice to God and to celebrate the Holy Eucharist both for the living and for the dead; in the name of the Lord. Amen."

The bishop and the priests cleanse their hands. The celebration is continued, one of the newly ordained priests going to the altar and reading the gospel as follows:

THE GOSPEL

"The holy gospel is taken from the twentieth chapter of the Gospel according to St. John, beginning at the nineteenth verse and from the twenty-eighth chapter of the Gospel according to St. Matthew, beginning at the eighteenth verse."

"The same day at evening, being the first day of the week, when the doors were shut where the disciples were assembled for fear of the Jews, came Jesus and stood in the midst and saith unto them: Peace be unto you. Then were the disciples glad, when they saw the Lord. Then said Jesus unto them again: Peace be unto you; as my Father hath sent me, even so I send you. And when He had said this, He breathed on them and saith unto them: Receive ye the Holy Ghost. Whose so ever sins ye remit, they are remitted unto them; and who so ever sins ye retain, they are retained.

Jesus spake unto them, saying: All power is given unto me in heaven and in earth. Go ye therefore and teach all nations, baptizing them in the name of the Father and of the Son and of the Holy Ghost, teaching them to observe all things whatsoever I have commanded you; and lo, I am with you always, even unto the consummation of the age."

Just before the offertorium, the new priests kneel before the bishop and each presents to him a lighted candle as a visible token of gratitude for the gift received and of the sacrifice of their lives for Christ's work. Thereafter the

new priests recite with the bishop the remainder of the holy Eucharist, word for word, taking particular care to say simultaneously with him the words of consecration with due intention to consecrate. The bishop shall communicate the newly ordained priests in both kinds.

IN THE PRAYER OF CONSECRATION

In the prayer of consecration the following clause is added after the words: "for all our bishops, clergy and faithful":

"Especially for these whom in Christ's Holy Name we have admitted to the order of the priesthood."

After the sentence, "Under the veil of earthly things, etc." the bishop is once more seated on the footstool; the new priests kneel before him and each one, placing his joined hands between those of the bishop, takes an oath of canonical obedience:

Bishop: Dost thou promise to myself and my successors due reverence and obedience in matters canonical?

New priest: I do promise.

If the bishop who is ordaining be not the Ordinary, he substitutes the name of the latter for the word "myself" and "his" for "my."

Bishop: Peace be to thee.

New Priest: And with thy spirit.

The bishop charges them thus:

Bishop: "Dearly beloved sons, as what you have to handle is not without its mischances, I warn you that you do most diligently attend to the course of the Holy Eucharist and especially to that which regards the consecration, the breaking and communion of the Host. Be you also careful that in everything which appertains to the administration of the sacraments of Christ's holy church, you do adhere to the form set forth by lawful authority and presume not to depart there from in any detail."

The bishop blesses the new priests kneeling before him, as follows:

"The blessing of God almighty, the + Father, the + Son and the Holy + Ghost, come down upon you, that you may be blessed in the priestly order and in the offering of sacrifice to almighty God, to whom belong honor and glory throughout the ages of ages. Amen."

The bishop is again seated upon the footstool and addresses the new priests as follows:

"Dearly beloved sons, consider attentively the order you have taken and be ever mindful of the sacred trust reposed in you. Since it hath pleased our Lord to call you thus closer to Himself, forget not the service of your brethren, which is the golden pathway to His most glorious presence. Freely ye have received, freely give."

The Communion is sung and the Holy Eucharist is continued to its close.

CHAPTER 5

FUNERALS AND MEMORIAL SERVICES

CHRISTWARD MINISTRY MEMORIAL SERVICE

(From "The Meaning and Value of the Sacraments" by Flower A. Newhouse.)

When a minister is asked to give a memorial service for one who has experienced transition, they should immediately inquire of the one making the arrangements as to the following information:

1. The time and address of the Last Service. (Preferably the Memorial Service should take place in a church where the body is not shown, and where only a large picture of the graduated member stands on an easel in the chancel area.)

2. Did the one for whom the service is to be given leave any written instructions as to his (her) wishes in regard to this service?

3. What music and poetry would he (she) have liked to have expressed or performed (played or sung)?

4. Are there favorite Bible verses that should highlight the memorial remarks?

5. Were there any causes, ideals, virtues or beliefs the loved one preferred and served?

6. What would the family and close friends describe as the

119

cardinal character qualities of the one who has been called into the Eternal Country?

7. Are there any written expressions of love and appreciation that the new Returned Member might enjoy hearing?

8. Would the loved one who is being remembered have liked flowers, young trees or contributions to be given in his (her) honor?

Music always inspires, but the preliminary compositions played on the organ, piano or from recordings should be played softly. Suggestions for this particular service are themes of such numbers as: **Death and Transfiguration** by Strauss, **The Grail Theme from Parsifal** by Wagner, **Elijah Chorus** by Haydn, **Pilgrim's Chorus** by Wagner, **Andante Religioso** by Thorne, **Calm As the Night** by Bohm, **It Is Morning** by Oley Speaks, **On The Holy Mountain** by Dvorak, **Jesu, Joy of Man's Desiring** by Bach, **Spirit Flower** by Campbell and Lifton, **Flower Song** by Lang, **Come Unto Me** by Handel, **Angel's Serenade** by Braga, **Largo** by Handel, **Nocturne** by Chopin.

THE MEMORIAL SERVICE

The Memorial Service begins with the minister reminding the gathered group:

During this sacred time we wish to honor (full name......) with the highest appreciation we can send him (her). We believe that he (she) is aware of this gathering and that it serves in its own way to be the ritual of commencement which concludes this incarnation.

The Bible assures us in its glorious way of the continuity of life. "Like as Christ was raised up from the dead by the glory of the Father, even so we also should walk in newness of life. For if we have been planted together in the likeness of His death, we shall be also in the likeness of His resurrection." Romans 6:4-5. "Peace I leave with you, my peace I give unto you; not as the world giveth, give I unto you. Let not your heart be troubled, neither let it be afraid." John 14:27.

From the world's great literature we may extract encouragement and inspiration regarding transition. Victor Hugo realized the purpose of physical releasement and describes his vision. "I feel in myself the future life. I am a forest once cut down; the new shoots are stronger and livelier than ever. I am rising, I know, toward the sky. The sunshine (of life eternal) is on my head. The earth gives me its generous sap, but heaven lights me with the reflection of unknown worlds...For half a century I have been writing my thoughts in prose and in verse; history, philosophy, drama, romance, tradition, satire, ode and song; I have tried all. But I feel I have not said the thousandth part of what is in me. When I go down to the grave I can say, like many others, 'I have not finished my life. My day's work will begin next morning. The tomb is not a blind alley; it is a thoroughfare. It closes on the twilight, it opens on the dawn.'"

Another glorious reminder of immortality is found in Sir Edwin Arnold's poem called:

The Song Celestial

Birthless and deathless and changeless remaineth
the spirit forever. Death hath not touched it at all,
dead though the house of it seems!
      Nay, but as when one layeth
His worn robes away, and, taking new ones sayeth,
      "These will I wear today!"
So putteth by the spirit lightly its garb of flesh.
      And it passes to inherit a residence afresh.

*****

An enlightened one said, "Death is not extinguishing the Light, it is putting out the lamp because the dawn has come."

Together in prayer let us ask Christ's renewal and blessing for this loved one.

"Divine Mother and Father Creator of us all, Lord Emmanuel the Christ, and Holy Comforter, receive our prayer for (full name ....) Receive him (her) into Thy world everlasting. Bless him (her) with inner peace, with trust and new dedication. May good attend every step our loved one shall take in Thy kingdom. May man, Angel and Master bless him (her) with their companioning. Enable him (her) to realize our love and devotion, and to have faith with us in eventual reunion in the higher dimensions. This we ask in the powerful name of Lord Emmanuel - the everliving Christ. Amen."

Following a musical interlude of a composition that is expectant and joyful, the minister summarizes Christian faith as it pertains to the belief in immortality:

"Today we honor the graduation of (full name.......) from this earthly school to the higher halls of learning in the world of God. Whatever it was that our friend was learning in the third dimensional world, the all wise Divine Benefactor knew that his (her) cycle of learning in this age had ended and now he (she) has earned a well-deserved respite from earthly duties or lessons."

(For the infant, young child, or youth, the minister would express his belief that though the outer body of the soul had been young in earth time, some lesson of specialization or of service had been gained or served according to the Divine Watcher's realization. He or she will return again to earth and realize a longer learning cycle in his length of years in the physical world.)

"As is true of all men, our friend was a pupil in the school of earth. This one we love believed in a higher existence and life everlasting. He (she) shall now reside in an environment of beauty, peace, refreshment and adventure. For some time he (she) will enjoy the welcome and association of persons and relatives with whom he (she) had ties. There will be periods of uninterrupted contemplation and periods of travel, and later, of absorbing creativity and higher learning.

After a long period has passed, the desire to return to the outer world to serve, to overcome, and to attain further development as only earth can provide will draw the soul to the formation of a new body in a set of new circumstances. He (she) will yearn to apply some of the instruction received in the Halls of Learning and the Schools of Wisdom. When he (she) returns to the outer life it will supply him (her) with the means of forming himself (herself) into a finer and more accomplished individual than he (she) has ever heretofore been.

This is not (first name .....'s) first separation from those he (she) knew and loved. There have been many reunions and separations from loved ones both in the outer and the inner worlds of experience. Love is the magnet which will draw souls who have loved one another together time after time. With each succeeding reunion souls have more in unfoldment and skills to share with one another."

(This is an appropriate place for a brief biographical sketch of the life just completed. A statement of the ideals, virtues and achievements can be included. Also, brief written expressions of appreciation for the deceased may be read.)

"Life is not only inexhaustible, but it is also eternal. With added experience and deepened consecration living becomes more refined, wise, and purposeful. Eventually the earth will have nothing more to teach the sons of men, so their grades here will be completed. Realizing the truth that life is continuous, we do not release (first name .....) into death, but into a state of fuller, freer, and richer consciousness and being. Our love and prayers will frequently ascend to our friend. We have been separated for only a temporary period. Let us prepare for our happy and interesting reunion."

Following a short musical selection, the minister closes the service with a prayer:

"Into Thy infinite care, Divine Mother and Father Creator, we release this one who is deeply loved. May our devotion be evident to him (her) during our temporal separation. Bless us with increased faith that we may accept his (her) absence from us as a necessary further-ance of (first name...'s) progress. Keep us attuned in love and awareness and prepare us for that momentous mo-ment of reunion. In Christ's Name and Spirit, so let it be. Amen."

(It is suggested that the soloist sing, "The Lord's Prayer" by Malotte, for as this great song is given, we know our friend will be lifted into the new residence of his (her) ongoing adventure in God.)

⤳

SERVICE BEFORE CREMATION

Following a musical prelude, the minister opens the service by saying:

"To you, O holy fire, we commit this body. You are the emblem of the invisible Spiritual Sun by whom we are all blessed. As you touch this form, purge it on all planes that the released Pilgrim may be freed from earthly forces and desires.

Out of this baptism of fire shall emerge a heaven-given freedom and a new vitality for the tasks confronting (first name....)."

While soft music is heard, the body is received by the fire. The minister says:

"Dust to dust and ashes to ashes, but the Spirit of this man (woman) walks free in his (her) invisible body which is fadeless, incorruptible and deathless."

In his (her) higher state, our friend is saying:

> From the walls of the powerful fortressed house,
> From the clasp of knitted locks–from the keep
> of well-closed doors,

124

Let me be wafted.
Let me glide noiselessly forth;
With the key of softness unlock the locks with a
whisper,
Set open the doors, O soul!

Walt Whitman

After a brief pause, the celebrant prays:

"Divine Trinity – God, the Mother-Father Spirit; God, the Son; and God, the Holy Comforter – may it be through Thy triune ensouling that our beloved is liberated from the bonds of earth. May the Light Eternal claim him (her) and shine everlastingly upon him (her).

We return to our homes confident in the knowledge that Thou watcheth and keepeth us in attunement with the spirit of our companion eternally. Amen."

SERVICE AT THE GRAVE

Following the opening musical selection (if available) the minister prays:

"Eternal Spirit, Thou hast known it wise to recall Thy son (daughter) into the Kingdom of Perpetual Light and Peace. We ask Thee to send forth Thy Angels to consecrate this resting place for the cast-off body of our loved one."

Flowers are dropped on the casket. As it is lowered the minister says:

"Dust to dust and ashes to ashes, the earth receives its own, while in a more glorious form the Graduate of earth witnesses his (her) freedom from earth's hold.

Birthless and deathless and changeless
Abideth the spirit forever.
Death has not touched it at all,
Dead though the house of it seems."

An appropriate vocal solo may be used at this point in the service after which the minister says:

"The Angel of Transition has visited our friend and released him (her) from a limited state into a wider and higher dimension of being. Death has robed (full name ...) in a new garment - a body of greater beauty - a form of enduring strength.

The veil that hangs between the three-dimensional world and the fourth dimension, into which (first name ....) has journeyed, is very thin to those who live an unselfish spiritual life.

Our inability to see (first name....) as he (she) now appears is due entirely to our limited senses and human viewpoints. Our loved one has been freed from his (her) prison house. Were he (she) able to speak to us across the chasm of consciousness he (she) would tell us of his (her) joyfulness and of the unspeakable wonders he (she) feels in being nearer the Presence of God.

There is no death. (First name....) has experienced but a change. He (she) lives and serves more widely and powerfully than he (she) has ever done in this world. And throughout his (her) pilgrimage in that spaceless world where his (her) spirit finds refuge, he (she) shall be attuned to us because love spans worlds and unites those who think and dream about one another."

Then the minister pronounces the closing benediction:

"Until we again meet, dear brother (sister) and friend, may your blessings be multiplied. Where you now are, we too shall someday be. Take with you our love and faith in reunion; and wherever you journey, remember we are blessing you and living to be more worthy of your watchful assistance. Our spirit calls to you, "Lo, I am with you always." Into God's love you are lovingly released. In Him lies your renewal and fulfillment. In Christ's Name we so speak. Amen."

NATIONAL SPIRITUAL SCIENCE

Before the funeral

Contact the Funeral Chapel concerning arrangements. When necessary, the minister may have to make arrangements. The Chapel usually supplies music. The Chapel supplies the funeral notice to the minister to be filed at the Center.

Funeral Service

Suggested Order of Funeral Service

Invocation: "I am now in the presence of pure Being, and immersed in the Holy Spirit of life, love and wisdom. I acknowledge Thy presence and Thy power, O blessed Spirit; in Thy divine wisdom now erase my mortal limitations and from Thy pure substance of love bring into manifestation my world, according to Thy perfect law."

Charles Fillmore

> or John 11:25,26
> Revelation 21:4,5,6,& 7
> Revelation 22:5

The Lord's Prayer

Summarize the purpose of the gathering and obituary (use the individual's name often)

Short sermon

Inspired reading (Bible or any inspirational source)

Solo (optional)

23rd Psalm

Prayer by the Minister

Announce interment details and invitation

Release of the Soul

"Father-Mother God, we thank Thee for the release of the soul of this Thy child (full name.....) as he (she) continues to walk in Thy Light; ever learning more of

Thee, to know Thee better and to love Thee more. Bless each and every one who knows him (her) with the realization that there is no death but that (first name....) lives and has being.

May each one realize that (first name....) is happy in Thy keeping. We thank Thee, Father-Mother God, for replacing all doubt, fear, loneliness, and selfishness in every mind, with harmony, peace and love. For this we thank Thee, forever and ever. Amen."

Inspired message
Eulogy, by minister or close associate of the departed
Benediction

After the Funeral

If cremation follows, the Minister remains and receives the guests, together with the family.

At the Cemetery

Invocation

Inspired reading (Bible or any inspirational source)

Brief inspired message

Benediction

The Minister offers his (her) personal service and the services of the Center to the family.

Immortality

Do not stand at my grave and weep
I am not there .... I do not sleep.
I am a thousand winds that blow,
I am the diamond glints on snow.
I am the sunlight on ripened grain,
I am the gentle autumn rain.
When you awake in the morning's hush,
I am the swift upflinging rush
Of quiet birds in circling flight.
I am the soft star-shine at night.

Do not stand at my grave and cry .....
I am not there. I did not die.

Unknown

༄ ༄ ༄

THE LITURGY OF THE LIBERAL CATHOLIC CHURCH

The Funeral Service

As burial customs vary in different countries and places, the clergy must use their discretion in re-arranging the several portions of the ceremony. Hymns may be introduced at suitable places, also addresses and readings from various sources.

According to the arrangements made, the portion of this ceremony preceding the burial itself will take place in the cemetery out of doors, in the cemetery or crematorium chapel, in a funeral parlour, in a private house, or in the church. The committal usually takes place at the crematorium or the cemetery.

The priest may either accompany the funeral procession or meet it at the church, the cemetery or the crematorium.

All stand.

As the body is carried through the cemetery or the church, some of the following passages are read by the priest or chanted by the choir:

"I am the resurrection and the life, saith the Lord; he that believeth in me, though he were dead yet shall he live; and whosoever liveth and believeth in me shall never die. Lay not up for yourselves treasures upon earth; where moth and rust do corrupt and where thieves break through and steal. But lay up for yourselves treasures in heaven; where neither moth nor rust doth corrupt and where thieves do not break through and steal. For where your treasure is, there will be your heart also."

✳✳✳✳✳✳

129

"I know that my redeemer liveth; whom I shall see for myself and mine eyes shall behold. Be not deceived; God is not mocked; for whatsoever a man soweth, that shall he also reap. For he that soweth to his flesh, shall of the flesh reap corruption; but he that soweth to the spirit, shall of the spirit reap life everlasting. And let us not be weary in well-doing; for in due season we shall reap, if we faint not. As we have therefore opportunity; let us do good unto all men."

******

"The souls of the righteous are in the hand of God; and there shall no torment touch them. In the sight of the unwise they seemed to die and their departure is taken for misery and their going from us to be utter destruction; but they are in peace. For God created man to be immortal; and made him to be an image of His own eternity. Glory be to the Father and to the Son, and to the Holy Ghost. As it was in the beginning, is now and ever shall be; world without end. Amen."

THE INVOCATION

When the priest has arrived at the chancel or grave and the above sentences are finished, he says:

"In the name of the Father + and of the Son and of the Holy Ghost. Amen."

THE CHARGE

The people are seated. The priest turns to the people and says:

"Brethren, we are met together here today on the occasion of the passing into a higher life of our dear brother (sister) (full name......). It is but natural that we who have known and loved him (her) should regret his (her) departure from amongst us; yet it is our duty to think not of ourselves, but of him (her). Therefore must we endeavour to lay aside the thought of our personal loss and dwell only upon his (her) great and most glorious gain. To this end I will call upon you to join with me in the recitation of:"

PSALM 23

"The Lord is my shepherd; therefore can I lack nothing. He shall feed me in a green pasture; and lead me forth beside the waters of comfort. He shall convert my soul; and bring me forth in the paths of righteousness, for His name's sake. Yea, though I walk through the valley of the shadow of death I will fear no evil; for Thou art with me; Thy rod and Thy staff comfort me. Glory be to the Father and to the Son, and to the Holy Ghost. As it was in the beginning, is now and ever shall be; world without end. Amen."

ANTIPHON

"The Lord gave and the Lord hath taken away. Blessed be the name of the Lord."

THE ABSOLUTION

During the following passages the priest encompasses the body and sprinkles it with holy water thrice on either side, after which he again encompasses it and censes it thrice on either side. If the body be not present, these ceremonies are omitted, but the words, nevertheless, are said. The absolution is omitted in the case of young children.

Priest: Rest in the eternal grant unto him (her), O Lord.
Congregation: And let light perpetual shine upon him (her).

Priest: Come forth to meet him (her), ye angels of the Lord.
Congregation: Receive him (her) into your fellowship, O ye saints of God.

Priest: May the choirs of angels receive him (her).
Congregation: And guide him (her) into eternal peace.

Priest: Rest in the eternal grant unto him (her), O Lord.
Congregation: And let light perpetual shine upon him (her).

Priest: O God, in whose unspeakable love the souls of the departed find rest and peace, in Thy name we + absolve from every bond of sin Thy servant who has cast off the garment of flesh. May Thy holy angels bear him (her) in their tender care, that he (she) may enter the brightness of the everlasting light and find his (her) peace in Thee; through Christ our Lord. Amen.

Priest: The Lord be with you.
Congregation: And with thy spirit.

THE COLLECTS

The following collects are recited, unless a special Requiem Eucharist is to be celebrated. In that event the Eucharist begins and the collects will be said in the usual place therein. In case of children, the words "this thy child" are used instead of "this thy servant".

Priest: Let us pray.

The people kneel.

Priest: Almighty God, who hast dominion over both the living and the dead and dost hold all Thy creation in the everlasting arms of Thy love, we pray Thee for the peace and repose of Thy servant, that he (she), being dead unto this world, yet ever living unto Thee, may find in Thy continued and unceasing service the perfect consummation of happiness and peace; through Christ our Lord. Amen.

Likewise, O Lord, we pray Thee for those who love Thy servant, those whom Thou hast called to sacrifice the solace of his (her) earthly presence; do Thou, O Lord, comfort them with the balm of Thy loving kindness that, strengthened by Thee and resting upon the surety of Thy wisdom, they may put aside their thoughts of sorrow and grief and pour out upon him (her) only such thoughts of love as may help him (her) in the higher life of service to which Thou hast now called him (her); through Christ our Lord. Amen.

The epistle, gospel, and communion from the Requiem

Eucharist may follow here if desired.

THE BURIAL OR THE CREMATION OR THE DISPOSAL OF THE ASHES

From this point onwards the ceremony is conducted either at the grave, in the crematorium chapel or at the place where the ashes are to be deposited. If the funeral service is held in a church and is to be followed by a Requiem Eucharist the committal may be said at the conclusion of the Requiem instead of at the cemetery or crematorium.

THE COMMITTAL FOR CREMATION

In the case of CREMATION the committal begins as follows:

Priest: Forasmuch as it hath pleased almighty God of His great love to take unto Himself our dear brother (sister) hence departed, we therefore commit this his (her) cast-off body to be consumed by fire, ashes to ashes, dust to dust, that in that more glorious spiritual body which now he (she) weareth, he (she) may be free from earthly chains to serve God as he (she) ought.

THE COMMITTAL FOR BURIAL IN A GRAVE

In the case of BURIAL IN A GRAVE, the procession bearing the coffin or casket goes to the grave. Before the coffin is lowered, the grave or ground is sprinkled with holy water and censed. The following prayer is said by the priest:

Priest: O God, Who in Thy providence hast appointed a wondrous ministry of angels, we pray Thee to + hallow this grave (or ground) and send down Thy holy angel from heaven to + bless and sanctify it; through Christ our Lord. Amen.

Forasmuch as it hath pleased almighty God of His great love to take unto Himself our dear brother (sister) hence departed, we therefore commit this his (her) cast-

133

off body to the ground, earth to earth **(here some earth is cast upon the coffin by the priest or someone standing by)**, ashes to ashes, dust to dust, that in that more glorious spiritual body which now he (she) weareth, he (she) may be free from earthly chains to serve God as he (she) ought.

THE COMMITTAL FOR DISPOSAL OF THE ASHES

In the case of DISPOSAL OF THE ASHES, the urn or casket containing the ashes is sometimes buried in a grave or sometimes deposited in a niche and sometimes the ashes are scattered on the ground. When the ashes are buried in a grave, the ground may be sprinkled with holy water and censed. The priest may bless the grave as in the case of burial of the body.

Priest: Forasmuch as it hath pleased almighty God of His great love to take unto Himself our dear brother (sister) hence departed, we therefore commit his (her) ashes to their resting place (or to the ground), ashes to ashes, dust to dust, that in that more glorious spiritual body which now he (she) weareth, he (she) may be free from earthly chains to serve God as he (she) ought.

For I say unto you: "Blessed are the dead which die in the Lord; for the souls of the righteous are in the hand of God and there shall no torment touch them. In the sight of the unwise they seem to die and their departure is taken for misery and their going from us to be utter destruction; but they are in peace. For God created man to be immortal and made him to be an image of His own eternity. The Lord sitteth above the waterfloods; the Lord remaineth a king forever. The universe is His temple. Wisdom, strength and beauty are about His throne as pillars of His works; for His wisdom is infinite, His strength is omnipotent and His beauty shines through the whole universe in order and symmetry. The heavens He has stretched forth as a canopy; the earth He has planted as His footstool; He crowns His temple with stars as with a diadem and from His hands flow all power and glory. The sun and the moon are messengers of His will and all His law is concord. If we ascend up into heaven, He is there. If we go down into hell, He is there also. If we take the wings of the morning and dwell in the uttermost parts of the sea, even there also His hand shall lead us and His right hand shall hold us. In His almighty care we rest in perfect peace and equally in His care rests this our loved one, whom He has deigned to draw nearer to the vision of His eternal beauty."

Ever praising Him therefore, in firm but humble confidence we call upon Him and say:

"O Father of light, in Whom is no darkness at all, we pray Thee to fill our hearts with calm and peace and to open within us the eyes of the soul, that we may see by faith the radiance and the glory that Thou art pouring upon us Thy servants. For Thou ever givest us far more than we can ask or think and it is only through our feebleness and faithlessness that we ever need crave any-thing from Thine omnipotence. But Thou knowest well the weakness of the human heart and in Thy limitless love Thou wilt make allowance for our human love when we pray Thee to grant eternal rest unto this our dear brother (sister) and that light perpetual may shine upon him (her). We thank Thee that in Thy loving providence Thou has drawn him (her) from the unreal towards the real, from the darkness of earth into Thy glorious light, through the gates of death into a splendor beyond our comprehen-sion. Our loving thoughts shall follow and surround him (her). O take Thou this our gift of thought, imperfect though it be and touch it with the eternal fire of Thy love, so that it may become for him (her) a guardian angel to help him (her) on his (her) upward way. Thus through Thy loving kindness may we in deep humility and reverence become fellow workers with Thy boundless power and may our weakness be supported by Thine infinite strength; that we, with this our dearly beloved brother (sister), may in due time attain unto the wisdom of the Spirit, who with the Father and the Son liveth and reigneth, God through-out all ages of ages. Amen."

135

The following prayer may be added:

"Almighty God, in Whose light do live the souls of them that depart hence in the Lord and with Whom the faithful, after they are delivered from the burden of the flesh, are in joy and felicity; we give Thee hearty thanks, for that it hath pleased Thee to deliver this our brother (sister) out of the miseries of this mortal world and do pray Thee that we may be found worthy, together with all those that are departed in the true faith of Thy holy name, to stand before Thee hereafter in the ranks of Thy glorious church triumphant; through Christ our Lord. Amen.

+ May the souls of all the departed through the love of God rest in peace. Amen.

+ The grace of our Lord Jesus Christ and the love of God and the fellowship of the Holy Ghost be with us all evermore. Amen."

THE UNIVERSAL SPIRITUALIST FUNERAL OR MEMORIAL SERVICE

OUR CONTINUING LIFE

Nowhere are the blessings of Spiritualism more evident than in the bringing of comfort and help to the bereaved. Indeed, the only possible message of comfort for those who are mourning the loss of their loved ones is the truth of the continuity of life beyond the change of death and the certainty of the unbroken link with those on earth.

The gloom which, in the past, has been associated with death has been due to ignorance concerning the afterlife. We know that physical life on earth is but one of countless stages of experience, and though the flesh may separate us in these present conditions there is no separation of spirit. We believe that death is but a gateway leading into a freer and happier life, and that spirit return is God's gift by which all spheres of life are linked in service together.

We cannot, in our limited human conditions, escape the

sadness which bereavement brings; but as we raise our thoughts to the glory of the heavenly life so the veil grows thinner and the truth of the co-operation and companionship of dear ones in the spirit world with those in the physical body is more clearly seen and felt.

It will be understood that this service can be modified as individual inspiration directs.

The Minister, meeting the coffin at the entrance to the church and going before it, may use one or more of the following sentences. Or, if the service takes place in a mortuary where the coffin is already in place, the Minister may begin the service with one or more of these sentences.

OPENING SENTENCES

I am the resurrection and the life, saith the Lord. He that believeth in me, though he were dead, yet shall he live; and whosoever liveth and believeth in me shall never die.

The Lord is my light and my salvation;
Whom shall I fear?
The Lord is the strength of my life;
O whom shall I be afraid?

Lord, Thou hast been our dwelling place in all generations. Before the mountains were brought forth, or ever Thou hadst formed the earth and the world, even from everlasting to everlasting, Thou art God.

He that dwelleth in the secret place of the Most High shall abide under the shadow of the Almighty. I will say of the Lord, He is my refuge and my fortress; my God, in whom I trust.

THE CHARGE

When the Minister has arrived at the chancel or when the above sentences are finished, he (she) says:

"Dearly beloved of our Father-Mother God; we are met together here today to celebrate the passing into a higher life of (full name...........). It is but natural that we who have known and loved him (her) should regret his (her) departure from amongst us; but on this occasion it is our duty to think not of ourselves, but of him (her). Therefore must we endeavor to lay aside the thought of our personal loss and dwell only upon his (her) great gain.

Let us remember that this physical life is but part of the greater life, and when each has accomplished his mission on earth he is called to continue that mission in a higher sphere. We give thanks for the knowledge of that continuing life, where there is neither death, nor pain, nor weeping. The physical body dies, yes, but that which inhabits the physical body – the soul, the spirit – never dies. And your loved one was not just that physical body that has died, his (her) real self, his (her) soul, his (her) spirit lives on.

I cannot say, and I will not say
That he (she) is dead. He (she) is just away.

With a cheery smile and a wave of the hand,
He (she) has wandered into the little known land.

And left us dreaming how very fair
It needs must be since he (she) lingers there.

And you—O you, who the wildest yearn
For the old-time step and the glad return—

Think of him (her) faring on, as dear
In the love of there as the love of here;

Think of him (her) still as the same, I say,
For he (she) is not dead – he (she) is just away!

Let us pray."

THE INVOCATION

In the Minister's own words, or one of the following:

"Almighty God our Father, from Whom we come and unto Whom our spirits return, Thou has been our dwelling place in all generations. Thou art our refuge and strength, a very present help in trouble. Grant us Thy blessing in this hour, and enable us so to put our trust in Thee that our spirits may grow calm and our hearts be comforted. Lift our eyes beyond the shadows of earth, and help us to see life in the light of the eternal. So may we find grace and strength for this and every time of need. Amen.

Eternal God, Father of all spirits, we come to Thee in this hour because we need Thy consolation and strength. Breathe Thy peace into our hearts and remove from us all fear of death. Help us to perceive that we are spiritual beings living in a spiritual universe and that while the things that are seen with the physical eye are temporal and pass away, things seen by spiritual vision are real and eternal. Give to us a blessed sense of Thine eternal love that holds us all. Amen.

Almighty God, Who art our refuge and strength, a very present help in time of trouble, grant us Thy light to shine through the shadows of this hour. Comfort the hearts that are heavy with sorrow, and have compassion upon our weakness. Give us the vision of the eternal realities, and solace us with the sure hope of the larger life beyond. Amen."

(HYMN, ANTHEM OR SOLO, if one is desired.)

SCRIPTURES

One or more of the following is to be said:

"The Lord gave and the Lord hath taken away. Blessed be the Name of the Lord."

*****

The 23rd Psalm

The Lord is my shepherd; I shall not want.
He maketh me to lie down in green pastures;
He leadeth me beside the still waters,
He restoreth my soul;

139

He leadeth me in the paths of righteousness for
His name's sake.
Yea, though I walk through the valley of the
shadow of death,
I will fear no evil; for Thou art with me;
Thy rod and Thy staff they comfort me.
Thou preparest a table before me in the pres-
ence of mine enemies;
Thou anointest my head with oil;
My cup runneth over.
Surely goodness and mercy shall follow me all
the days of my life;
And I will dwell in the house of the Lord forever.

*****

"Let not your heart be troubled, said Jesus, ye believe
in God, believe also in me. In my Father's house are many
mansions; if it were not so, I would have told you; for I go
to prepare a place for you. And if I go and prepare a place
for you, I will come again, and will receive you unto
myself; that where I am, there ye may be also. And whither
I go, ye know. Thomas saith unto Him, Lord, we know not
whither Thou goest; how can we know the way? Jesus saith
unto him, I am the way, the truth and the life; no one
cometh unto the Father, but by Me.

Now hath Christ been raised from the dead, and
become the first fruits of them that slept. For since by
man came death, by man came also the resurrection of
the dead. For as in Adam all die, so also in Christ all be
made alive. But someone will say, How are the dead
raised? and with what manner of body do they come?
That which thou sowest is not quickened except it die; and
that which thou sowest, thou sowest not the body that
shall be, but bare grain, it may chance of wheat, or of
some other kind; but God giveth it a body even as it
pleased Him, and to each seed a body of its own. So also is
the resurrection of the dead. It is sown in corruption; it is
raised in incorruption. It is sown in dishonor; it is raised

in glory. It is sown in weakness, it is raised in power. It is sown a natural body, it is raised a spiritual body. There is a natural body, and there is a spiritual body. And as we have borne the image of the earthly, we shall also bear the image of the heavenly. For this corruptible must put on incorruption, and this mortal must put on immortality. But when this corruptible shall have put on incorruption, and this mortal shall have put on immortality, then shall come to pass the saying that is written: Death is swallowed up in victory. O death, where is thy victory: O grave, where is thy sting?"

*****

I heard a great voice out of heaven saying: "Behold the tabernacle of God is with men, and He will dwell with them, and they shall be His people; and God Himself shall be with them and be their God. And God shall wipe away all tears from their eyes; and there shall be no more death, neither sorrow, nor crying, neither shall there be any more pain; for the former things are passed away."

POEMS

One or more of the following may be said, or may be incorporated into the address that follows.

There is No Death

There is no death! The stars go down
To rise upon some other shore;
And bright in heaven's jeweled crown
They shine forevermore.

There is no death! The dust we tread
Shall change beneath the summer showers
To golden grain, or mellow fruit,
Or rainbow tinted flowers.

There is no death! An angel form
Walks o'er the earth with silent tread;
He bears our best loved ones away,
And then we call them "dead".

Born unto that undying life,
     They leave us but to come again;
With joy we welcome them – the same
     Except in sin and pain.

And ever near us, though unseen,
     The dear immortal spirits tread;
For all the boundless universe
     Is life – there are no dead.

John Luckey McCreery

*****

The Beyond

It seemeth such a little way to me
     Across to that strange country, the beyond,
And yet not strange, for it has grown to be
     The home of those of whom I am so fond;
They make it seem familiar and most dear,
     As journeying friends bring distant countries
       near.

So close it lies that when my sight is clear
     I almost think I see the gleaming strand;
I know that those who have gone from here
     Come near enough to sometimes touch my
       hand.

I never stand above a bier and see
     The seal of death set on some well-loved face,
But to think – one more to welcome me
     When I have crossed the intervening space
Between this world and that one over there;
     One more to make the strange beyond seem
       fair.

And so for me there is no sting to death,
     And so the grave has lost its victory;
It is but crossing with abated breath
     And white-set face a little strip of sea,

To find our loved ones waiting on that shore,
More beautiful, more precious, than before.

Ella Wheeler Wilcox

*****

My Prayer

Hold fast my hand, dear God, and never let it go.
Tho' night descends, and rolling clouds of storm
Sweep o'er the sky with mists that blot the glow
Of stars and blurs the giant oak tree's massive form
    from sight;
Tho' lightning flash and thunder roll, I know
The stars still shine beneath the gloom.
My hand in Thine, I shall not fear to stand
And watch the breaking clouds that loom
To billowing heights to make the dawn more glorious.
With radiant hues, the rainbow, to a tear drenched
land,
Proclaims its promise of an end victorious.
And so is life. While on this rock of faith I stand,
I shall not fear, dear God, if you hold fast my hand.

Isabelle Gale

*****

OBITUARY (If one is desired- should be short)

THE PRAYER FOR THE DEPARTED

Almighty God, Who hast dominion over all souls everywhere and dost hold all Thy creation in the everlasting arms of Thy love, we pray Thee for the peace and repose of Thy servant (full name.....) that he (she), ever living unto Thee, may find in Thy continued and unceasing service the perfect consummation of happiness and peace.

Rest in the eternal grant unto him (her), O Lord.
And let light perpetual shine upon him (her).
Come forth to meet him (her), ye Angels of the Lord.
May the choirs of Angels receive him (her).

And guide him (her) into perpetual peace.

O God, in whose unspeakable love the souls of the departed find rest and peace, absolve from every bond Thy servant who has cast off this garment of flesh. May Thy holy Angels bear him (her) in their tender care, that he (she) may enter the brightness of the everlasting light. Amen.

HEBREW PRAYERS FOR THE DEAD

RULES FOR MOURNERS

1. Mourning ceremonies are observed in honor of parents, husband, wife, son, daughter, brother, or sister.

2. To indicate grief the mourner makes a rent of about four inches in length, in his garment, to the right hand side, and at the death of his parents to the left. This ceremony is known as **K'riah.**

3. During the first seven days, including the day of the funeral, the mourner stays at home. There usually prayer meetings are held and Kaddish is said for the demised. This seven day mourning is known as **Shivah.** During shivah the mourner must not wear shoes, must sit on a low seat, and must not do any business or work. When the mourners are poor persons compelled to work for their daily bread, three days of mourning are sufficient.

4. During the week of Shivah a candle or lamp for the deceased is kept burning.

5. The Kaddish prayer shall be recited for departed parents every day at a prayer meeting or at the synagogue, during eleven months from the day after death. At the expiration of the year, Kaddish is to be said on Yahrzeit and repeated at every anniversary. The Yahrzeit (anniversary of one's death) is to be observed on the day when the death took place. Yahrzeit is kept according to the Hebrew date of death. The light is burned the evening before the Yahrzeit date.

6. The time for the unveiling of monuments is any time after the traditional period of mourning, namely, thirty days after the day of death.

7. One must wait thirty days, the period commonly called **"Shloshim"** before one may visit the grave of a deceased relative. After that it can be visited at any time.

THE MOURNER'S KADDISH
(English Translation)

Reader and Mourners: Extolled and hallowed be thy name of God throughout the world which He has created, and which He governs according to His righteous will. Just is He in all His ways, and wise are all His decrees. May His kingdom come, and His will be done in all the earth.

Congregation: Praised be the Lord of life, the righteous Judge for evermore.

Reader and Mourners: To the departed whom we now re-member, may peace and bliss be granted in life eternal. May they find grace and mercy before the Lord of heaven and earth. May their souls rejoice in that ineffable good which God has laid up for those who fear Him, and may their memory be a blessing unto those who treasure it.

May the Father of peace send peace to all who mourn, and comfort all the bereaved among us. Amen.

THE MEMORIAL OF DEPARTED SOULS

For the Father

May God remember the soul of my honored father (name) who is gone to his repose; for that, I now solemnly offer charity for his sake; in reward of this, may his soul enjoy eternal life, with the souls of Abraham, Isaac, and Jacob; Sarah, Rebecca, Rachel, and Leah, and the rest of the righteous males and females that are in Paradise; and let us say, Amen.

For the Mother

May God remember the soul of my honored mother (name) who is gone to her repose; for that, I now solemnly offer charity for her sake; in reward of this may her soul enjoy eternal life, with the souls of Abraham, Isaac, and Jacob; Sarah, Rebecca, Rachel, and Leah, and the rest of the righteous males and females that are in Paradise; and let us say, Amen.

For the Dear Departed Ones

May God remember the souls of my father and mother, my grandfathers and grandmothers, my uncles and aunts, my brothers and sisters, whether paternal or maternal, who are gone to their repose; for that, I now solemnly offer charity for their sake; in reward of this, may their souls enjoy eternal life with the souls of Abraham, Isaac, and Jacob: Sarah, Rebecca, Rachel, and Leah, and the rest of the righteous males and females that are in Paradise; and let us say, Amen.

MEDITATION AND PRAYERS AT THE GRAVES OF OUR DEAR DEPARTED

Lord, Thou has been our dwelling place in all generations. Before the mountains were brought forth, or ever Thou hadst formed the earth and the world, even from everlasting to everlasting, Thou are God. Thou turnest men to contrition; and sayest; "Return, ye children of men." For a thousand years in Thy sight are but as yesterday when it is past, and as a watch in the night.

Psalm XC

Humility and sadness fill my soul when I enter this mournful abode of the dead. Here all human projects and desires, all passions of pride and power end. Wealth and poverty, love and hate, all are here leveled within the bosom of mother earth.

Faith alone can save us from anguish and despair. Faith can reveal to us the immortal destiny of the soul. It inspires in us holy affections, of lofty sentiments and a high sense of duty. Faith knows no death, since it is the key that unlocks the gates of eternal life.

Thus wilt Thou strengthen and guide me, O Heavenly Father, so that when my earthly pilgrimage is ended, and Thou shalt call me hence, my soul may be found worthy of Thy salvation. Amen."

On the Anniversary of a Parent's Death

(Yahrzeit)

O Lord, Thou has searched me, and known me. Thou knowest my downsitting and mine up rising. Thou understandest my thought afar off. Thou measurest my going about and my lying down. And art acquainted with all my ways." Psalm CXXXIX

O day of sacred, solemn and sorrowful memories! Annually Thou renewest the painful recollection of parting with the soul of my dearly beloved (father – mother). Somehow I feel this day in close communion with the soul of my dear parent. (His/her) sainted spirit seems to hover over me. (His/her) memory penetrates my heart and my soul. Yea, as long as I live, I shall keep sacred this Yahrzeit, this annual Day of Memorial, as a tribute to (him/her) whom I loved with a love everlasting.

O God of Life, grant rest and peace unto the soul of my sainted (father – mother). May (his/her) spirit have found the ineffable good which Thou hast prepared for Thy children in Eternity. And may I (his/her) earthly child, be permitted to share in that holiness of (his/her) sainted spirit that I may become more worthy and more acceptable in Thy sight, O Lord, who givest and takest away. Praised be Thy name forever and ever. Amen.

On Setting a Tombstone

A mere shadow are our days upon the earth. Naught is left to me of him who has gone to the valley of the shadow of death but a stone bearing his name. This is all we have to mark the spot where his mortal remains are laid, to remind us what we too shall soon become. In the grave all our efforts end. Here is nothing but a fragile stone or a nameless grave, to recall to us the memory of those whom we leave behind, unless we sow the seed of goodness and useful deeds in our earthly career, the fruits of which we shall reap in heaven.

O thou who sleepest in the dust, this monument was not needed to recall thy name, for thy precious memory is enthroned in the hearts of many; but thy gentle qualities and kind friendship have so endeared thy image to my soul, that death alone can efface the remembrance of the loss I have sustained in thy decease.

May the body rest in peace. Lord, in setting this stone to the memory of (name....), I beseech Thee to grant repose to (his/her) soul, give (him/her) the peace of the righteous, and admit (him/her) to the joy of contemplating Thy divine presence.

Vouchsafe Thy mercy to me, O Lord, that my spirit may one day also enjoy eternal beatitude, and make my memory worthy of being honored and preserved among those whom I shall leave behind. Amen.

CHAPTER 6

CANDLELIGHTING SERVICES

The midwinter festivals of Hanukkah, Winter Solstice, and Christmas celebrate the return of light and the promise of spring to come. These follow celebrations of the return of light that were from pre-history in pagan times (Winter Solstice). The Christian and Jewish winter festivals both arise from the fundamental religious experience that there is in this mysterious universe a promise of forgiveness and a hint of renewal. The Hanukkah menorah is not the same as the advent candles and the Christmas tree, but it is not totally different from them either. (The Kwanzaa Kinara is very similar to the Kanukkah memorah.) All of these represent the light of God's love shining in the darkness of the world. In the preconscious imagination, they stand for the triumph of light over darkness in the middle of winter and the human instinct that light and life are stronger than darkness and death. The lights on the tree and the candles on the menorah both tell us that God is the light of the world, a light that can never be extinguished.

SUNDAYS OF ADVENT

First Sunday of Advent

To use this service on the Sundays of advent, on the first Sunday, light one candle, The Candle of Expectancy, from a large candle on the altar. Then say:

The Prayer for The Dedication of the Light

I kindle the Candle of Expectancy on the Earth plane, looking forward to the birth of Christ. This light represents the light within my heart and I dedicate myself to the service of the Spirit. I guard and cherish this flame as a living symbol and an act of faith in the reality of the Powers of Light.

You may then go on with a communion service or other Sunday ritual.

*****

Second Sunday of Advent

On the second Sunday of advent, the first candle is already lighted before the service, so the second candle, The Candle of Purification, is lighted from a large candle on the altar. Then say:

Prayer

I light the Candle of Purification looking forward to the birth of the Christ. May the Beings from Higher Worlds see this flame and kindle its counterpart on the ethereal plane. May this ethereal light be a channel for the inflow of the healing and purifying powers of the Spirit. May the Light and Love of the Divine permeate this building and protect it, warming the hearts and enlightening the understanding of all who live in it or enter it. May the homes of all persons here be blessed. May the hearts of all here be purified.

(Go on with the regular Sunday service.)

*****

Third Sunday of Advent

The two candles are already lighted before the service begins, so light the third candle, The Candle of Hope and Joy, from the large candle on the altar. Then say:

150

Prayer

I light the Candle of Hope and Joy looking forward to the birth of the Christ within my heart and the hearts of all humanity. May the blessing of light be on you, light without and light within. May the blessed sunlight shine upon you and warm your heart till it glows like a great peat fire so that the stranger may come and warm himself at it. And may the light shine out of the eyes of you, like a candle set in the window of a house, bidding the wanderer come in out of the storm. **(Go on with the regular Sunday service.)**

*****

Fourth Sunday of Advent

The three candles are already lighted before the service, so light the fourth candle, The Candle of Identification, from the large candle on the altar. Then say:

Prayer

I light the Candle of Identification looking forward to the birth of the Christ within my heart and the hearts of all humanity. (Soul mantra) "I am the Soul and also love am I. Above all else I am both will and fixed design. My will is now to lift the lower self into the Light Divine. That Light am I. Therefore I must descend to where that lower self awaits my coming. That which desires to lift and that which cries aloud for lifting are now at one. Such is my will." I am a child of God and look to the example of my brother, Jesus, as a role model for my life.

(Go on with the regular Sunday service.)

∽∽∽∽

WINTER SOLSTICE

Before the service begins, choose four people to be CANDLELIGHTERS. Give each person a card with the prayer for the Advent

candle they are to light (see below). Then choose four more people to be the Archangels and give them a card with their reading on it (see page 156).

WELCOME

INTRODUCTION

(This ceremony is taken from "THE BOOK OF RITUALS" by Reverend Carol E. Parrish-Harra, published and available through Sparrow Hawk Press, Sparrow Hawk Village, 11 Summit Ridge Drive, Tahlequah, Oklahoma 74464.)

"Heaven and Earth rejoice as we enter the Christmas winter solstice days. Colorful flowers, lit candles, and music in abundance reflect the joy of the celebration. The drama of the winter solstice festival of light and love allows our open hearts to be touched. We receive love at the festival of the birth of the Christ—the Historical Christ for humanity and the Mystical Christ within ourselves. This event is indeed a mystery that we penetrate by contemplation and inner expansion."

Celebrant: LET THE CELEBRATION BEGIN! **(Play music and/or sound a gong.)** The time has come! The festival of the Christ is here. We celebrate the Word made matter. Amid presents and parties, we listen to the proclamation, "Christ is Born!" and ponder with new appreciation the affirmation, "The Lord is my light."

Here have each of the four CANDLELIGHTERS in turn light their advent candle from other candles on the altar and read their prayer from their card.

First Candlelighter

I kindle the Candle of Expectancy on the Earth plane, looking forward to the birth of the Christ. This light represents the light within my heart, and I dedicate myself to the service of the Spirit. I guard and cherish this flame as a living symbol and an act of faith in the reality of the Powers of Light.

Second Candlelighter

I light the Candle of Purification looking forward to the birth of the Christ. May the Beings from Higher Worlds see this flame and kindle its counterpart on the ethereal plane. May this ethereal light be a channel for the inflow of the healing and purifying powers of the Spirit. May the Light and Love of the Divine permeate this building and protect it, warming the hearts and enlightening the understanding of all who live in it or enter it. May the homes of all persons here be blessed. May the hearts of all here be purified.

Third Candlelighter

I light the Candle of Hope and Joy looking forward to the birth of the Christ within my heart and the hearts of all humanity. May the blessing of light be on you, light without and light within. May the blessed sunlight shine upon you and warm your heart till it glows like a great peat fire so that the stranger may come and warm himself at it. And may the light shine out of the eyes of you, like a candle set in the window of a house, bidding the wanderer come in out of the storm.

Fourth Candlelighter

I light the Candle of Identification looking forward to the birth of the Christ within my heart and the hearts of all humanity. (Soul Mantra) "I am the Soul and also love am I. Above all else I am both will and fixed design. My will is now to lift the lower self into the Light Divine. That Light am I. Therefore, I must descend to where that lower self awaits my coming. That which desires to lift and that which cries aloud for lifting are now at one. Such is my will." I Am a child of God and look to the example of my brother, Jesus, as a role model for my life.

Then the celebrant reads the following:

At this enchanted time there occurs a threefold birth: First, the cosmic birth of the Christ Spirit that has been

153

quietly waiting ignites into new life deep within the planet, quickening all nature into a cycle of new birth–awareness and enlightenment.

Secondly, we honor the historic births of all great world teachers who selected winter solstice as the time to enter the earth plane with the blessing of the higher world, as did Master Jesus, the bearer of the Christ Light.

Third, the metaphysical birth of the Christ within each disciple occurs. The birth of the Mystical Christ – the first initiation – manifests within those who have met the challenges of the probationary path. They are already stimulated in the inner temple to aid the continued unfolding of this Christ Within that moves toward further illumination. The birth is beheld everywhere.

The spiritual power of winter solstice culminates on December 24, Christmas Eve. Orthodox Christians pay homage to the birth of the Master Jesus in Bethlehem at this time. Mystical Christians, however, observe a three-fold devotion to the Christ Child, the Christ Light and the Christ Spirit during the holy days of December 21 through 24:

- We pay homage to the Christ Child of Bethlehem.

- We give forth praise and thanksgiving for the awakening Christ Light within ourselves. As we grow day by day and live the highest truth we can grasp, we know this Christ Light expands in power and radiance.

- Most importantly, at this festival we offer devotion, love and recognition to the glorious Cosmic Christ, the light of God brought to earth. On this occasion the greater Christ Light presses into the heart of the planet to regenerate, redeem and restore the Plan on Earth.

What beauty we would behold if we could view the planet at midnight on this holy night – from space and with spiritual eyes! As the Christ reaches the heart of the planetary sphere, the earth would seem to be a radiant, luminous ball, filled with the glory light which only the love and power of the Lord Christ can generate.

Winter solstice, the Festival of Lights, is the time for rejoicing in the light of the cosmos. We welcome the light to the planet! We welcome the Cosmic Christ! On winter solstice we celebrate the cycle of the coming of the Christ impulse. The planetary keynote changes. The universe expresses joyous fellowship.

The keynote changes from Sagittarius to Capricorn – from a bouncing, moving energy to one of stability, anchored within the earth plane. The earth is submerged in the white light of consecration. These forces increase until the holy night of December 24. The powerful solstice radiations of the Cosmic Presence envelop the earth with intense love. Between this celebration and the morning of December 25 – the interval most sacred to early Christians and the mystical tradition – the movement in the heavens is almost still, as cosmic energy penetrates the earth.

*****

Rama of India, one of the first known avatars, is said to have received his illumination on the night of winter solstice and through its power healed all who came to him. Rama created the first sacred ceremonies in observance of the blessed period, it is said, and first called this "the holy night."

The Christ Mass of the early Christians also was celebrated on winter solstice, acknowledging Jesus, the long-promised advanced initiate of the Hebrew tradition, as the Holy One sent to earth to prepare the way for the Planetary Christ. He imparted the revelation of the Christ mystery to his followers, teaching humanity how to develop the living tree of spiritual light within the self.

A magical event occurs in the inner world on this holy night, we are told. The temple doors of the inner halls

155

open. Altar lights gleam. Hymns and the chiming of bells resound. A call, the long-awaited invitation, is issued to the neophyte esteemed worthy (because of the Christ's birth within) to enter the Path of Initiation.

The Christmas season is marked by a profound inner stillness for the sensitive aspirant. Each has waited for the birth of the new self, and at this sacred time, those who are ready enter the portals of initiation. The world is wrapped in white light – a benediction to aid the transformation that can occur in the coming cycle.

Earth's desire currents become quiet as spiritual forces dominate. Heaven bends low, and earth is lifted in the outpouring of love. Angels and archangels tread a pathway of light connecting heaven and earth – singing, chanting and rejoicing.

Celestial forces sweep to earth in long, swirling lines of symmetrical beauty. Mother Earth's work is held symbolically before us in the symbol of the Madonna and Child to remind us that earth is to produce divine heirs.

*****

Each year, four great archangels touch and bless planet earth as it moves in its cycles of awakening, we are told. During their respective reigns, these four beings dispense their angelic forces to humanity and to the planet through the ethers in which the planet floats.

As each annual cycle ends, we prepare to receive the holy touch of the Cosmic Christ, and we speak the sacred names of the archangels with love. We recognize the blessing we and our earth have received from their celestial assistance through the past year.

Drama of the Archangels

The four people chosen as ARCHANGELS now prepare to read their parts.

Celebrant: The drama begins. The holy cycle is about to

change. Are we prepared? An open gateway in the heavens appears – with stars below and above. Starlight outlines the Madonna and Child. A being stands, a tender smile on his lips and in his hand a branch of green. He lives among the stars. His holy name is Gabriel, the angel of love, the angel of winter.

Gabriel speaks: Gabriel, I am. I have stood in the presence of God, and I serve His Holy Name. I touch the earth each year at solstice. With me, multitudes of heavenly hosts praise God, saying, "Glory to God in the highest; peace and good will to all on earth." Last December I set into motion the cycles of this year that is passing, and I blessed them. Then I gently released the light into the hands of Raphael. The archangel of spring, Raphael, stirs the fires of resurrection and of immortality. Every spring he brings healing to earth. Spring erupts into the joy of new life and all of nature sings, "He is risen." Vitality and renewal sweep the earth. Known for the shining aura about the head, the fervor of the heart, the igniting of fervor, the blending of water and fire, the days and nights do pass. The light is passed to Raphael.

Raphael speaks: Raphael, I am, the Angel of Healing – healing of every situation of humankind and every condition of the blocked spirit. Each must be opened. Each heart that fears must find hope and joy and new love. Healing must happen for all kingdoms of the earth. Rich friendship must be built again between the kingdoms. The lion and the lamb must lie down together. Each human must seek friends among the plants, the animals, the crystals, and the gems, as well as among the stars. The heart that closes itself to the light of others closes itself into darkness. Uriel showers the fields with green grass. Abundance is everywhere. Vitality, sunlight and power abound. Life knows no limitations. Uriel stands with a crown of light, brilliant as a star. From the hands fall blessing that take the form of flower petals. Blue and silver lights radiate purification through the atmosphere. I pass the light to Uriel, the archangel of summer.

Uriel speaks: Uriel, I am, the Angel of Beauty. With my angels to help, we paint the faces on every flower and every cloud; we cloak earth in colors soft and sweet. We sweep earth with summer breezes and pure love. Beauty radiates in the air, and everyone displays sweetness and grace. Midsummer marks the perfect fruition of nature's annual work, calling all to produce its finest. The vision of the Christ enfolds humankind, inspiring disciples to fervor. The forces of purification prepare for Michael and his assistants. Michael, the archangel of autumn, carries the flaming blue sword of protection for all of humanity. Michael would integrate the forces of light and encourage all to unite as one force against the tides of negativity. Michael brings celestial realms close to the earth to dispense protection and tender care.

Michael speaks: Michael, I am. The angels of God stand beside the children of light wherever circumstances place them. I am the guardian and protector of the sons and daughters of God. Let no fear be found among you. Fear finds no room in the heart filled with love and light. Stand in faith, call upon the angels of God, and invoke the forces of light. Until the tests pass, I am with you–provided by the higher world to be invincible armor. I walk with you–sword uplifted in my hand, courage upon my face, as I return you to Gabriel. Gabriel is as tender as I am strong, as gentle as I am fierce. He is at the head of the ministering angels who are guardians of all mothers and the newly born – in both the human and animal kingdoms. Gabriel was the constant companion and teacher of the Blessed Mary during her life on earth. Therefore, it is fitting that he rule earth while currents of new birth flood the inner planes with vibrancy and power. I return the light to Gabriel, the archangel of winter.

Gabriel speaks: I, Gabriel, touch earth with truth and light. Heaven and earth shall see great joy. Angelic hosts come close to bless the hearts of those who would find their way into temples made ready. Streams of love pour upon the earth with mighty strength these holy days. The angelic hosts under my command prepare the way; that those who seek the light may find it, that those who would love might love, that those who would serve the Christ might serve. I bring to earth the love that underlies the happenings of the time.

Celebrant: This concludes the drama. We continue now with a meditation.

Entering the Temple Meditation

We turn our attention inward, to penetrate the holy silence and patiently await the thoughts that come to guide us. We breathe and relax, entering the silence of the holy night.

PAUSE

The inner world is bathed in light, quiet. The hush of the Christmas blessing has spread over the world, nurturing and uplifting it, energizing the physical plane. Hear the angelic chorus, "Peace on Earth, Good Will to All."

PAUSE (CAN PLAY MUSIC HERE)

The chorus of angels strengthens our lives. Their energy sustains us in our challenges and heals our pain. Bathed in the love of the Ever-Present and Timeless, we travel an upward spiral to higher and higher consciousness. We seek the realizations of the higher nature.

PAUSE

See a white temple, high on a hill. A mist of holy light surrounds it. We are going from darkness of night into a lighted space. Observe the temple.

PAUSE

Notice the large doors. The patterns on twelve windows filter holy energies to the denser world.

PAUSE

We let it be known by the knocking of our hearts that we wish to be admitted. With our thoughts, we ask to enter, and the doors open. The altar blazes with lights; candles and flowers fill the air with sweetness.

PAUSE

While you know that many are in this pure space, you are also here in the inner chamber alone. Walk to the altar and kneel. "Ask and you shall receive. Knock for it shall be opened unto you."

PAUSE

In the clarity of this moment, know your life and your tests. Strength and growth progress as they should under the guidance of those watching over you. The work of the Inner Brotherhood reaches its zenith; the energy builds hour by hour over these last days. On the large cross over the altar the White Rose is fully open. Its sweet fragrance pervades the senses. Streams of energy shine, stimulate, uplift and flood each being. Gabriel and his angels sing their holy song. Each heart is a chalice, being filled, as the song inspires and comforts us.

PAUSE

(CAN CONTINUE PLAYING ANGELIC CHORUS MUSIC)

You sense a Golden Presence in the luminescence of this white and holy setting, and you bow your head to be blessed by the Lord Christ. He is born anew to the planet, to humanity, to your awareness. His holy hand touches your head, and your heart and mind quicken. You resolve to live, to love, and to learn. In the privacy of this moment, your inner spirit is renewed. The holy night is here. You resolve to begin again, born anew in hope, joy, and beauty, that you might express a vibrant Christ Consciousness to humankind. Open and receptive, we birth the Christ.

PAUSE

Affirm in your heart: "My preparation is done. I have

looked at my life. I prepare my heart and open my mind. I ask the Christ to bless and guide me in the year ahead. May angelic songs comfort and lift me as I discover my continued service and seek to do all that I can. Keeping my feet upon the path, my heart embraces the holy way. The words, 'I have come that they may have life and have it more abundantly,' come unto me. May the Christ be born in me. I know abundant life."

WE WILL NOW SPEND SOME TIME IN SILENCE
(Allow from 5 to 10 minutes of silence)

And now begin to return your awareness to the outer reality. Feel the love in your heart. Breathe. Center yourself in love. The inspiration in your mind focuses on the Christ. Perceive and center yourself in that Holy Presence within. Again, take a deep breath. Resolve to remember this renewal and these feelings, knowing you can return to this peace whenever you choose. We now turn our attention to the outer, renewed and blessed by our inner contact. Be gentle with yourself as you bring the love within to the physical, so that your spirit can endow the world with Christ's love and light. Feel the abundance within as it blesses the world. Allow it to form within you and be a point of strength for the environment you have chosen in the dense world.

PAUSE

Again, take a deep breath, as we shift back to this room. Feel eager now to express the Inner Spirit ever more vibrantly as you live and move and have your being, more firmly a part of the inner and the outer. Amen. Go in peace.

BENEDICTION

I am a source of Endless Love
Centered in the light of Love Divine.
I seek this source in You,
That in humanity we may together build

A point of Love Divine
And send it forth that all who recognize its Light
May build anew. Amen.

SUGGESTED CLOSING SONG

"O Holy Night," considered the song of winter solstice, would be appropriate music to conclude this meditation.

᠙᠙᠙

CHRISTMAS EVE SERVICE

Before the service begins, prepare a tray with candles (bottoms covered with foil), a tray of small cups of wine or grape juice and a chalice of hosts for communion. If you are using the option of having a child put the statue of the Infant Jesus in the manger during the reading of the gospel, put the statue on the altar.

WELCOME: **(Use any appropriate greeting then the following:)**

Today we stand at the very verge of the birth hour of the racial Christ, and out from the darkness of the womb of matter the Christ Child can enter into the Light of the Kingdom of God. Another crisis is upon us, and for this Christ has prepared the race. When He was born at Bethlehem, it was not simply the birth of another Divine Teacher and Messenger, but the appearance of an individual Who not only summed up in Himself the past achievements of the race, but Who was also the forerunner of the future, embodying in Himself all that it was possible for humanity to achieve. The appearance of the Christ in the cave at Bethlehem was the inauguration of the possibility of a new cycle of spiritual unfoldment for the race, as well as for the individual.

Bathe now your Soul in holy Light until Christ's quickening power immerses you in His pure love, and hallows you this hour.

OPTION 1: Light all four advent candles at this service.

162

Before beginning the service, choose four persons, one to light each of the four advent candles and assign a candle to each. It helps to type, on a card, the prayer for each of the candles (shown under "Sundays of Advent") and give it to each person so they can easily read the particular prayer for their candle. Then the celebrant(s) light the Christmas candle, and say(s) the following prayer:

I (WE) light the candle of new birth tonight—The Christ is born! We have beheld His glory, glory as of the Son from the Father and from His fullness have we all received, grace upon grace.

The time has come! The festival of the birth of Jesus Christ Our Lord is here. We celebrate the Word made flesh. And amid presents and parties listen to the proclamation 'Christ is Born!' We pause to ponder with new appreciation the affirmation: "THE LORD IS MY LIGHT."

Eternal God Who is everpresent; Lord Emmanuel, the living Christ; and Divine Comforter; Spirit of Truth, bless this service with Thy mantling and Thy gifts of quickening. Clear our minds, elevate our feelings, and help us to more fully realize the increase of our dedication to Christ. May this night reveal to us how to be better lightbearers. Let the Spirit of the Divine and His Power pour into us and through us into the stream of the whole world.

Now go directly to having all light their candles and say the "Dedication to the Light Prayer."

*****

OPTION 2: If you keep the advent candles burning on your altar, start with the lighting of the Christmas candle. Choose three people to read the three paragraphs of "The Great Invocation, Stanza Two" after the celebrants(s) light the Christmas Candle and say the following:

I(We) light the candle of new birth tonight—The Christ is born! We have beheld His glory, glory as of the Son from the Father and from His fullness have we all received, grace upon grace.

The time has come! The festival of the birth of Jesus Christ Our Lord is here. We celebrate the Word made flesh. And amid presents and parties listen to the proclamation "Christ is Born!" We pause to ponder with new appreciation the affirmation: "THE LORD IS MY LIGHT."

Eternal God Who is everpresent; Lord Emmanuel, the living Christ; and Divine Comforter; Spirit of Truth, bless this service with Thy mantling and Thy gifts of quickening. Clear our minds, elevate our feelings, and help us to more fully realize the increase of our dedication to Christ. May this night reveal to us how to be better lightbearers. Let the Spirit of the Divine and His Power pour into us and through us into the stream of the whole world.

Now have the three people chosen before the service, each read one of the following paragraphs:

THE GREAT INVOCATION, STANZA TWO

Let the Lords of Liberation issue forth,
Let Them bring succor to the sons of men.
Let the Rider from the Secret Place come forth,
And coming, save.
Come forth, O Mighty One.

Let the souls of men awaken to the Light,
And may they stand with massed intent.
Let the fiat of the Lord go forth;
The end of woe has come!
Come forth, O Mighty One.
The hour of service of the Saving Force has now
    arrived.
Let it be spread abroad, O Mighty One.

Let Light and Love and Power and Death
Fulfill the purpose of the Coming One.
The will to save is here.
The Love to carry forth the work is widely spread
    abroad.
The Active Aid of all who know the truth is also

here.
Come forth, O Mighty One, and blend these three.
Construct a great defending wall.
The rule of evil now must end.

*****

**THE SERVICE IS NOW THE SAME FOR BOTH OP-
TIONS. ALL ATTENDEES TAKE A CANDLE FROM A
TRAY THAT HAS BEEN PREPARED BEFORE THE SER-
VICE, AND LIGHT IT FROM THE CHRISTMAS
CANDLE ON THE ALTAR. ALL STAND IN A CIRCLE
AND RECITE THE FOLLOWING PRAYER:**

PRAYER FOR THE DEDICATION OF THE LIGHT

(ALL) I kindle this little light on the Earth plane. I
dedicate it to the service of the Spirit. I guard and cherish
this flame as a living symbol and an act of faith in the
reality of the Powers of Light.

THE GREAT INVOCATION, STANZA ONE

"Let the Forces of Light bring illumination to man
    kind.
Let the Spirit of Peace be spread abroad.
May men of goodwill every where meet in a spirit
of cooperation.
May forgiveness on the part of all men be the
    keynote at this time.
Let power attend the efforts of the Great Ones,
So let it be, and help us to do our part.

Celebrant does a Benediction: The reach of Thy Light is
endless, its influence enduring, its power loving, its potency healing. Each of us offers Thee a gift - the gift of
ourselves. May Thy Light live in us as love. Amen.

**Now have everyone place their candle on trays that have
been covered with foil. Tell them to pull off the foil from
the bottom of their candle, tip the candle so a little wax falls
on the tray then place the bottom of the candle into that**

165

wax to hold it upright. (You may have several trays in different areas of the room or church if there is a large number of people attending.)

READING OF THE GOSPEL

Choose someone to read the gospel. (AN OPTIONAL RITUAL: If you have a nativity scene, ask a child to take the statue of the infant Jesus from the altar and put it into the manger when that part of the gospel is read.) The congregation may stand or sit as you choose.

The holy gospel is taken from the second chapter of the Gospel according to St. Luke, beginning at the first verse.

*****

"It came to pass in those days that there went out a decree from Caesar Augustus that all the world should be enrolled. And all went to be enrolled, everyone into his own city. And Joseph also went up from Galilee, out of the city of Nazareth, into Judaea, unto the city of David, which is called Bethlehem (because he was of the house and lineage of David) to be enrolled with Mary his espoused wife, being great with child. And so it was that, while they were there, the days were accomplished that she should be delivered. (**HERE THE CHILD TAKES THE STATUE OF THE INFANT JESUS FROM THE ALTAR**) And she brought forth her first-born son and wrapped him in swaddling clothes and laid him in a manger (**THE CHILD PUTS THE STATUE INTO THE MANGER**) because there was no room for them in the inn. And there were in the same country shepherds abiding in the field, keeping watch over their flock by night. And lo, the angel of the Lord came upon them and the glory of the Lord shown round about them and they were sore afraid. And the angel said unto them: 'Fear not, for behold, I bring you good tidings of great joy, which shall be to all people. For unto you is born this day in the city of David a saviour, who is Christ the Lord. And this shall be a sign unto you; ye shall find the babe wrapped in swaddling clothes, lying in a manger.' And suddenly there was with the angel a multitude of the heavenly host praising God and saying: "Glory to God in the highest and on earth peace, good-will toward men."

COMMUNION SERVICE

Celebrant reads the esoteric meaning of communion (by Flower Newhouse from her book "The Meaning and Value of the Sacraments" published by The Christward Ministry).

"Provided we have fittingly prepared ourselves, Communion becomes a stepping-up in consciousness. When no negative powers inwardly oppose the unfolding of our Latent Christ, the Divine Spirit and the human Soul are wondrously united. Out of this inner experience comes a conception of regeneration which increases with each highly received Communion.

Esoterically, during the total ceremony a great Angel of the Christ Presence ensouls the aura of the entire assembly. By His purified will and activity an emanation of the Christ Spirit is released which strongly acts upon the celebrant and communicant during the taking of the wafer and juice. The whole mystical service brings the Christ within every person closer to outer awareness. It empowers the God Self to broadcast Its Light, message and peace to the lesser bodies that comprise our multiple faculties."

Blessing of the Bread and Wine

(Over the bread) In receiving this bread, O Christ, we are infused with currents from Thy Life Spirit which works within us to strengthen us. **(Over the wine)** In this juice is symbolized the flowing into expression more of Thy influence which we absorb and live. Amen.

Prayer

Eternal Presence of God, Lord Emmanuel, The Christ, Holy Comforter, Divine Spirit of Grace and Mercy, and Cloud of Silent Witnesses before the Throne—enfold, mantle, purify and bless us in this significant service that we may receive Thy Spirit and more ably glorify Thy

Presence and Cause. May our worship of Thee this night deepen our relationship with Thee, that we may more radiantly live for Thee. Amen.

We come to Thy table, Lord Christ, to Thy truth-giving nourishment spread before us eternally. We receive this bread as Thy eternal substance, and this drink as the symbol of Thy life to which Thou wilt awaken us. All power is Thine, Almighty Spirit of God. Thou didst send us Thy perfected Son to experience the drama of initiation into Christhood here upon the Earth. He inspired the custom of communion as an ever-renewing oneness with those who revere and love Him. As He said to His disciples: "Take, eat (**extend hands over bread**), this is My Life which I give you. Do this in remembrance of Me." He then took the cup (**extend hands over cups of juice**) and said, "Drink ye all of this, for this is My regenerating Life Spirit which I give to you, and to all, for the mastery of self. Do this as oft as ye shall drink it, in remembrance of Me."

The celebrant(s) receive the bread and juice, then all others. The celebrant(s) give the host to each communicant, either onto their outstretched tongue or into their cupped hands, saying, "Receive the body of Christ."

ENDING PRAYER

Everliving Christ, Thou has fed and blessed us through the mysterious beauty of Thy sacrament. May we be ever more conscious of Thy Holy Presence. May we be attuned to Thy ever-present nearness, and to the grace of Thy helpfulness. And so shall it be. Amen.

BENEDICTION

The celebrant extends hands over congregation and says:

"May the peace of God which passeth all understanding bless you, and may His love and wisdom enrich you within continually. Amen."

OPTIONAL ENDINGS:

1 - Sing hymn ("Silent Night," or "O, Holy Night")

2 - (More appropriate for a small group) Do a sharing—have each person share the meaning of Christmas from their heart. This could be a poem, song, experience, etc. Then sing Christmas carols. This can be followed by a covered dish meal or snacks.

HANUKKAH

This Hanukkah information is taken from "THE PEREN-NIAL DICTIONARY OF WORLD RELIGIONS" published by Harper and Row, 10 East 53rd Street, New York, New York 10022.

The origins of Hanukkah are post-biblical and are recorded mainly in rabbinic literature and such contemporary sources as the books of the Maccabees and Josephus. It dates to the Hellenist oppressions under Antiochus Epiphanes (168 B.C.) who decreed that images were to be worshiped in the Jerusalem Temple. A revolt, led by Judas Maccabee and his brothers of the priestly Hasmonean family, ejected the Hellenists from the city after three years of battle. Hanukkah is celebrated on the twenty-fifth of Kislev (December) during which there are no restrictions on labor or food preparation. Hanukkah commemorates the renewal and rededication of the Temple in Jerusalem in the year 165 B.C. by Judas Maccabee, three years to the day after it had been profaned.

Lights are kindled for each of the successive eight days of the festival on a special candelabrum called a **hanukiah**. In addition special prayers are used to commemorate the day. Several traditions surround the eight-day celebration and the kindling of lights. The most popular tells that upon entering the Temple, the Judeans found that the supply of oil used for lighting its gold candelabrum was defiled. Only one vial with an unbroken seal could be found. Though sufficient for only one day, the oil miraculously fueled the candelabrum for eight days, enough time to prepare a fresh supply and rededicate the Temple. Other customs include eating potato pancakes and jelly doughnuts, betting on the spins of a four-sided top (called a dreidel) and offering coins to young children. (**Bibliography: "The Perennial Dictionary of World Religions" and "From Ezra to the Last of the Maccabees" by E. Bickerman; print pages 3-9.**)

KWANZAA: AN AFRICAN-AMERICAN SERVICE

The Kwanzaa information is taken from Modern Maturity magazine (December 1991-January 1992). It is excerpted from an article titled "A Family Festival - Kwanzaa: An African-American Original" by Ken Wibecan.

The word "Kwanzaa" comes from a phrase that means "first fruits" of the harvest in Swahili. The seven-day festival, which begins on December 26 and ends on New Year's Day, has been steadily growing in popularity since it originated in 1966. The creator of the Kwanzaa festival is Maulana Karenga, Ph.D., chair of the Department of Black Studies at California State University, Long Beach. Dr. Karenga says, "This is a holiday based on traditions surrounding the first fruits; it adopts practices prevalent throughout Africa. First-fruit celebrations are a bringing together of a living human harvest, a time for renewing and strengthening the bonds between people. Kwanzaa teaches respect for the family, for the community, and our traditions. Its values are one of our contributions to the best of human culture."

The heart and soul of Kwanzaa are the "Nguzo Saba" (seven principles) guidelines for year-round living. These principles are:

Umoja (unity) – to strive for and maintain unity in the family, community, nation and race.

Kujichagulla (self-determination) – to define ourselves, name ourselves and speak for ourselves instead of being defined and spoken for by others.

Ujima (collective work and responsibility) – to build and maintain our community together and to make our brothers' and sisters' problems our problems and to solve them together.

Ujamaa (cooperative economics) – to build and maintain our own stores, shops, and other businesses and to profit together from them.

Nia (purpose) – to make as our collective vocation the building and developing of our communities in order to restore our people to their traditional greatness.

Kuumba (creativity) – to do always as much as we can, in the way we can, in order to make our community more beautiful and beneficial than when we inherited it.

Imani (faith) – to believe with all our hearts in our parents, our teachers, our legitimate leaders, our people and the righteousness and victory of our struggle.

******

Additional information about Kwanzaa follows and is taken from "Afrikan People and European Holidays: A Mental Genocide, Book 1" written by Rev. Ishakamusa Barashango, published by IV Dynasty Publishing Co., 7706 Georgia Ave., NW, Suite 4, Washington, DC.

Kwanzaa observances often include art shows, poetry readings, musical concerts, dancers, drummers and plays. Nearly every Kwanzaa celebration has a Karamu (feast) on December 31, the sixth night of the holiday.

Finally on the seventh day of Kwanzaa, January 1, the Zawadi (gifts) should be opened. Moreover, it is important that a large family meal be prepared the last day and at the table the seven principles be explained and discussed and the children's commitments for the coming year be heard. Please note that the children should do as much in preparation and celebration of the holidays as they are able to (i.e., decorate, cook, rearrange items, etc.).

Greetings: On each day of a the seven-day holiday, a special greeting is given. When greeted with "Habari gani" (what is the news?), the answer will be one of the Nguzo Saba (seven principles of Blackness).

Decorations: Approximately one week before December 26th, the house should receive a good cleaning so as to welcome the positive forces and your Kwanzaa decorations put up and arranged. A red, black and green color scheme should be dominant for these are the colors of our nation. **Red** stands for the **blood** our ancestors, which has not been shed in vain; the life force which binds us together eternally, **black** is the color of our **skin**, and **green** is symbolic of our rich, **green homeland**, Mother Afrika.

The main table should have as its centerpiece a straw basket or a cornucopia (Horn of Plenty) filled with mixed tropical fruits and vegetables (the mezao-crops or fruits of our labor). Either the floor or a low table should be used to place the mkeka (the straw mat of tradition) and the other items. Place the kinara (seven lamp candle holder) in the center. Then place the ears of muhindi (an ear of corn for each child) around it. Place the zawadi (presents) on the mkeka in any arrangement that is artistic. Finally, the mshumaa (seven candles) should all be placed at the far right of everything else so that they might be available for daily lighting.

The family ceremony: As a further means of drawing the family together, on each evening of Kwanzaa the family should eat together. Following dinner all should form a unity circle around the Kwanzaa setting and each night take turns in the primary portion of the ceremony, which is lighting the candles. The candle is lit and placed in the seven-branch "kinara" (candleholder) to symbolize giving light and life to the seven principles and to the ancient African concept of raising up light to lessen both spiritual and intellectual darkness. Each candle symbolizes one of the principles of the Nguzo Saba. As each night's candle is lit, the candles from the previous nights are lit also. The person lighting the candle should explain the table setting and its symbols to everyone gathered in the unity setting, and give an explanation of the Nguzo Saba principles for that night. It is very important to have the children participate in this part of the celebration.

Following the candle lighting, the Kikombre (unity cup) is passed around. The kikombre should contain unfermented wine (grape juice). Each person within the circle sips from the cup and says "Harambee" which means "we are pulling together" as the cup is passed to the next person. When the cup has completed the circle, the person who lit the candle should lead the circle in seven "Harambees." The seventh and final

"Harambee" should be held as long as possible to symbolize the unity of our people. After that a song or songs of Black unity and love should be sung, while the family prepares to attend community sponsored services and activities in areas where such functions are being observed.

On the last evening of Kwanzaa, January 1, many have found it edifying and revitalizing to have a special ecumenical (that is all Afrikan faiths) spiritual service to strengthen us for the struggles ahead in the coming year.

There is a seriousness of purpose; a sense of belonging not just to a family, but to a culture with rich ancient traditions. By discussing these principles each day with the knowledge that it is not just for one day but is to be incorporated into the entire life, Kwanzaa teaches the children the spiritual aspects of the season and gets them away from the commercial aspects.

While most Kwanzaa activities are family affairs, on December 31st family and friends join with other members of the community for the "karamu" (feast). This final event is particularly festive. The karamu site is decorated in the rich red, black, and green that has come to symbolize Africa, adults and children wear colorful African garments, and all present contribute dishes to the karamu table. It is a time for good fellowship, a time for learning, a time for sharing.

CHAPTER 7

HEALING SERVICES

$\mathcal{H}$ealing services have been conducted since the beginning of civilization. All healing comes from changes within the person. The minister acts as a channel for the Divine energies of healing but it is up to the receiver to accept and work with it. That person must change the attitudes or circumstances which caused the disease.

THE LAW OF CURE

There can be instantaneous healing but this is a rare occurrence. The normal reaction is a gradual improvement of the problem over time. It is helpful for you to understand and be able to explain the Law of Cure to the person receiving healing in case of a reoccurrence of their symptoms. The natural Law of Cure is:

- Healing occurs from the inside to the outside. There will be improvements in attitudes and feelings before physical symptoms change. (Healing also takes place on an upward spiral, usually reaching its peak three days after the initial healing session. It would thus be advantageous to schedule another healing session in a week.)

- Healing moves from the top downward or from head to foot. Example: A rash will start clearing from the top of the body first.

- Symptoms will reappear and clear in the opposite order that they appeared, so recently occurring conditions respond more quickly than chronic conditions. (All disease or discordant energy that has lodged in the cellular memory of the body must be released in order to be cured. When these symptoms are experienced after a healing session, it is called a "healing crisis" and will last a very short time. However, it is a good sign that the problem has been eliminated.)

In this chapter we will cover such types of services as laying-on-of hands, absent healing and exorcism of persons and places.

LAYING-ON-OF-HANDS

The Ministers or Healing Practitioners should be in touch with their own inner guidance. They should channel God's energy and **NOT USE THEIR OWN ENERGY.**

How to Channel Energy

First ask God to use you as a channel of His healing energies. Then visualize God's white light coming down from infinity, flowing through the top of your head into your heart and connecting with the God essence within you. Breathe in deeply and FEEL the energy coming in, then breathe out and FEEL the energy coming from your heart and out of your hands. When the energy is flowing well, place them on the person needing healing. Ask within for guidance as to where to place your hands and what to do for the highest good of the person requesting healing. Listen within for inspiration.

*****

Following are Healing Services from various religions.

HEALING SERVICES
Universal Spiritualist

If the Healing Service is a separate and complete service it shall be begun by the Minister of Healing with an appropriate call to worship and hymn.

The Minister of Healing shall then say:

Let us pray.

Most merciful Father, we Thy children approach Thee with humbleness of heart, beseeching Thee that Thou wilt send down upon us gathered here a manifestation of healing power. We ask for the presence of ministering angels, with healing in their wings. We reach up in faith to touch the hem of the garment of Him who taught us to pray.

ALL SAY "THE LORD'S PRAYER"

The Minister of Healing shall then say:

We humbly follow the example of Jesus the Christ and His holy apostles in the Cure of Sickness by the Laying On of Hands. Let those who have need come forward in faith.

If other Servers are to assist, chairs for each of them and one for the Minister of Healing have previously been placed in the front of the church, facing the congregation. The healers take their places behind each chair. The supplicants (those who wish to receive individual healing treatments) come forward and sit in the chairs. Music may be played during the healing treatments or the congregation may sing an appropriate hymn such as "The Great Physician." The healer places both hands, palms down, over the head of the supplicant, saying:

In the name of God the Father, God the Son, and God the Holy Spirit; be thou made clean, be thou made whole, be thou made well. Amen.

When all treatments are finished, the Minister shall close the Healing Service with this prayer:

O divine Master, we turn to Thee in deep humility, thanking Thee that Thou art so willing to give, that Thou art so patient, that Thou art so understanding. And as we thank Thee, there descends upon us something of gladness and peace, so that we can return to the tasks of daily

177

life renewed, replenished, recharged with virtue bestowed by Thee. Thy grace indeed is sufficient for each and every one. Amen.

Prayers for Healing Services

O Thou Who art our life, we humbly seek to draw closer, and to hold sweet and pure communion with Thy Spirit. May we realize the truth of the words, "Breathe on me, Breath of God." For indeed our souls can breathe in Thy life, Thy love, Thy peace. May our inner vision open to the life eternal and to those angelic beings who of Thy bidding come to this service to bring healing, inspiration, courage, and strength, and that deep peace which is not of this earth but of Thy heaven. May the presence of the Lord Christ be felt and seen during this service. Amen.

*****

Almighty Spirit, our Father-Mother God, we bring our hearts to Thee, in prayer, asking to be cleansed and healed of all conflict and all ills. We feel the presence of Thy ministering angels, O Lord. We are enfolded in Thy peace, and we pray humbly that the healing waters may be stirred, and that we may so be restored to harmony, to health, and to Thy life which is perfect. O God, we pray that all present in this service may receive the healing touch, may receive balm to their souls and strength to their bodies. May the vision open for us all so that we see clearly the truth of Thy life and the presence of the company of shining spirits who are Thy messengers and servers of humanity. So may the glorious presence of the Cosmic Christ be made clear and real to our souls. Amen.

*****

FOR THE RECOVERY OF HEALTH

O Father of mercies, and God of all comfort, our only help in time of need, we lift up our hearts unto Thee on behalf of this Thy servant. Look graciously upon him (her) we beseech Thee, and strengthen him (her) with Thy grace. We know, O

Lord, that all things are possible with Thee. In keeping with Thy will, restore him (her) to health and strength, and to Thy name shall be the praise forever. Amen.

The Liturgy of the Liberal Catholic Church
A Service of Healing

The purpose of the Service of Healing is twofold: first, to bring spiritual upliftment to those who are in sore need thereof; secondly, to give some relief, when possible, to those who are suffering from various physical ills.

At the outset, by means of the asperges, the thought atmosphere of the church is purified and made ready for the coming of a healing angel, who is immediately thereafter invoked. The confiteor follows and the attitude of those who join in this confession should result in an earnest desire to rise above the imperfections of their nature and to live a higher and nobler life. Such an attitude arouses our spiritual powers to activity. The priest then pronounces the absolution; it must be remembered that this does not relieve a man of responsibility for the consequences his wrong-doing, because it is only by paying each debt which he contracts that he can learn the great lessons of life. Absolution does make it easier, however, to do what is right after a mistake that has been made, by clearing away the mental and emotional entanglements which blind the inner nature and by straightening our distortions in the etheric body.

The people rise and sing a hymn which is intended to incline their hearts to the Christ and to enable them to feel the nearness of His presence and the wonder of His love. The words of this hymn should be felt as well as sung by those who desire help. St. James' instructions as to the anointing of the sick are then read and the **Veni Creator**, which is the traditional call for the aid of God the Holy Ghost, is sung by His kneeling worshippers. While this is sung, for eyes that can see, the whole church slowly fills with that glorious glow of fire which is the outward manifestation of the presence of the Third Person of the Blessed Trinity; and in the strength of that Presence the priest sends forth a cleansing current of exorcism which is intended to clear anything that might hinder the working of the healing power.

This next step is to follow the apostolic custom of anointing the patient with consecrated oil, invoking the mighty leader of the hosts of the healing angels, the Archangel Raphael. The possibility of angelic assistance is unsuspected by the vast majority of people in this age, but it is nevertheless a wonderful and beautiful fact which will be comprehended more and more fully as the years roll on. Then the priest lays his hands upon the patient's head and pours into him, with all the strength which God has given to him, the uplifting and healing power of the Lord Christ. He has been specially prepared by his ordination to be a channel for this, and for the power of God the Holy Spirit. In doing this he is exercising one of the functions of his ministry. If a bishop is present at the service he has the additional opportunity of helping by the imposition of his crozier, the healing power of which has long been recognized.

During the anointing and the laying on of hands the attitude of the patient should be that of love for our Lord Christ and confidence in His mighty power. The whole nature should be opened to the downpouring spiritual influence, even as a flower opens its petals to the sun. The less the thoughts of a person are centered upon himself at this moment, the more the depths of his nature are responsive to the compassionate presence of the Christ, and the greater is the possibility of cure.

The greatest means of spiritual aid and physical healing is now given to the patient in the holy communion. No greater help both for body and soul can be offered than this, for with the reception of the sacred Host the human body becomes for a few hours a veritable shrine, radiating the glowing love and power of the Christ.

It is not expected that those instantaneous cures which are commonly (though wrongly) called miraculous will often occur at these services. They may and they do happen in certain cases; but we are not yet sufficiently conversant with the method of working of these stupendous powers to be able to predict results. Many patients, especially chronic cases, feel considerable temporary improvement, but gradually relapse either partially or entirely. Such patients should try again. Where there is a slight amelioration, only temporary at the first attempt, second and subsequent attempts may well carry it much further. Even Christ Himself had to apply His treatment twice in the case of the man born blind.

If a patient is not restored to health even after repeated attempts it must not be thought that Christ cannot heal, that the Holy Spirit cannot heal. It may be that there are circumstances and factors, not known to us, which may prevent or hinder the desired result. The priest will do his best to help; the patient will do his best to prepare himself to be helped; what will come of it is in higher hands than ours, in the hands of Christ the Healer and the King.

If it be desired to hold a special intercessory service for sick persons, the Holy Eucharist may be offered for that intention, the collect, epistle and gospel of St. Raphael being used, and the names of the sick being mentioned in the usual place.

When the healing service is celebrated immediately after the Holy Eucharist, the asperges, confiteor and absolution should be omitted, but the invocation of the healing angel should be said immediately after the invocation of the Blessed Trinity. Patients should receive communion at the service of healing rather than at the Eucharist.

THE INVOCATION

All stand. The priest wears a red stole or, if the Veni Creator be omitted, a green stole. The people stand. The priest says:

"In the name of the Father + and of the Son and of the Holy Ghost. Amen."

ASPERGES

Receiving the aspergill the priest makes the sign of the cross over himself with it saying:

"May the Lord purify me that I may worthily perform His service."

Sprinkling the altar in the middle, then the chancel to his left and to his right, he continues:

"In the strength of the Lord do I repel all evil from this His holy altar and sanctuary:"

Then turning to the people and sprinkling them with the same triple motion, he continues:

"and from this house, wherein we worship Him:"

Turning back to the altar and resigning the aspergill:

"and I pray our heavenly Father that He will send His healing angel to minister unto these His servants here present, that they may be restored to health of mind and body; through Christ our Lord. Amen."

CONFITEOR

All kneel and say together:

"O Lord, Thou has created man to be immortal and made him an image of Thine own eternity; yet often we forget the glory of our heritage and wander from the path which leads to righteousness. But Thou, O Lord, hast made us for Thyself and our hearts are ever restless till they find their rest in Thee. Look with the eyes of Thy love upon our manifold imperfections and pardon all our shortcomings, that we may be filled with the brightness of the everlasting light and become the unspotted mirror of Thy power and the image of Thy goodness; through Christ our Lord. Amen."

THE ABSOLUTION

The priest rises, goes to the altar and, turning to the people, who remain kneeling, says:

"God the Father, God the + Son, God the Holy Ghost bless, preserve and sanctify you. The Lord in His loving kindness look down upon you and be gracious unto you; the Lord + absolve you from all your sins and grant you the grace and comfort of the Holy Spirit. Amen."

A hymn may be sung here and the people are seated.

READING FROM SCRIPTURE

Hear the words of the apostle James: "Is any sick among you? Let him call for the elders of the church; and let them pray over him, anointing him with oil in the name of the Lord. And the prayer of faith shall save the sick and the Lord shall raise him up; and if he have committed sins, they shall be forgiven him. Pray for one another that ye may be healed. The effectual fervent prayer of a righteous man availeth much."

All kneel while the following appeal is sung:

VENI CREATOR

Come, Thou Creator Spirit blest,
And in our souls take up Thy rest;
Come with Thy grace and heavenly aid,
To fill the hearts which Thou hast made.

Great Paraclete, to Thee we cry,
O highest gift of God most high;
O living fount, O fire, O love,
And sweet anointing from above.
Thou in Thy sevenfold gift are known,
Thee, finger of God's hand, we own,
The promise of the Father, Thou
Who dost the tongue with power endow.

Kindle our senses from above,
And make our hearts o'erflow with love;
With patience firm and virtue high
The weakness of our flesh supply.

Far let us drive our tempting foe,
And Thine abiding peace bestow;
So shall we not, with Thee for guide,
Turn from the path of life aside.

O may Thy grace on us bestow
The Father and the Son to know,
And Thee, through endless times confessed,
Of both eternal Spirit blessed.

All glory while the ages run
Be to the Father and the Son,
Who gave us life; the same to Thee,
O Holy Ghost, eternally. Amen.

THE UNCTION

Priest: Let us pray.

The people kneel.

183

Priest: O Lord, Who hast given unto man bodily health and vigor wherewith to serve Thee, we pray Thee to free Thy servants from their sickness (or imperfections or weakness) so far as may be expedient for them and by the might of Thy + blessing to restore unto them full health, both outwardly in their bodies and inwardly in their souls; through Christ our Lord. Amen.

The people are seated. Those who desire to be anointed come forward and kneel at the communion rail. The priest now says over each one:

Priest: In the Name which is above every name, in the power of the + Father and of the + Son and of the Holy + Ghost, I exorcise all influences of evil, that thou mayest be rightly purified to receive this sacrament of Holy Unction.

Taking upon his thumb some of the holy oil for the sick, the priest anoints the person in the form of a cross upon the forehead saying:

"In the Name of our Lord Christ and invoking the help of the holy Archangel Raphael, I + anoint thee with oil, that thou mayest gain refreshment both of soul and body."

The priest proceeds to anoint, in the same manner as before but in silence, the center at the top of the head, the front of the throat and the nape of the neck. He then places both hands upon the head of the person with the definite intent to heal, saying:

"Christ the Son of God pour down His healing power upon thee, and enfold thee in the light of His love."

When all desiring the sacrament of holy unction have been anointed, the priest cleanses his hands and turning to the people, says:

"As with this visible oil your bodies are outwardly anointed, so may almighty God, our heavenly Father, grant of His infinite goodness that your souls may be anointed inwardly with the Holy Ghost, Who is the Spirit of strength, relief, and gladness. And may He so replenish you with the spirit of His wisdom and strengthen you with His mighty power, that you may persevere in the way of holiness and ever serve Him joyfully in the course that He hath appointed for you, through Christ our Lord. Amen."

THE COMMUNION

The priest turns to the altar and says:

"O God, who in the wonderful sacrament of the altar has left us a living memorial of Thine eternal sacrifice; grant us, we beseech Thee, so to receive the sacred mystery of Thy Body and Blood that we may ever perceive within ourselves the power of Thine indwelling life and thus, by the glad pouring out of our lives in sacrifice, may know ourselves to be one with Thee and through Thee with all that lives; Who livest and reignest with the Father in the unity of the Holy Spirit, God throughout all ages of ages. Amen."

Those who have been anointed kneel at the chancel rail and the priest administers holy communion to them, saying to each:

"The Body of our Lord Christ keep thee unto life eternal."

When all have partaken, the people rise. A hymn may be sung here.

Priest: Let us pray.

The people kneel.

Priest: We who have been refreshed with Thy heavenly gifts do pray Thee, O Lord, that Thy grace may be so grafted inwardly in our hearts, that it may continually be made manifest in our lives; through Christ our Lord. Amen.

THE BENEDICTION

The priest turns to the people and says:

"Unto God's gracious love and protection we commit you; the Lord + bless you and keep you; the Lord make His face to shine upon you and be gracious unto you; the Lord lift up the light of His countenance upon you and give you His peace, now and for evermore. Amen."

If Benediction of the Most Holy Sacrament is to follow, the priest turns towards the altar and says, instead of the benediction, the following prayer:

"+ The grace of our Lord Jesus Christ and the love of God and the fellowship of the Holy Ghost be with us all evermore. Amen."

⌒

ABSENT HEALING

(This explanation is taken from "An Outline of Spiritual Healing" by Gordon Turner, a great British healer.)

"The healer, in absent healing, is an agent of transmission. Distance prevents him from assisting the healing power by the easy movements of locked joints or the soothing away of pain in conjunction with the healing power. Thus it would appear that spirit intervention is direct. It would seem that a spiritual influence requires a material agency through which it can manifest upon a physical plane. Even though thousands of miles may separate patient and healer, the healer is still the medium through which the healing is translated. Absent healing, despite its apparently nebulous character is, in fact, carried out on as personal a level as possible.

A mental link has to be made with each patient. This link is essential for spirit workers to make the contact they need. One possible explanation could be that the healing force needs a medium, acting as does a catalyst in a chemical process, before it can be used to any specific purpose. A sick person requests a healer to make contact with the spiritual sphere. The healer projects his thoughts both towards the sick person and towards the spiritual realm. A link is formed which permits a direct contact to be made. A state of auric attunement is built up between the patient and healer. Stage by stage, spiritual stimulus is translated into mental and physical reaction and the health of the patient gradually improves."

How to Send Absent Healing

Sit quietly, breathe deeply, and ask to be a channel for Divine Light, Love and healing energies. If you know what the sick person looks like, visualize them standing in front of you. Always see them as whole, healthy, and happy. Breathe in the Divine Light, and as you breathe out, see white light fill and surround the person who requested the healing. Ask the healing angels to wrap the person in wings of love and healing energies.

If you do not know what the person looks like, you can simply see yourself writing their name in golden light while asking that what is for their highest good will happen.

〜

Universal Spiritualist Absent Healing Service

The Healing Service shall be begun by the Minister of Healing with an appropriate Call to Worship and Hymn.

The Minister of Healing shall then say:

"Let us pray. Most merciful Father, we Thy children approach Thee with humbleness of heart, beseeching Thee that Thou wilt send upon us gathered here a manifestation of healing power. We ask for the presence of ministering angels, with healing in their wings. We reach up in faith to touch the hem of the garment of Him who taught us to pray."

All say the Lord's Prayer. The Minister of Healing shall then say:

"Dearly beloved, speak now clearly the names of the suffering absent."

The people do so.

After the names are called, he shall say:

187

"We offer unto Thee, O Father, the names of Thy children who stand in need of Thy care. Amen."

This may conclude the Healing Service or be a prelude to a Communion Service.

༄༅༄

THE EXORCISM AND BLESSING OF A PERSON

The following is taken from "Exorcism The Report of a Commission Convened By the Bishop of Exeter" edited by Dom Robert Petipierre, O.S.B. in London 1972.

Exorcism of human beings was a normal, frequent, and repeated routine liturgical action for all candidates for Christian initiations, from the end of the second century at least. In less emphatic form than in the earlier centuries it still remains so in the Eastern orthodox Churches, and in the newly-reformed baptismal rite of the holy Roman Church. Realization of this fact helps to reduce the present unfortunate emphasis on exorcism as an action concerned exclusively with so-called demonic "possession" exorcisms. It cannot be overstressed that, as it is usually understood, the concept of demonic "possession" is extremely dubious.

In the first place it should be assumed that the patient's illness has a physical or mental cause, and the case should be referred by his general practitioner to a competent physician in psychological medicine. The exorcism of a person must not be performed until possible mental or physical illness has been excluded in this way, and furthermore until a thorough investigation has been made of the patient in terms of spiritual values by a duly licensed exorcist. Only in an extreme emergency should either of these safeguards be omitted. The need for exorcism, however, when all other steps have been taken, may still arise. The testing and decision about this should be undertaken only by a priest (or minister) with experience in such matters.

*** <u>AN INEXPERIENCED MINISTER SHOULD ASK THE HELP OF AN EXPERIENCED MINISTER BEFORE ATTEMPTING AN EXORCISM AND ON NO ACCOUNT TRY THIS ALONE.</u>

Rules for Exorcism

1. The priest should only undertake the exorcism of a person if he himself is in a state of recollection and confident of our Lord's victory over evil in general and in the situation confronting him.

2. It is wise to share such situations with another priest experienced in this aspect of the ministry. (The more strong spiritual persons present, the safer it is to do an exorcism.)

3. The priest should prepare himself, and those who he selects to be present, by confession, prayer, and fasting, and if possible, communion together.

4. Those present should consist only of mature Christian people who are sympathetic to this ministry. If the afflicted person is a woman, at least one other woman should be present willing to restrain or help her as occasion demands.

5. People unknown to the priest should not be present. This includes those "interested" reporters, and so on, not least because of the spiritual danger in which they place themselves.

6. If the exorcism takes place in a house, animals and children should be removed, and the latter given a prayer of protection and a blessing before the service begins.

7. The service should, if possible, take place in a church or sacred space, or at least in a place chosen by or agreeable to the exorcist.

8. Appropriate steps should be taken to ensure that no unscheduled exit on the part of the person is possible before the ministration is complete.

9. It is recommended that doctor and psychiatrist are aware of the steps that are being taken by the Church, and that, if they are not excluded by the demands of (4) above, they be invited to attend.

10. Prayers of a select number of other Christians not present should be encouraged, not only for the sufferer but also for those present and the exorcist. Such imparted knowledge need not include personal details, and must not be such as

would break confidences or cause gossip.

11. As, occasionally, a prolonged period is necessary, two hours or more should be made available, so that if the case is of this nature the person will not be left in a state of acute distress by an uncompleted ministry.

12. If the sufferer is brought into church, he should on no account be left alone, but at least two people, capable of restraining violent activity, should stay with him. (If these people are to attend the exorcism itself, it will mean that separate arrangements may have to be made for their spiritual preparation.)

13. The priest should not hesitate at any time prior to the exorcism itself to dismiss any person or persons whose presence, for any reason, he feels to be inappropriate. The presence of another priest makes it possible for the would-be exorcist, if inexperienced, to exclude himself should he, for example, experience sudden doubt or fear. This is not a trivial point.

14. Because of the possibility of self-injury, the patient could well be seated in a deep armchair throughout the service.

15. The exorcist should be open to the possibility that after the exorcism other sacramental means of grace would be appropriate: e.g. Holy Communion, Holy Unction, and perhaps even Baptism. It is wise to arrange things so that these are readily available without the need for extensive preparations.

The Immediate Preparation

Candles, incense, and sacred music will help create a protected atmosphere. All attending should be anointed with blessed oil on the forehead, front of throat, nape of neck, back of ears, and front and backs of the wrists and sprinkled with holy water. All should pray that the Angels and Beings of Light be there for protection and to take in hand any lost souls and show them the way to the Light. (This should be done before the person requiring the exorcism is brought into the room.)

Now bring in the person needing exorcism, anoint them with blessed oil and sprinkle them with holy water and

place them in a chair in the center of the circle of people attending.

The exorcist then creates a sacred space by making a circle of lighted candles, sprinkling holy water around the circumference of the circle and praying to the Archangels of the four directions as follows:

Face north and say:

I call on **MICHAEL**, the Archangel of the North to seal the portal to this place and make it a sacred space. Bring Beings of Light here to guard and protect and heal.

Then face south and say:

I call on **GABRIEL**, the Archangel of the South to seal the portal to this place and make it a sacred space. I call on all the Healing Agnels and Beings of Light to come here now and transmute all negative energies.

Then face east and say:

I call on **RAPHAEL**, the Archangel of the East to seal the portal to this place and make it a sacred space. Bring Beings of Light and Healing here to help with this healing now.

Then face west and say:

I call on **URIEL**, the Archangel of the West to seal the portal to this place and make it a sacred space. Bring all the Healing Spirits, Angels, and Beings of Light here to join in on freeing this soul from all harmful attachments and take any lost soul to the Light.

All now say the Lord's Prayer, after which someone should read John I:1-14. After this shall be a pause for silent prayer, which could conclude with the following:

O God, whose nature and property it is ever to have mercy and to forgive, grant that the chains of evil binding this person may, by your mercy, be loosed, and let no evil power harm any one. Through Jesus Christ your Son our Lord. Amen.

The Exorcism of a Person

Prior to the ceremony, ask inwardly for guidance as to which exorcism prayer to use for this particular person.

O Holy Lord, Almighty Father, Who has sent Your only begotten Son into the world that He might destroy the works of the devil, speedily hear us we pray You. Grant strength to Your servants to fight valiantly against the evil one. May the strength of Your right hand make Satan loose Thy servant (name of person....) so that he no longer dares to hold captive him (her) whom You have made in Your image and redeemed in Your Son; Who lives and reigns with You in the unity of the Holy Spirit, world without end. Amen.

The exorcist then puts a rosary around the neck of the person and/or gives them a crucifix to hold. The exorcist then stands firmly in front of the person, holding a crucifix at arm's length so it is about one foot in front of the person's face and says one of the following prayers according to inner guidance:

1. I command you, every evil spirit, in the Name of God the Father Almighty, in the Name of Jesus Christ His only Son, and in the Name of the Holy Spirit, that harming no one you depart from this creature of God, (name of person....) and return to the place appointed you, there to remain forever.

2. I command you, every unclean spirit, in the Name of God the Father Almighty, in the Name of Jesus Christ His Son our Lord and our Judge, and by the power of the Holy Spirit, that you go from this image of God, (name of person...) whom our Lord of His goodness has called to become a temple of the living God, that the Holy Spirit may dwell in him (her). Through the same Christ our Lord. Amen. (From the Roman Ritual.)

3. I command you, unclean spirits, in the name of the Father and of the Son and of the Holy Spirit, that you come out and depart from this person (name....) whom our Lord

Jesus Christ has vouchsafed to call to Baptism and so to be made a member of His Body and congregation. Therefore, thou cursed spirit, remember your sentence and your judgement, remember the day to be at hand wherein you shall burn in fire everlasting prepared for you and your angels. And presume not hereafter to exercise any tyranny towards this person whom Christ hath bought with His precious blood, and by His Holy Baptism called to be of His flock. Amen. (From First Prayer Book of Edward VI.)

4. I command you, O evil spirit, through God the Father Almighty, and through Jesus Christ His Son, and through the Holy Spirit the Paraclete, that you depart, through His power, from this His vessel, (name..) whom you hold captive. (From the East Syrian Rite.)

If, as occasionally happens, there are somewhat violent physical reactions, the patient should be firmly held down, and another form of exorcism (one of the above) should be repeated.

It can be helpful, if this occurs, to use also some form of Saint Patrick's Breastplate, such as:

Christ be with you; Christ within you; Christ before you; Christ behind you; Christ on your right hand; Christ on your left hand; Christ above you; Christ beneath you, Christ round about you. (**This can well be said with both hands on the patient's head.**)

When it appears that the person has been released, give them a blessing as follows. (If any of the inhabitants of the house has been seriously disturbed, frightened, or damaged by the past events in the place, it is of considerable value for them to also receive the Laying on of Hands. The form given here, taken with slight adaptation from that issued by the Guild of St. Raphael, is suitable:)

In the Name of God most High may release from your pain be given you, and your health be restored according to His holy will.

In the Name of Jesus Christ the Prince of life, may new life surge through your mortal body.

In the Name of God the Holy Spirit may you receive inward health and the peace that passes understanding.

And may God, who gives us peace, make you completely His, and keep your whole being, spirit and soul and body, free from all fault at the coming of our Lord, Jesus Christ. Amen.

FINAL PRAYER

O God, the creator and defender of men, look upon this your servant, (name..). Drive back from him (her), O Lord, the power of the demons and banish forever their treacherous deceits. May the wicked tempters flee away. May your servant, (name..) be fortified in mind and body by the power of your Name.

Guard his (her) inner life, rule his (her) desires, strengthen his (her) purposes. May the powerful temptations of the enemy vanish from his (her) soul.

Grant grace, O Lord, by this invocation of your Name, that the prince of this world, who has struck terror until now, may himself flee in terror to his own place. And may this your servant be enabled to do your will with a firm heart and undivided mind; through Jesus Christ your Son our Lord. Amen.

THE FINAL BLESSING

This can be given in any form which is acceptable. It is good that hands should be lain on the person's head. The following form is possible for such use:

God the Father, Who creates you, preserve and keep you. God the Son, Who bought you with His blood, bind you to Himself. God the Holy Spirit, the Giver of life, grant you the new and eternal life.

May all the Saints pray with you. May the holy Angels

and Archangels guard, guide, and protect you; and the Blessing of God Almighty, the Father, the Son, and the Holy Spirit be upon you now and always. Amen.

IN AN EMERGENCY

The exorcist must make a quick, deep act of Recollection calling upon the help and power of the Holy Spirit, and then speak the Command, using perhaps the form, "God, the Son of God" as in the exorcism of places, or else a brief command to the effect:

In the Name of Jesus Christ our Lord, I command you, evil spirit, to harm no one, but depart to the place appointed you.

THE EXORCISM AND BLESSING OF A PLACE

It is a good idea for a minister to have prepared ahead of time items needed for the exorcism of a house. Forms for preparing the holy water and oil are given below. It is suggested that you have a large bag or briefcase in which to put everything needed. A kit should have: holy water, blessed oil, candles and candleholders, incense and incense holder, matches, several crucifixes, a rosary, and papers with the appropriate prayers and gospel reading.

Forms for Blessing Holy Water and Salt

Salt, in quantity enough to cover a two-penny piece, is placed on a piece of paper. Water, in suitable quantity in a bowl or jug, stands beside the salt. The salt is exorcised and blessed first and then the water. After this they are mixed by pouring the salt into the water, and the last prayer is said.

It is well, when a house or place is being dealt with, to carry out this blessing in the presence of those concerned so that they come to understand that Holy Water is not a "Christian Magic" but the symbol of the prayers that are offered to God as it is blessed.

EXORCISM OF THE SALT

I exorcise you, creature of salt, by the living God, so that you be fit for the healing of mind and body of all who use you. Wherever you are sprinkled may all evil and wicked thoughts depart, all works and deceits of the evil one be driven away, and all unclean spirits be cast out, by Him who is ready to judge the living and the dead. Amen.

BLESSING OF THE SALT

Almighty and eternal God, graciously bless and make holy this creature of salt. May it give health of body and mind to them that use it. Let all touched or sprinkled with it be protected against all that is sinful and against all attacks of spiritual wickedness. Through Jesus Christ your Son, our Lord. Amen.

EXORCISM OF THE WATER

I exorcise you, creature of water, in the Name of God the Father Almighty, in the Name of His Son our Lord, and in the power of the Holy Spirit, that you be fit to put to flight all the power of Satan and to root out and expel Satan himself and his fallen angels; through the power of the same Lord Jesus Christ Who shall come to judge the living and the dead. Amen.

BLESSING OF THE WATER

Almighty God, Father Eternal, hear our prayers and bless and make holy this creature of water, that it may serve you for the casting out of devils and the driving away of sickness of mind and body. Grant that whatever is sprinkled with this water may be cleansed from all that is foul or harmful. Let no sickness abide there, and cause all the power of the unseen enemy, with his cunning and deceits, to go away.

Through this water dispel all that is contrary to the health and peace of your people, so that, protected by the invocation of your Holy Name, they may be secure against every adversary; through Jesus Christ your Son our Lord. Amen.

The officiant then pours the salt into the water, saying:

May this mixing of salt and water be done in the Name of the Father and of the Son and of the Holy Spirit. Amen.

After this mixing, he shall say:

Almighty Father, look with mercy on this creature of salt and water and of your loving kindness sanctify it. Wherever it shall be sprinkled with the invocation of your holy Name may the attacks of evil spirits be repelled and the fear of evil be kept far away.

May the presence of the Holy Spirit be given to all who seek your mercy; through Jesus Christ your Son our Lord, who lives and reigns with you and the same Holy Spirit, ever one God, world without end. Amen.

Rules for Exorcising a Building

1. **At all exorcisms it is well to have one or two committed and instructed Christians present to help in prayer, since exorcism is an act of the Church and not simply of an individual.**

2. **If an outside site has to be exorcised and blessed, it is better that the assistants stand within sight of the exorcist, but do not walk round with him, as this might attract undesirable attention and publicity.**

3. **When a building is to be exorcised the assistants would normally accompany the exorcist from place to place within it. If the building is a house, then the congregation would normally include some members of the household. In such case all should be gathered in one room, which would be exorcised and blessed at the start. The congregation would remain in that room until the end of the operation.**

4. **When all is ready, the officiant will lead in prayers.**

These should include the Lord's Prayer, a confession and absolution, a short reading from the Gospels with a request to our Lord for His help, and an invocation of the Holy Spirit. After this it may be useful to add some portion of the Mozarabic form as follows:

Preparatory Prayer - Mozarabic Rite

O God, the Author of blessing and Fount of salvation, we earnestly pray and beseech You to pour the manifold dew of Your grace and the abundance of Your blessing upon this place. Amen.

May You grant it prosperity and drive out adversity. Amen. May You drive out Satan, the author of evil. Amen.

May You place herein the angel of light, the guard and defender of good. Amen. By the multitude of Your mercies may peace abound for those who dwell in this place and may there always be present here, O Lord, those of Your gifts which are profitable to all. Amen.

AND/OR

Send, O Lord, to this dwelling Your good and holy angel, as watchman, sentinel, and guard to resist evil things and provide good things so that all disquiet and disaster may be banished from this house. Amen.

May Your Presence always keep far from here need, pestilence, sickness, and the attacks of the evil ones so that, where your holy Name is invoked, abundant good may follow and the attacks of the demons be driven back and Your protection and the help of the Saints take their place. Amen.

Our Father, Who art in heaven, hallowed be Thy Name. Thy Kingdom come, Thy will be done on earth as it is in heaven. Give us this day our daily bread and forgive us our trespasses as we forgive those who trespass against us; and lead us not into temptation, but deliver us from evil; for Thine is the kingdom, the power, and the glory forever and ever. Amen.

May the Lord bless and sanctify this tabernacle of His servants and grant to them the riches of the kingdom of heaven. Amen.

5. **The exorcist shall then pronounce the form of exorcism in this main room. A possible form runs as follows:**

God, the Son of God, Who by death destroyed death, and overcame him who had the power of death, beat down Satan quickly.

Here the officiant makes the sign of the cross over the place and exhales deeply, then continues:

Deliver this place (room, house, church) from all evil spirits; all vain imaginations, projections and phantasms; and all deceits of the evil one; and bid them harm no one but depart to the place appointed them, there to remain forever. God, incarnate God, Who came to give peace, bring peace.

6. **Having said the form of exorcism, the exorcist then goes round the room sprinkling it with holy water. When he returns to his place a blessing should be given on the congregation and the room by the exorcist:**

The Blessing of God Almighty, the Father, the Son, and the Holy Ghost, be upon this place and upon all here present, now and always. Amen.

7. **The exorcist then goes round the rest of the house or building, repeating the form of exorcism as he goes and sprinkling with holy water. The assistants should go with him, carrying candles and incense, opening doors of rooms and cupboards, dealing with lights if need be, and helping to maintain a spirit of prayer. It is important to pause a while at each stage (each room or passage) to renew the awareness of the presence and the power of God. If at any stage some opposition makes itself known, there should be a period for such recollection lasting for one or two minutes.**

8. **When the exorcism has been completed, all those in the**

house should be gathered together, either in the main hall or in the main room, the other doors being left open. The officiant then says either or both of the following prayers and gives the blessing:

Visit, we beseech you, Lord, this place and drive far from it all the snares of the enemy. May Your holy angels dwell here to keep us in peace, and may Your blessing be upon us evermore. Through Jesus Christ your Son our Lord. Amen.

The following may also be used:

O God, the Father Almighty, we humbly entreat You for this house (place); for all who live here; and for all things in it. Grant, Lord, to those living here such earthly and heavenly blessings as are necessary for the maintenance of life; and so control what they desire that they may be able to receive Thy mercy. Bless and hallow this place (house) and let Angels of Light dwell within it to guard it and all its inhabitants through Christ our Lord. Amen.

The officiant will then pronounce a blessing on the house:

The blessing of God Almighty, the Father, the Son, and the Holy Ghost, be upon this place and upon all here present, now and always. Amen.

9. **After the blessing, the officiant will again sprinkle the congregation and the room with holy water, and then with his assistants, go round the rest of the house. In each main section he will repeat the blessing, and sprinkle with holy water.**

10. **CONCLUSION -- After this is done, the whole group will meet together for a short act of thanksgiving. This might be informal, or take the form of saying together the "Te Deum" or the "Gloria in Excelsis."**

11. **If any of the inhabitants of the house has been seriously disturbed, frightened, or damaged by the past events in**

the place, it is of considerable value for them to receive the Laying on of Hands. The form given here, taken with slight adaptation from that issued by the Guild of St. Raphael, is suitable:

In the Name of God most High may release from your pain be given you, and your health restored according to His holy will.

In the Name of Jesus Christ, the Prince of life, may new life surge through your mortal body.

In the name of God the Holy Spirit may you receive inward health and the peace that passes understanding and may God, Who gives us peace, make you completely His, and keep your whole being, spirit and soul and body, free from all fault at the coming of our Lord Jesus Christ. Amen.

When there is no indication of an evil presence or negative energies, the following house blessing might be preferred. It is taken from: "The Meaning And Value of the Sacraments" by Flower A. Newhouse and published by The Christward Ministry, Rt. 5, Box 206, Escondido, CA 92025.

DEDICATION AND BLESSING OF A HOME

The type of service which is suggested here inaugurates the use of a place, a home (or business building) with which a family (or workers) will be involved. One who realizes the value of a permanent thought atmosphere and who can pray effectively and self-forgetfully is able to idealize and thereby create a permanent archetype which shall steadily influence the site as well as the building (or complex) that is being dedicated. This ritual is written especially for a home, but it can easily be adapted to the blessing of a monument, carillon bells, or any place or building. Anyone who meditates or prays successfully can act as celebrant, though in this chapter a Minister is envisioned as officiating.

Prior to the gathering of relatives and friends for the House Blessing, the home has been ideally and thoroughly cleaned. Flowers beautify at least one room (the living room) and soft music and incense are appropriate. A bowl of clear, fresh water should be on a table awaiting blessing.

The House Dedication Service

The Minister begins the ceremony by stating the inner value of such a service. He (she) might say:

Friends, we have gathered together to celebrate the dedication of this home. Each of us should add our thoughts of interest and goodwill to the general benediction of the home and grounds by envisioning the family as realizing this place as a home whose steadfast spirit always renews, heals and uplifts everyone who steps over its threshold. Pray inwardly with me:

Eternal God Presence, in Christ's Powerful Name we ask for Thy permanent blessing to ray forth into every room in this home, and into every atom of the whole place. May Thy Light cleanse whatever currents of negativity might be in the atmosphere. Let Thy Ray of Benediction in permanent activity, bless, cleanse, renew, and protect every atom of the home and grounds on every plane of being. May Thy Light forever cheer and inspire everyone who enters its radius. So let it be; so is it now established in order and beauty. Amen.

The Minister blesses the water.

The Minister goes to the bowl of waiting water, lifts it and blesses it verbally or silently. He (she) makes the sign of the Cross slowly and thoughtfully in this manner: with both hands he (she) raises the water to the level of his (her) eyebrows in a straight line with the center of the body and prays.

Eternal Spirit, source of our lives, bless this water with cleansing, vitalizing, and ever-active spiritual powers.

Then the bowl is lowered slowly to the naval area from

which it is raised again in a straight line to the center of the chest in the region of the heart. From this position the left bar of the cross is drawn by extending the bowl toward the left side.

Let Thy healing, regenerating and transforming forces permeate this water, O Christ Emmanuel.

The sign of the cross is now drawn to the right side as the celebrant concludes the blessing.

Holy Comforter, Spirit of Truth, quicken this water with Thy gifts of wisdom, guidance and illumination. For the continual activities of these energies, we thank Thee, Holy and Everpresent Trinity. Amen.

The Minister dips fingers into the blessed water and sprinkles the water in the directions of north, south, east, and west. Should the family wish each room blessed, the minister does so alone with the members waiting in the living room. In each room all the corners are sprinkled with the water and these words may be said.

I ask the blessings of the Father, Son, and Holy Spirit to remove any negative energies and to fill every corner of this room with heavenly protection and healing.

The Minister gives an explanation of the ceremony.

This custom originated with Jesus, who said on His first visit to the home of a friend, "Peace be to this house." He taught His disciples the inner meaning of such a blessing and He encouraged them to use it. This particular ceremony has two main benefits. It causes a descent of power to enter the home from the Causal Level which radiates a charging of renewal. These energies help every occupant of the home. It also attracts an Angel to the dwelling who becomes known to the family as the Angel of the Home. Her work is to ensoul, protect, and harmonize the home and grounds. (She is not present all the time, but this One interested Angel remains in constant telepathic communication with the family.) When trees are planted on the grounds other intelligences, such as Tree Devas, will make their regular visitations.

The Minister concludes the service praying:

May the Spirit of Peace rest upon this home. May the Presence of Love dwell here steadily. May the inflow of happiness and laughter be here centered. May the beauty of friendship grace this home. May the impetus of progress be expressed in this family.

Dipping fingers again into the water bowl, the celebrant invokes the name of the dwelling that the family has chosen, sprinkling the water at the same time in the direction of the fireplace or toward the East (if there is no hearth.)

And now in awareness of the Presence Who observes us, we pray. In the names of the Divine Mother-Father Spirit; Lord Jesus, the Christ; and the Holy Comforter we christen this home (.....Name..........). May Divine Powers faithfully hallow, purify and sanctify the safety of this blessed place, bringing to everyone who crosses its threshold attunement to the Eternal Watcher Who is also our Divine Benefactor. Through the grace of the Lord Christ we ask this. Amen.

PART III

MEDITATION

CHAPTER 8

MEDITATION

WHAT IS MEDITATION?

Meditation is making an inner contact with your God-consciousness, aligning yourself with the higher energies, listening to inner guidance, and being in touch with your conscious creativity. It is a way to align your body, mind and spirit.

HOW TO MEDITATE

There are many different methods of meditation available. The easiest one is simply to sit quietly, with hands and feet uncrossed and spine straight, then just watch your breathing. Do not control your breath, just pay attention to how your breath flows in and out. **FEEL** where it flows into and out of your body. Then count your in breath and your out breath. Finally, adjust your breathing so the in and out breaths are the same length. This will bring about a relaxation of the body and an alertness of the mind.

At this point you may just relax in the stillness or you can ask questions and listen for the answer to come into your mind. You can contemplate – think about a subject, or quality like love, joy, peace, health – then imagine everything you can about that subject. Do this for 10 or 15 minutes. Write down everything you imagined about the subject. You may not get answers at the time of meditation. They may come into your daily conscious mind at a later time. It may take some time before you feel that you "get something" but do not be discouraged. Just keep making that inner contact every day and you will obtain many benefits such as:

- Better health
- Peace of mind
- A feeling of being protected and guided every day
- Getting good intuitive "hunches"
- It makes you attractive and magnetic
- You obtain knowledge
- You obtain self-actualization

Meditation is a vertical penetration into another dimension. It enables one to extend one's beingness into a higher level, to become an expression of beauty, goodness, and truth. You should develop a discipline of meditating at the same time and place every day. It will be the most valuable time you ever spent.

There are four levels or steps to meditation:

1. Have a seed thought or object or idea in your concrete mind and examine it.

2. Discover the quality of the object. Is it good, bad or indifferent? Is it fast, slow or motionless? What does it do?

3. Discover the purpose by using inspiration. Why was it created? Inspiration is a higher level of the mind where you get in touch with your Inner Guide and the purpose of your Soul is revealed. You become soul-infused and have energy.

4. Discover the cause. You tune into the frequency or soul of the object and identify with it. The real cause is then revealed to you.

∽∽∽

DAILY PRACTICES

There are many different disciplines that one can practice to stay close to the Divine Essence. In addition to meditation, I offer a few that have been particularly helpful in my life. Over the past 20 years I have given out thousands of copies of these prayers. People keep telling me of the miracles that have happened in their lives from using them.

The following prayer was given to me in 1973 by James V. Goure from <u>UNITED RESEARCH</u>, Black Mountain, North Carolina.

Effective Prayer

1. I **release** all of my past, present, future, negatives, fears, human relationships, human desires, sex, money, judgement, communication, and identity to the Light.

2. I am a Light Being.

3. I radiate the Light from my Light Center throughout my being.

4. I radiate the Light from my Light Center to everyone.

5. I radiate the Light from my Light Center to everything.

6. I am in a bubble of Light, only Light can come to me and only Light can be here, nothing can ever harm me.

7. Thank you, God, for everything, for everyone, and for me but mostly, God, thank you for Thee.

This prayer can become an evolution from being the victim of circumstances to becoming the creator of our own lives. You do this by changing your attitudes of mind and heart. In Step 1 of the Effective Prayer, use the word "release" for a month then instead use the word "replace." After another month, substitute the word "change" as shown below:

1st month use "I release all my past, present, future, (etc.) to the Light."

2nd month use "I replace all my past, (etc.)with the Light."

3rd month use "I change all my past (etc.) to the Light."

4th month use "I create Light in all my past, etc."

5th month use "I declare from the I Am Presence within me that all my past, (etc.) are Light."

We have angels, masters, teachers and guides working with us from the heavenly realm. They are there to help us but we must ask for that help or under Universal Law they cannot interfere in our lives." **From Gene Davis, LIFE RESEARCH FOUNDATION, INC. P.O. Box 653, McMinnville, Oregon 97128, we have been given the following calls.**

Gene Davis Calls

To Be Used Upon Awakening:

I call on the I AM Presence and the CHRIST SELF to thank you for a good night's sleep and for taking me to the retreat to study with the Masters. May the knowledge that I received be brought into my outer consciousness as it is needed. I call to the Beloved Ascended Master Saint Germain, Chohan for the Seventh Ray, to radiate into my consciousness His Divine Plan for my part in the transformation into the Golden Age. And I make the call to the Beloved Ascended Lady Master, Mother Mary, to hold in consciousness, the Immaculate Conception for this Great Plan.

A Morning Call:

I AM the Light of the world because I AM a CHRIST! Every day in every way I AM getting younger, healthier and happier because I AM thinking with love in the moment of the present. And I AM releasing love and pure energy to all those who are troubled and to all those who have come into the world and to all those who have passed over in the last 24 hours. (I call on the I AM Presence and the CHRIST SELF to invoke the Violet Flame of Freedom's Love – **say 3 times**) to transmute all the karma from my Etheric, Mental, Emotional and Physical Bodies and all of the discordant belief patterns in my Belief System – and I AM filling it with love so that I can do all my thinking with love. I love myself and my new identity of consciousness because I AM perfect as the CHRIST that I AM. I approve of what I AM doing because I AM the creator of my own reality. I AM doing the best I can with the Light that I have at the moment. I turn all of my decisions, desires, wants and needs for this day over to the CHRIST SELF, and I accept everything that happens to me, or comes into my life, as the workings of the CHRIST SELF. I AM now FREE to carry out the Divine Design of my life.

A Rejuvenation Call:

I FEEL the electro-magnetic currents of energy flowing from my open Heart Center and pulsating through my body and into my hands. I AM regenerating my physical body and reversing its aging process. I AM experiencing, each hour, the Love, Wisdom and Power of my CHRIST SELF!

Calls to Bring Additional Energy into the Third Dimension:

I call on the Lord Maha Chohan, Lord of Energy for the Earth, to release additional energy to my Higher Self and I AM qualifying that energy with my own love for life. And I AM condensing it with love and storing it in my aura and my Causal Body to be used for peace, healing, and perfection of my four lower bodies—and to radiate to others as it is needed. I call on the I AM Presence to draw from the Sun, the Great Solar Ring-Pass-Not, to surround me for protection, and I visualize it as an armor of White Light to absorb and trans-mute all negative and discordant energy with which I may come in contact this day. I turn it over to the CHRIST SELF to be held in the Immaculate Conception, and to be anchored in my consciousness and energy of proximity. I call on the Beloved Lady Master Astrea, Feminine aspect of the Elohim of Purity, to tangibly infuse the Feminine Ray of infallible purity into my daily thinking. I call on the Beloved El Morya to unite his Great Power of Light with my consciousness so that I can build and sustain a constant stream of Pure Energy flowing into my daily activities. I call on the Beloved Saint Germain at the Cave of Symbols Retreat to saturate my consciousness with the Violet Flame of Freedom's Love so that I may master the process of thinking without creating destiny.

We create with a clear thought powered by an emotion. During our waking hours, we think many thoughts and have many emotions. These create karma but it takes 24 hours for these thought-forms to move out to the boundaries of our area of influence and come back into our energy field. Therefore, if

we withdraw and cancel out all negative, discordant and unkind thoughts within the 24 hours, we no longer accumulate negative karma. Then we just have to deal with the karma already existing. The following call was created to free us from additional karma. Do it every night before going to sleep.

Just Before Going to Sleep:

I call on the I AM Presence and the CHRIST SELF TO INVOKE THE VIOLET FLAME OF FREEDOM'S LOVE (say 3 times) to transmute, withdraw, and cancel out all of the negative, discordant, and unkind thoughts that I might have issued in the last 24 hours. I call on the CHRIST SELF and the I AM Presence and the Angel of the I AM Presence to take me in my Soul Consciousness to the Royal Retreat in the Grand Tetons where I will receive the instructions for the use of the Precipitation Energy (Energy of Manifestation). And I AM drawing energy from the retreat so that I can be taken to the retreat on that energy and study "at the feet of the Masters" and attend the Table Councils and sit in on the Floor Classes and actually study at the feet of the Masters.

You may use these "calls" or design others. The main thing is that they stem from a sincere energy of need. They should be issued diligently every day.

Another valuable technique for clearing the debris of past negative thoughts is the "Brush-Down with the Violet Flame" which is given here.

Violet Flame Brush-Down

Stand in your room and call the Violet Transmuting Flame into action up, through, and around you for at least nine feet in every direction. Raise your hands and ask your Higher Self, your "I AM" Presence, and Saint Germain to qualify your hands with the Purifying Power of the Violet Transmuting Flame. Visualize your hands blazing with Violet Light.

Then, starting at the head, pass your hands down over your body to the feet, taking in as much of the body surface as you can reach with your hands. Now, with the left hand, sweep down over the right shoulder, arm and hand, and with the right hand give the left shoulder, arm and hand the same treatment.

Repeat this activity in its entirety four times, once for each of the four lower vehicles (physical, etheric, mental and emotional). Periodically shake your hands from the wrist to cast off the heavy, discordant energy that is being removed from your bodies and visualize the vehicle being transmuted in the surrounding Violet Fire.

If not just yet, eventually you will be able to see with the inner sight what takes place during this exercise. In the first part of the exercise, it is as though a close fitting garment of black substance were being removed from the body with the hands. The second time you go over the body, the "garment" removed is of a dark grey substance, the third time, it is of a lighter grey color and so on. Night after night, as you proceed with the exercise, this astral substance gets lighter and lighter in color and texture until it is entirely removed from the body and actual purification takes place. This is real substance with actual color, vibration and feeling.

On completion of the exercise, visualize the Violet Transmuting Flame expanding through your Heart Flame flooding the entire planet and affirm:

> MY WORLD IS A WORLD OF VIOLET FIRE!
> MY WORLD IS THE GOD-WORLD I DESIRE!
>
> MY BODY'S A PILLAR OF VIOLET FIRE!
> "I AM" THE PERFECTION THAT GOD DESIRES!
>
> OUR EARTH IS A PLANET OF VIOLET FIRE!
> OUR EARTH IS ALL THAT GOD DESIRES!

Torkom Saraydarian has written an inspiring booklet entitled "A Daily Discipline of Worship" from which the following prayers are taken. The booklet can be ordered from:

Aquarian Educational Group
P.O. Box 267
Sedona, Arizona 86336

Saraydarian's Daily Worship

Sunrise

O Giver of light, The Cosmic Beauty,
Permeate my whole nature with Thy Rays.
Kindle the flame on the altar of my temple.
So that I may live as a beam of light, in beauty,
Until the sunset of the day...of my life.

9 a.m.

O Sphere of Light advancing
　　　　and elevating Goodness,
May my soul rise with You,
　　　　expressing goodness in
All its contacts.

Noon

The flame of the Great Presence in me,
Let me stand as a radiant fire
of righteousness today and during
The days of my life.
Let me think, act and speak
in the spirit of righteousness.

Sunset

My Lord, thank you for the joy of living today
in the spirit of beauty, goodness and righteousness.
May Your joy radiate in other parts of the world
As the Sun disperses the night and brings the joy
of the day.
My Lord, You are the joy of my heart.

Bedtime

My Lord, in Your perfection permeate my whole
being.
Let me be free from all worries and anxieties,
From all painful memories of the day,
From all attachments and identifications,
So that my soul freely soars in Your temple of
beauty.

Let me realize freedom from my physical, emo
tional and mental crystallizations
And be with You as a free soul.

෴෴෴

Another wonderful daily practice is taken from the book
"The Next Step" by Patricia Diane Cota-Robles which can be
ordered from:

The New Age Study of Humanity's Purpose
P.O. Box 41883
Tucson, Arizona 85717

Seven Steps to Change & Personal Empowerment

Begin by centering yourself in the present moment, then say:
"I AM" here now!
"I AM" Happy and Balanced!
I Love myself and I enjoy what "I AM" doing!
"I AM" having fun!

STEP ONE

"I AM" LETTING GO OF ATTACHMENTS AND RELEASING
OLD PATTERNS AND BELIEFS.

1. I Love and accept myself as "I AM."
2. I release any belief or pattern that does not support my highest good.
3. I recognize the moment of my new beginning and my right and ability to change.
4. I move into change easily and joyously.

STEP TWO

"I AM" TRUSTWORTHY AND HONEST TO MYSELF.

1. "I AM" experiencing the true integrity of myself.
2. "I AM" willing to know the Truth of who "I AM."
3. I trust the Truth, and the Truth sets me FREE!

STEP THREE

"I AM" WORTHY AND DESERVING OF CHANGE.

1. I Love and Forgive myself for any perceived transgression.
2. "I AM" a Child of God, and I deserve to be Loved and Forgiven.
3. "I AM" willing and able to restore every aspect of my Life.
4. "I AM" Healing myself physically, mentally, emotionally and spiritually.

STEP FOUR

"I AM" CHANGING THROUGH GRACE AND JOY.

1. Buoyant Joyous energy interpenetrates every aspect of my Life.
2. Laughter and relaxation are continually present through my growth.
3. "I AM" willing to experience Joy and feel good about my changes.

STEP FIVE

I HAVE FAITH AND TRUST IN MY POWER TO CHANGE.

1. "I AM" in the Divine flow of my true God Reality.
2. "I AM" experiencing a patience, silence, and inner calm through my changes.
3. "I AM" One with the Infinite Intelligence inside of me.
4. The Infinite Intelligence within me always makes correct choices.

STEP SIX

I LOVE MYSELF AND "I AM" GRATEFUL FOR MY GROWTH AND CHANGE.

1. I Love myself unconditionally right now.
2. I accept each opportunity with Gratitude and Love.
3. "I AM" Loveable, and all that is less than Love in me, I Love FREE!

STEP SEVEN

I ACCEPT RESPONSIBILITY FOR THE CHANGES IN MY LIFE, AND I ACCEPT THE POWER TO SUSTAIN THE CHANGES.

1. I support my Power within and know it is available as I accept my true God Self.
2. I choose to know now that "I AM" creating my own Reality moment by moment.
3. I choose to create only that which supports my highest good.
4. I choose to be my God Presence, NOW!

The following World Healing Meditation is also by Patricia Diane Cota-Robles. I use this on December 31st each year.

WORLD HEALING MEDITATION

In the beginning God created heaven and the Earth. And God said "Let there be light" and there was light.

Now is the time of the **new** beginning. I am a co-creator with God, and it is a new Heaven that comes, as the Good Will of God is expressed on Earth through me. It is the Kingdom of Light, Love, Peace, and Understanding. And I am doing my part to reveal its Reality.

I begin with me. I am a living Soul and the Spirit of God dwells in me, as me. I and the Father are one, and all that the Father has is mine. In Truth, I am the Christ of God.

What is true of me is true of everyone, for God is all and all is God. I see only the Spirit of God in every Soul. And to every man, woman and child on Earth I say, "I love you, for you are me. You are my Holy Self."

I now open my heart, and let the pure essence of Unconditional Love pour out. I see it as a Golden Light radiating from the center of my being, and I feel its Divine Vibration in and through me, above and below me.

I am one with the Light. I am filled with the Light. I am illumined by the Light. I am the Light of the world.

With purpose of mind, I send forth the Light. I let the radiance go before me to join the other Lights. I know this is happening all over the world at this moment. I see the merging Lights. There is now one Light. We are the Light of the world.

The one Light of Love, Peace, and Understanding is moving. It flows across the face of the Earth, touching and illuminating every soul in the shadow of the illusion. And where there was darkness, there is now the Light of Reality.

And the Radiance grows, permeating, saturating every form of life. There is only the vibration of one Perfect Life now. All the kingdoms of the Earth respond, and the Planet is alive with Light and Love.

There is total Oneness, and in this Oneness we speak the Word. Let the sense of separation be dissolved. Let mankind be returned to Godkind.

Let peace come forth in every mind. Let Love flow forth from every heart. Let forgiveness reign in every soul. Let understanding be the common bond.

And now from the Light of the world, the One Presence and Power of the Universe responds. The Activity of God is healing and harmonizing Planet Earth. Omnipotence is made manifest.

I am seeing the salvation of the planet before my very eyes, as all false beliefs and error patterns are dissolved. The sense of separation is no more; the healing has taken place, and the world is restored to sanity.

This is the beginning of Peace on Earth and Good Will toward all, as Love flows forth from every heart, forgiveness reigns in every soul, and all hearts and minds are one in perfect understanding.

It is done. And it is so.

CHAPTER 9

FULL-MOON MEDITATIONS

The following information about the three Festivals of Spring was given by Alice A. Bailey in her book, "The Reappearance of the Christ."

In the ancient wisdom teachings there is information about certain major festivals in relation to the Moon and in a lesser degree to the zodiac. The truth lying behind all invocation is based upon the power of thought, particularly in its telepathic nature, rapport and aspect. The unified invocative thought of the masses and the focussed, directed thought of the New Group of World Servers constitute an outgoing stream of energy. This will reach telepathically those spiritual Beings Who are sensitive and responsive to such impacts. Their evoked response, sent out as spiritual energy, will in turn reach humanity after having been stepped down into thought energy and in that form will make its due impact upon the minds of people, convincing them and carrying inspiration and revelation. Thus has it ever been in the history of the spiritual enfoldment of the world and the procedure followed in writing the world Scriptures.

The establishment of a certain uniformity in the world religious rituals will aid humankind everywhere to strengthen each other's work and enhance powerfully the thought currents directed to the waiting spiritual Lives. At present, the Christian religion has its great festivals, the Buddhist keeps his different set of spiritual events, and the Hindu has still another list of holy days. In the future world, when organized, all humans of spiritual inclination and intention everywhere will keep the same holy days. This will bring about a pooling of spiritual resources, and a united spiritual effort, plus a simultaneous spiritual invocation. The potency of this will be apparent.

There will be three major Festivals each year, concentrated in three consecutive months and leading therefore, to a prolonged annual spiritual effort which will affect the remainder of the year. These will be:

THE THREE SPRING FESTIVALS

1. The Festival of Easter

This is the Festival of the risen, living Christ, the Teacher of all men and the Head of the Spiritual Hierarchy. He is the Expression of the love of God. On this day the spiritual Hierarchy, which He guides and directs, will be recognized and the nature of God's love will be emphasized.

This Festival is determined always by the date of the first Full Moon of spring and is the great Western and Christian Festival. Easter is always the first Sunday after the first full moon after the Vernal equinox so is usually near the Full Moon of April (Aries). It is the great Western and Christian Festival.

Behind all the reconstruction with which humanity is faced is the potency of inevitable resurrection, the constant flow of enlightened thinking into and directing the mass consciousness. There is a growing realization that humanity is NOT alone, that the spiritual values are the only real values, and that the Hierarchy stands immovable in its spiritual strength, steadily oriented towards world salvation, and acting ever under the direction of that great divine yet human leader, the Christ. The Christ has passed through all human experiences, and has never left us. With His disciples, the Masters of the Wisdom, He is drawing closer to humanity decade after decade. When He said at the Ascension initiation, "Lo, I am with you always even until the end of the age," He meant no vague general idea of helping humanity from some distant location called "the Throne of God in Heaven." He meant just what He said – that He was staying with us.

2. The Festival of Wesak

This is the Festival of the Buddha, the spiritual Intermediary between the highest spiritual center, Shamballa, and the Hierarchy. The Buddha is the expression of the wisdom of God, the Embodiment of Light and the Indicator of the divine purpose.

This feast is celebrated annually at the Full Moon of May (Taurus). It is the great Eastern Festival.

3. The Festival of Goodwill

This is the Festival of the spirit of humanity aspiring towards God, seeking conformity with the will of God and dedicated to the expression of right human relations. This is celebrated at the Full Moon of June (Gemini). It is a day when the spiritual and divine nature of mankind will be recognized. On this Festival for two thousand years the Christ has represented humanity and has stood before the Hierarchy and in the sight of Shamballa as the God-Man, the Leader of His people, and "the Eldest in a great family of brothers" (Romans VIII:29). Each year at that time He has preached the last sermon of the Buddha, before the assembled Hierarchy. This is a festival of deep invocation and appeal, of a basic aspiration towards fellowship, of human and spiritual unity, and represents the effect in the human consciousness of the work of the Buddha and of the Christ.

The three Festivals are a part of the unified spiritual approach of humanity although they are not yet sufficiently related to each other. The time is coming when all three Festivals will be kept throughout the world and by their means a great spiritual unity will be achieved and the effects of the Great Approach, so close to us at this time, will be stabilized by the united invocation of humanity throughout the planet.

The remaining full moons will constitute lesser festivals but will be recognized to be also of vital importance. They will establish the divine attributes in the consciousness of man, just as the major festivals establish the three divine aspects. These aspects and qualities will be arrived at and determined by a close study of nature of a particular constellation or constellations influencing those months. For instance, Capricorn (late December) will call attention to the first initiation, the birth of the Christ in the cave of the heart, and indicate the training needed to bring about that great spiritual event in the life of the individual. Thus, the twelve annual festivals will constitute a revelation of divinity. They will present a means of bringing about relationship, first of all, during three months with the three great spiritual Centers, the three expressions of the divine Trinity. The minor festivals will emphasize the interrelation of the Whole, thus lifting the divine presentation out of the individual and the personal, into that of the universal divine Purpose; the relationship of the Whole to the part and of the part to that Whole will be thereby fully expressed.

Humanity will, therefore, invoke the spiritual power of the Kingdom of God. Hierarchy will respond, and God's plans will be worked out on Earth. The Hierarchy, on a higher turn of the spiral, will invoke the "Center where the Will of God is known," thus invoking the Purpose of God. Thus will the Will of God be implemented by Love and manifested intelligently. For this mankind is ready, and for this the Earth waits. On the basis of the fundamental truths will the new world religion be built. The definition of religion which will in the future prove of greater accuracy than any yet formulated by the theologians might be expressed as follows:

"Religion is the name given to the invocative appeal of humanity and the evocative response of the greater Life to that cry."

THE WESAK STORY

There is a valley, lying at a rather high altitude in the foothills of the Himalayan Tibet ranges. It is surrounded by high mountains on all sides except towards the northeast, where there is a narrow opening in the mountain ranges. The valley is, therefore, bottle-shaped in contour, with the neck of the bottle to the northeast, and it widens very considerably towards the south. Up towards the northern end, close to the neck of the bottle, there is to be found a huge flat rock. There are no trees or shrubs in the valley, which is covered with a kind of coarse grass, but the sides of the mountains are covered with trees.

At the time of the full moon of Taurus, pilgrims from all the surrounding districts begin to gather; the holy men and lamas find their way into the valley and fill the southern and the middle parts, leaving the northeastern end relatively free. There, so the legend runs, gathers a group of those great Beings Who are the Custodians on Earth of God's Plan for our planet and for humanity. By what name we call these Beings does not greatly matter. The Christian believer may prefer to speak of Christ and His church, and regard Them as constituting that great Cloud of Witnesses Who guarantee to humanity ultimate salvation. The esoterists of the world may call Them the Masters of the Wisdom, the planetary Hierarchy, Who in Their varied grades are ruled and taught by the Christ, the Master of all Masters, and the Teacher alike of angels and of men. Or we can call Them the Rishis of the Hindu scriptures, of the Society of Illumined Minds, as in the Tibetan teaching. They are the Great Intuitives and the Great Companions of our more modern presentation, and are the aggregate of perfected humanity who have followed in Christ's steps and have entered for us within the veil, leaving us an example that we should do as They have done. They, with Their wisdom, love and knowledge, stand as a protective wall around our race, and seek to lead us on, step by step (as They Themselves were led in Their time) from darkness to light, from the unreal to the real, and from death to immortality.

This group of knowers of divinity are the main participants in the Wesak Festival. They range Themselves in the northeastern end of the valley, and in concentric circles (according to the status and grade of Their initiatory development) prepare Themselves for a great act of service. In front of the rock, looking towards the northeast, stand Those Beings Who are called by Their disciples "the Three Great Lords." These are the Christ, Who stands in the center; the Lord of living forms, the Manu, Who stands on His right; and the Lord of Civilization, Who stands on His left. These three face the rock, upon which there rests a great crystal bowl, full of water.

It is an interesting sidelight upon this ceremony and its reality, that all who have dreamt of participating in it are always well aware of the exact position in the lower part of the valley where they themselves stood. One who described it to me spoke of standing well off to one side, close to a tree to which a horse was tethered; and others seemed to know where they found themselves. Some few realized that the place and the position, within the body of onlookers, indicated quite clearly the evolutionary status of the participant.

Behind the grouped Masters, adepts, initiates, and senior workers under God's plan, are to be found the world disciples and aspirants in their various grades and groups (either "in the body or out of the body" to quote the words of St. Paul), who constitute at this time the New Group of World Servers. Those present in their physical bodies have found their way there by ordinary means. Others are present in their spiritual bodies and in the dream state. The "dream" which they later relate, may it not be the physical recognition and the recollection of an inner spiritual happening?

As the hour of the full moon approaches, a stillness settles down upon the crowd, and all look towards the northeast. Certain ritualistic movements take place, in which the grouped Masters and Their disciples of all ranks take up symbolic positions, and form on the floor of the valley such significant symbols as the five-pointed star, with the Christ standing at the highest point; or a triangle, with the Christ at the apex; or a cross, and other well known formations, all of which have a deep and potent meaning. This is all done to the sound of certain chanted words and esoteric phrases, called mantras. The expectancy in the waiting, onlooking crowds becomes very great, and the tension is real and increasing. Through the entire body of people there seems to be felt a stimulation or potent vibration which has the effect of awakening the souls of those present, fusing and blending the group into one united whole, and lifting all into a great act of spiritual demand, readiness, and expectancy. It is the climax of the world's aspiration, focussed in this waiting group. These three words – demand, readiness and expectancy – best describe the atmosphere surrounding those present in this secret valley.

The chanting and the rhythmic weaving grows stronger, and all the participants and the watching crowd raise their eyes towards the sky in the direction of the narrow part of the valley. Just a few minutes before the exact time of the full moon, in the far distance, a tiny speck can be seen in the sky. It comes nearer and nearer, and grows in clarity and definiteness of outline, until the form of the Buddha can be seen, seated in the cross-legged Buddha position, clad in His saffron colored robe, bathed in light and color, and with His hand extended in blessing. When He arrives at a point exactly over the great rock, hovering there in the air over the heads of the three Great Lords, a great mantra, used only once a year, at the Festival, is intoned by the Christ, and the entire group of people in the valley fall upon their faces. This Invocation sets up a great vibration or thought current which is of such potency that it reaches up from the group of aspirants, disciples or initiates who employ it, to God Himself. It marks the supreme moment of intensive spiritual effort throughout the entire year, and the spiritual vitalization of humanity and the spiritual effects last throughout the succeeding months. The effect of the Great Invocation is universal or cosmic, and serves to link us up with that cosmic center of spiritual force from which all created beings have come. The blessing is poured forth, and the Christ, as the Representative of humanity, receives it in trust, for distribution.

Thus, so the legend runs, the Buddha returns once a year to bless the world, transmitting through the Christ renewed spiritual life. Slowly then the Buddha recedes into the distance, until again a faint speck can be seen in the sky, and this eventually disappears. The whole ceremonial blessing, from the time of the first appearance in the distance until the moment the Buddha fades out of view, takes just eight minutes. The Buddha's annual sacrifice for humanity (for He comes back only at great cost) is over, and He returns again to that high place where He works and waits. Year after year He comes back in blessing; year after year the same ceremony has taken place. Year after year He and His great Brother, the Christ, work in the closest cooperation for the spiritual benefit of humanity. In these two great Sons of God have been focussed two aspects of divine Life, and They act together as Custodians of the highest type of spiritual force to which our humanity can respond. Through the Buddha, the wisdom of God is poured forth. Through the Christ, the love of God is manifested to humanity; and it is this wisdom and this love which pour forth upon mankind each Wesak full moon.

When the Buddha has again disappeared the crowd rise

to their feet; the water in the bowl is distributed in tiny portions to the Masters, initiates and disciples, and They then go Their way to the place of service. The crowd, who have all brought their little cups and vessels of water, drink of them, and share with others. In this beautiful "water ceremony of communion" we have presented for us, in symbol, an indication of the New Age which is today upon us, the Aquarian age, the age of the Water Carrier. It is the age of the "man bearing a pitcher of water," as Christ said in that episode preceding the communion service which He initiated. In this ceremony is perpetuated for us the story of the universality of God's love, the need for our individual purification, and the opportunity to share with each other that which belongs to all. The water, which has been magnetized by the presence of the Buddha and of the Christ, carries certain properties and virtues of a healing and helpful nature. Thus blessed, the crowd silently disperses; the Masters and the disciples return with renewed strength to undertake another year of world service.

Suggested Ceremony for Wesak

Prepare the meeting place with lighted candles, incense, flowers (if possible) and chairs in a circle. Have inspiring music playing. Place a table in the center upon which rests a large crystal bowl filled with pure water and a stack of small cups. If you wish the Wesak story to be read by several people, prepare papers for them with their part of the story. Put a sign on the door asking everyone to enter in silence.

1. Start on time. If the exact time of the full moon is not convenient, start at 7:30 p.m. and time-slot (have the intention that the ceremony takes place at the full moon time) the ceremony. Welcome everyone.

2. Make any necessary announcements. Then say:

The Christ Mantra

In the Name of the Christ, by the power of His Name and Sword, His Love, His Joy, His Divinity, let the reality of His Presence govern our every thought and His truth be the master of our lives.

3. Have everyone sit up straight, with hands and feet uncrossed and be in a meditative state. Lead them into the valley in the Himalayas and tell them to go to their place there. Ask them to see what they are wearing and where they are located. Then they will visualize the ceremony happening to them.

4. Read the Wesak Story. (You can have several persons take turns reading portions of it.) Then tell everyone that you will leave them in the silence for a time.

5. After about 15 minutes of silence, bring them back to the present. Have them stretch and gradually open their eyes.

6. All stand in a circle. The celebrant then goes to the crystal bowl and asks each person as they walk around the circle past the bowl to take a cup. The celebrant fills the cup with water from the bowl. When all have filled their cups and returned to their places, the celebrant asks God's blessing on everyone and all drink their energized water together.

7. All sit. The cups are collected and thrown away. Ask them to share their experiences.

8. When all sharing has been completed, have all say:

The Great Invocation

From the point of Light within the Mind of God,
Let Light stream forth into the minds of men.
Let Light descend on Earth.

(Pause 3 seconds.)

From the point of Love within the Heart of God,
Let Love stream forth into the hearts of men.
The Christ returns to Earth.

(Pause 6 seconds.)

From the center where the Will of God is known
Let purpose guide the little wills of men,
The purpose which the Masters know and serve.

227

(Pause 6 seconds.)

From the center which we call the race of men,
The Plan of Love and Light works out
And has sealed the door where evil dwells.

(Pause 9 seconds.)

Light and Love and Power restores the Plan on Earth.

9. **All stand and hold hands. Can sing "Let There Be Peace On Earth" or any other appropriate song or chant "OM."**

Rainbow Bridge Meditation

1. **Play a tape of "The Great Invocation."**

2. **Welcome everyone and make any announcements.**

3. **Ask everyone to sit with their spine straight and hands and feet uncrossed. Then say "The Christ Mantra."**

4. **Ask them to visualize themselves as a connection between Heaven and Earth by reaching up with their left hand to the Masters and Teachers and reaching back with their right hand to humanity. Then say:**

The Mantra of Unification

The sons of men are one and we are one with them. We seek to love, not hate. We seek to serve and not exact due service. We seek to heal, not hurt.

Let pain bring due reward of Light and Love. Let the Soul control the outer form and life and all events, and bring to light the love which underlies the happenings of the time.

Let vision come, and insight. Let the future stand revealed. Let inner union demonstrate and outer cleavages be gone. Let love prevail. Let all men love.

5. Say the Soul Mantra:

We focus our attention in the Soul Star (**6 inches above our head**), becoming one with that radiating sphere and declare our true identity by saying: **WE ARE THE SOUL.**

(Pause)

We unify with each other at this level by linking soul star to soul star with every other group member, present or not, and to the point at the center.

(Pause)

From this center of light move down the antahkarana to the earth star (**6 inches below our feet**) and find each other at this level. We move further down the antahkarana to connect with the center of the Earth and with each other at this level.

We ascend the group antahkarana and focus our attention on the highest level of the mental plane, the abstract consciousness, the plane of ideas and concepts. Here we declare: **WE ARE LIGHT DIVINE.**

(Pause)

We link with each other at the level and link ajna center to ajna center and to the group ajna center.

We move further up the antahkarana to the Buddhic plane and here we declare: **WE ARE LOVE.**

(Pause)

We link heart center to heart center and to the heart of the Christ at the center of the group. From this plane of union we reach out into the network and link with all other soul groups meeting and meditating with common purpose; we link with all the lightworkers, the great devas, with the planetary energy stations whether known or unknown, and with the Buddhic columns placed all over the planet. Here at the Buddhic level we invoke the Epsilon-One (or etheric sieve) to move down through our

229

energy bodies and remove all distortion from our energies and align our vehicles so we can carry the higher energies as we move up into the higher planes.

We rise further on the group antahkarana, within the planetary antahkarana, to that point of Will, the Atmic plane and here we declare: **WE ARE WILL.**

(Pause)

We reach out horizontally to each other at this level and link throat center to throat center and to the group throat center. We stand welded together in integrated purpose. The leader says: "In the center of the Will of God we stand. Naught can remove us from that Will. We implement that Will with loving, intelligent activity, and turning, serve our fellow man."

Now we move up to the Monadic plane and here we declare: **WE ARE FIXED DESIGN.**

(Pause)

Here we are fully identified with the Life known as inspiration and integration, and we connect with each other crown chakra to crown chakra, to the crown center of the group and with the center of the group crystal. Gently we allow this pure and rarified energy to descend to meet and merge and blend with the center of the Earth, the heart of the planet. We say the words of power for the 7th Ray – **THE HIGHEST AND LOWEST MEET.**

6.   **Energy Work: Depending on the group at this point you can either do Phase I work (triangulations over the chakras) or reach up to the level of the Divinity and bring down energies through the great triangle of the constellations of Sirius, the Great Bear, and the Pleides. Then step down the energy through the triangle of solar system planets according to the month involved. These are:**

Full moon of Capricorn (January): Mercury, Venus, Saturn
Full moon of Aquarius (February): Moon, Jupiter, Uranus
Full moon of Pisces (March): Neptune, Pluto, Jupiter
Full moon of Aries (April): Uranus, Mars, Mercury
Full moon of Taurus (May): Moon, Vulcan, Venus
Full moon of Gemini (June): Venus, Jupiter, Mercury
Full moon of Cancer (July): Neptune, Mars, Moon
Full moon of Leo (August): Sun, Uranus, Neptune
Full moon of Virgo (September): Venus, Jupiter, Mercury
Full moon of Libra (October): Uranus, Saturn, Venus
Full moon of Scorpio (November): Saturn, Pluto, Mars
Full moon of Sagittarius (December): Sun, Mercury, Jupiter

Then bring the energies down from the triangle of planets through the great triangle of the Avatars: The Buddha, The Spirit of Peace and Equilibrium, and the Avatar of Synthesis with the chalice of the Christ at the center and then down upon the Earth. See the Earth filled and surrounded with light. See people of all nations joining hands around the planet in peace and brotherhood. Send the energies out to the crisis points on the planet to nurture it, heal it and transmute Earth into a sacred planet.

7. Say:

The Disciples Mantra

We are points of light within a greater light.
We are strands of loving energy within the stream
of Love Divine.
We are sparks of sacrificial Fire, focussed within
the fiery Will of God.
       And thus we stand.

We are ways by which men may achieve.
We are sources of strength, enabling them to stand.
We are beams of Light, shining upon their way.
       And thus we stand.

And standing thus, revolve
And tread this way, the ways of men,
And know the Ways of God.
       And thus we stand.

231

8. **Say:**

The Great Invocation

From the point of Light within the Mind of God,
Let Light stream forth into the minds of men,
    Let Light descend on Earth.

From the point of Love within the Heart of God,
Let love stream forth into the hearts of men,
    May Christ return to Earth.

From the center where the Will of God is known,
Let purpose guide the little wills of men,
    The purpose which the Masters know and
    serve.

From the center which we call the race of men,
The Plan of Light and Love works out
And seals the door where evil dwells.

Light and Love and Power restore the Plan on
    Earth.

9. **End standing in a circle, holding hands. Say a prayer of thanksgiving and feel the energy running around the circle when you breathe in the light and send it to the person on your right. When all feel energized, you can end with hugs.**

PART IV

BLESSINGS AND PRAYERS

CHAPTER 10

THE SCIENCE AND SERVICE OF BLESSING

This chapter is taken from a little booklet by Roberto Assagioli which was published by Sundial House, Nevill Court, Tunbridge Wells, Kent, England TN4 8NJ.

RADIATION AND BLESSING

The value of the age-old service of Blessing needs to be reaffirmed. It is a conscious and deliberate use of radiation and is one of the greatest contributions we can make to the well-being of our fellow men.

Blessing is therefore a service which is based on the laws that govern energy and radiation, and to bless effectively we should have some understanding of radiation, its nature and its laws.

In general terms, radiation is an outward projection of energy from some originating source. It is a subject which is today being increasingly studied by scientists, and the extensive explorations in this field now being undertaken by, for example, the Radiation Laboratory of the University of California, are an indication of its growing importance as the New Age science emerges.

As a result of these investigations, we may expect to learn a great deal more about this ancient means of distributing benefi-cence. In the meantime, let us remember that radiation is mag-netic, and similarly that Blessing is an act which blesses those who give as well as those who receive. When we seek to bless, we place ourselves in a divine circulatory flow of benediction.

What is Radiation?

Active, or conscious, human radiation finds a close analogy in the projection of radio or television waves from a transmitting station. It can be put into operation in two ways:

1. **In all directions**, with no specific aim or target as in broadcasting, and addressed to "all it may concern," to all who may be able and willing to receive the message or impression. In order to be effective this type of radiation demands a considerable degree of inner power, a high spiritual "voltage."

2. **Specific Radiation,** directed towards a definite target. This is analogous to those etheric waves which are projected in only one direction. This method does not demand so high a "voltage" because the effect is increased by the focussing of the energy, much as the heat of the sun's rays can be sufficiently amplified by concentration through a lens to kindle a fire.

What We Can Radiate

By means of mental and spiritual telepathy we can radiate **ideas**; either pure abstract ideas, or ideas formulated into thought-forms. We can also radiate qualities, aspects, and attributes (such as love, light, joy, strength, will). These two forms of radiation can be combined, that is, we can radiate ideas or thought-forms conditioned or vitalized by spiritual qualities.

Each of us necessarily and inevitably radiates **what he (she) is.** It is time that we realized this and became aware of the opportunity it offers and the responsibility it entails, so that we may consciously utilize this power to the full and use it only in constructive and helpful ways. Radiation can be considered a form of telepathy; it is a way of "impressing," and it has both general and specific aspects. It expresses what we really are, which, in both a higher and a lower sense, is much more than we are aware of.

Techniques of Radiation

Let us consider **how** to radiate. This is important for the success of our endeavor.

1. First comes a general preparation in which we concentrate on what we want to radiate. In the case of a spiritual quality, an

effective preparation consists in **arousing in ourselves** that quality, of **identifying ourselves** with the idea, the feeling, the qualified energy. Then it radiates spontaneously. In this way we can combine both spontaneous and purposeful, directed radiation.

Another factor which increases the effectiveness of radiation is **joy**. This may cause surprise at first, but we can easily become convinced of it by realizing that joy has always a stimulating and vivifying effect, so that it facilitates and enhances the effectiveness of every action.

2. After this preparation comes the exact **formulation or visualization** of the idea. It can be a word or a phrase and, whenever possible, an image or a picture.

3. In the third stage we link up with and tune in to the recipient. This is accomplished in two ways:

    a. By visualizing the person, nation, world, etc.

    b. By sending a wave of love in the same direction. Love is a great linking and unifying energy.

4. In the fourth stage comes the actual **projection**. This is best done by visualizing a channel or beam of light projected towards the target; or, in the case of a general radiation, beams of light in all directions.

Responsibility

A real danger arises when, prompted by our will-to-power, we are tempted to impose our radiatory influence on others. Even if we do this with the best motives, it may be harmful. Let us remember that we never have the right to infringe on the freedom of others, and we must beware not to project on others **our ideal** image of them, or what we think they should be.

This very common mistake is often made by parents. It is committed either by an outward display of authority, or by means of "persuasion" and suggestion, but it can be just as harmful in a subtle way if it is done through radiation. Therefore, let us realize our responsibility in this respect and never try to influence in any specific direction.

The same warning may be given concerning "prayers" or projected thoughts used for influencing political or religious leaders in specific directions.

Radiation may also be too intense, and this may have two effects: it may repel the recipient, evoking a contrary reaction, or it may "burn" and be destructive. The effects of the sun's rays provide a good example. The sun is the source of all life, and its rays are beneficent, healing, and life-giving; but when they are too intense, we retreat into the shade, or, if we persist in remaining exposed to them, we may get sunburnt and even suffer sunstroke. But that is not the fault of the sun, but of our own stupidity.

Radiation and Magnetic Attraction and their Redemptive Effect

Radiation and magnetism appear at first to be contradictory. Radiance, however, evokes magnetism, its effect is magnetic and the recipient of radiation is attracted towards the radiating center or source. A clear example of this is the response of a plant to sunlight; the sun radiates light to the plant, which is attracted and reaches up towards the sun. The radiation of the sun is thus magnetic.

The same is true of the light of the Soul or Self playing upon the personality. The Soul radiates its light and the right reaction of the personality is a yearning towards this source of light. It is its response to the magnetic attraction of the Soul. But the personality does not always react in this positive way; sometimes it is not aware of or repels the Soul's influence.

Magnetic attraction also takes place in inter-personal relationships. If a person radiates light and love towards other human beings, they are attracted. The normal effect of radiation, therefore, is attraction-magnetism. It attracts towards the source of radiation.

Spiritual Radiation

Spiritual Radiation is a redemptive process, producing what might be called almost a "chemical change" in the substance of humanity and of the planet. Each of us is contributing to it all the time, and the **group contribution** (the radiation of groups gathered for specific purposes) is a growing factor in life on Earth today.

As we progress, we become increasingly radiatory and magnetic, and we have to respond to those who are attracted by this magnetism. It is inspiring to realize that each step we take upward changes, heightens, and intensifies our spiritual emanation.

The conscious projection of thoughts and the active radiatory work of **blessing** are **specific** types of radiation. To be effective, this radiation must flow from the soul-infused personality – at least soul-infused to a certain extent.

A blessing or benediction might be regarded as "**a transfer of spiritual energy.**" This illuminates the concept of radiation. When someone with spiritual power blesses another, and the blessing is not formal or perfunctory, it is a transmission of energy, a form of radiation.

Blessing and **healing** are also linked and a real blessing can have a healing effect. This is not necessarily physical, but can be psychologically and spiritually beneficial. Also in healing, however, there is need for caution. For instance, concentrating the attention on the patient's illness, or on the parts of the body affected, might have undesirable effects.

Under the Law of Cause and Effect the release of divine energies emerges as radiation, and the **redemptive** process of evolution is thus carried out. So blessing becomes part of the redemptive process of evolution.

When radiation has a spiritual quality, when it emanates from a person who has achieved a high point of Self-realization, its effects are potent. A modern psychologist, A.H. Maslow of Brandeis University, has recognized the reality of such radiation and has described it as follows:

"....in self-actualizing, creativeness is 'emitted,' like radioactivity, and hits all of life, regardless of problems, just as a cheerful person 'emits' cheerfulness without purpose or design or even consciousness. It is emitted like sunshine; it spreads all over the place; it makes things grow (which are growable)." (**Creativity in Self-Actualizing People, p.12.**)

Keyserling has stated the same truth in a strong way:

"...the mere existence of a saint is a blessing—the mere existence of a hero gives strength and courage; the mere existence of a great believer creates faith; and that of one who greatly trusts generates confidence. Moreover, it is the silent effortless **radiance** of deep being which ensures the most powerful action at a distance. This has proved itself true thousands of times, in space as well as in time." (Hermann Keyserling, **From Suffering to Fulfillment, p. 90.**)

From the angle of human evolution, it might be stated that only when the soul aspect is dominant does the response apparatus (the form nature of man) fulfill its destiny, and only then does true radiation and the pure shining forth of light become possible.

The **creative** faculty works by means of radiation and magnetism. These bring to its possessor the material for creation and a magnetic capacity which arranges in due form and beauty that which radiation has evoked. Creativity is a consequence of a particular state of mind and a specific state of being; it signifies a point in evolution wherein the person is definitely "radioactive."

Radiation and magnetism are an expression of the energetic or dynamic aspect of **love**, and our attempts to realize spiritual love may be helped by the recognition that it is a magnetic energy.

Each of us can and should be a "center of radiation," affecting other centers and lives and in this way fulfilling our part in the redemption of the planet. We each have **our** sphere of radiation; it is our area of responsibility, and within that sphere (which is larger than we think) we can serve in an effective way the Purpose of Divinity.

"The sense of the Earth opening and exploding upwards into God; the sense of God taking root and finding nourishment downwards into Earth; a personal, transcendent God and an evolving Universe no longer forming two hostile centers of attraction, but entering into hierarchical conjunction to raise the human mass on a single tide: such is the sublime transformation which we may with justice foresee, and which in fact is beginning to have its effect upon a growing number of minds, freethinkers as well as believers: the idea of the spiritual evolution of the Universe; the very transformation we have been seeking." (Pierre Teilhard de Chardin in, **The Future of Man.**)

TECHNIQUES OF BLESSING

A problem continually facing us is **what use to make** of the energies aroused or received through meditation, prayer, affirmation and invocation. These energies must be used for two reasons:

1. To avoid congestion and overstimulation in ourselves.

2. Because they are most valuable, and it is our duty and privilege to utilize them for the benefit of humanity.

It is possible to emanate or radiate these energies on spiritual, mental and emotional levels. The reality of such a radiation has always been acknowledged, except perhaps in the modern, materialistic cultural interlude from which we are beginning to emerge.

Modern physical processes and technical achievements help us to realize both the possibility and the procedure of radiation. Two examples are the phenomena of spontaneous radioactivity, like that of radium, and of induced radioactivity through bombardment of atoms in cyclotrons. Radio and television also demonstrate the possibility of transmitting sound and images on the ether without any material means in the sense of visible matter.

If these things are possible on etheric levels and with etheric energies, it is not surprising that they occur on more subtle levels, in the psychological and spiritual worlds or realms. Here we find the phenomena of spontaneous telepathy which so frequently occurs, and also the experimental telepathy which has been scientifically studied in recent years and its validity sufficiently ascertained for few to have reason to doubt it.

Blessing Through Meditation

An important fact that should be realized is that the Soul or Self is endeavoring to infuse the personality all the time. We do not have to "storm" the Soul; it is ever reaching out towards the personality. This infusion can be considered the blessing of the personality by the Soul.

The thinking, loving soul, which tightens its hold over its response apparatus, avails itself upon every possible occasion of every advance made by the form, and employs every influence for the perfecting of its great work...Soul infusion produces joy.

Meditation is obviously the great means of transmitting the radiation or blessing of the soul and the spiritual realms. Various forms of blessing are given on the following pages, and these suggest the many different directions in which blessing may be sent.

We cannot, of course, carry out all of them every day, but it will add to our power to bless if we learn to practice the different techniques, and to develop a habit of blessing is to put ourselves directly in the line of its divine descent.

In meditation the aim is to pass quickly through the stages of concentration (using the will), through rapid alignment of the quieted physical, emotional, and lower mind, to soul levels; this can be visualized as an upward moving to the Soul. Then we should remain poised in a receptive attitude.

We should not look for conscious results, but do the work daily with confidence. Sensitivity to the Soul has to be cultivated; so many earthly energies clamor for attention that we are not aware of the energy of the Soul, but if we persist, just "keep on keeping on," Soul infusion will be attained. Every technique has to be consistently practiced to attain efficiency. Witness our great musicians, artists, scientists, athletes, and all who attain success on the material level.

Every potent blessing requires the use of the will. Its first use is to eliminate obstacles; this can be expressed as "making room" in **time and consciousness.**

"Making room in time" means consecrating regularly a certain span of time to blessing meditation, protecting it from all the "pulls" and claims which try to induce us to outer activity.

"Making room in consciousness" means pushing out of the field of consciousness all that normally occupies it or tries to invade it; sensations, emotions, images, thoughts, anticipations, memories, etc.

Much will is needed for concentrating on active blessing, avoiding a negative, dreamy condition. Above all, let us seek an enlightened fusion of our individual will with the divine Will, and this for the greater good of the Whole – for all humanity.

Blessing the Lower Kingdoms

This blessing is based, first of all, on recognition of the gifts of the lower kingdoms to us and is an expression of the **gratitude** we owe to them. In a wider sense, from a universal point of view, it is prompted by the realization that they are all part of Divine manifestation, that they are unconsciously proceeding on the way of evolution, and that the function of humanity is to help them on that way, and finally to redeem them. An effective means towards this is **blessing**.

Our closest relationship with the other kingdoms of nature is that created by our using them as food. In this way they give us a needed service for which we should be grateful. On our part we transmute them by incorporating them into ourselves. This is the basis (even if unrecognized) of the old custom or ritual of blessing food and saying grace. At present food is generally taken in a hurried, absent-minded way, but eating and drinking with gratitude and appreciation would bring added benefit to us.

There are many forms for the blessing of food, but here is one which incorporates gratitude to the lower kingdoms:

> The food of which we are going to partake is your gift, O God, and the fruit of the labor of many beings. We are grateful for it and bless it. May it give us strength, health, joy and may it increase our love.

The Blessing of Money

This blessing has a special significance, purpose and usefulness owing to the peculiar nature of its object.

Money can be regarded as materialized or condensed Divine energy. In its essence it is therefore something good and pure. But in the course of its use money becomes polluted by the evil passions, the low desires, the worries and fears, the selfish attachment of all to whom it temporarily belongs.

This is not merely a symbolical or psychological connection. Evil forces become attached to money and possessions. This is one of the chief causes of the trouble, individual and collective strife, and maladjustment and unjust distribution connected with material goods, and particularly with money. If this cause has a subjective character, the true solution, the effective remedy should be of the same kind; primarily subjective, psychological and spiritual. In fact, the right use of money depends on **right motivation**, which is a subjective psychological urge, determining **right choices**.

But there is a more specific way of counteracting what can be considered the "curse" attached to money. (This "curse" forms the central theme and the deep meaning of Wagner's series of musical dramas, "The Ring of the Nibelung.") The spiritual purification and redemption of money can be achieved by the conscious use of our spiritual and psychological energies. It can be accomplished by the use of concentrated thought, animated by right feeling (or emotional force) and projected by will, through the use of affirmation formulated in words.

If we subject all money which passes through our hands to such a "treatment," and if an increasingly large number of people deliberately did so, many problems which find no external and technical solution would be done away with. This may seem surprising, so little are we accustomed in this materialistic civilization to give true practical consideration to the reality and the power of subjective forces. Yet it is so, and if we are consistent in our spiritual convictions, we cannot but admit it.

It is in reality an act of **blessing**. Any apt formulation of it can be effective. The following, which is being used by many groups as well as individuals, is suggested:

> May this money be blessed. It is a symbol of divine substance and energy.

> May it be redeemed from every impure influence, from every attachment and craving.

> I appreciate it and keep it as a divine gift.

> I will use it only for good, right, appropriate purposes.

> In using it, again I **bless** it and give thanks for it.

This blessing can be extended to all material possessions and objects. A blessing can also be addressed to those who give money or other possessions for spiritual purposes and uses; this may also include future, unknown "givers."

The Blessing of Obstacles

This might seem to be the most difficult kind of blessing. Our first natural reaction to obstacles is generally one of rebellion or resentment. According to psychological type, it manifests as irritation or self-pity. Yet there are good reasons, first for graciously accepting obstacles, and then for blessing them.

The first reason is that negative reactions increase the difficulty and have bad effects on our psychological and physical health. A recommended consideration lies in the recognition of the universality of, and humanity's totality of, obstacles. Alfred Adler, the well-known psycho-therapist, has expressed it:

"I am in a world full of difficulties and my difficulties belong to me. Why should I quarrel with them?" (Alfred Adler, p.3)

It has been said that the purpose of obstacles is to draw upon the latent will. "Blessed be the obstacles, they teach us unity and resistance" we read in the book **Heart** (Agni Yoga Series).

The positive function of obstacles is often unconsciously recognized, particularly by the young; they resent the easy life and look for adventure and risk, with their accompanying hardships. In a more general way we might say that in sport and games people create **obstacles** for the satisfaction of overcoming them.

Moreover, the willing acceptance of obstacles and the recognition of their usefulness helps to overcome or destroy them, sometimes in a surprising way.

Therefore we can well say, when confronted by difficulties:

"Blessed be Obstacles."

∽

GENERAL BLESSINGS

General blessing has been called "the radiation of a rainbow of blessings to the world." Here is a form used daily by many:

Morning Blessing

May all things and all beings with whom I am, or shall come in contact today, be blessed, now and forever.

∽

Another short form of **Morning Blessing** is:

Blessed be this day towards the perfect consummation of the Divine Plan.

∽∽∽

Blessing Meditation for the World

245

I. Alignment

This requires quieting the personality so that there is no obstruction to Soul union, for it is the Soul, the Self, that blesses. Its three stages are:

1. The body sits relaxed.

2. The emotions are stilled, so that they do not interfere ("quiet as a mountain lake").

3. Then we observe the "monkey" mind (as it has been called because it jumps around). This, too, must be quieted and, if it leaps away, be brought back to stillness, to face the Soul.

II. Meditation

So aligned, we raise our center of consciousness towards the Soul and endeavor to enter into communion through a chosen seed-thought or consideration of a spiritual quality, such as good-will, joy, peace, or the realization of world need.

III. Radiation

"Breathe out" the ideas as formulated thought-forms into the great stream of mental substance which is ever playing upon the human consciousness.

❧❧❧

VISUALIZATION AND USE OF THE HANDS IN BLESSING

Visualization is of particular value in blessing. It not only aids concentration, but brings to the blessing we are seeking to bestow the power of creative imagination and the positive factor of "seeing" the blessing we are sending out reaching the recipient. The following exercise is an example of this:

Visualize a sphere of golden light and place yourself within it. From that center, holding your consciousness as high and steady as possible, say:

"I stand in spiritual Being and, as a Soul, I serve.
I stand within the Light, and as the Light shines
through my form, I radiate that Light.
I stand within the Love of God, and as that love

246

streams through and from my heart, I bless all whom I seek to aid."

Visualize this blessing going out to:

a.   Your immediate circle of family and friends.
b.   All those with whom you come in contact.
c.   Those in places of responsibility all over the world.
d.   Humanity as a whole.

See this beneficent light and blessing streaming forth as you hold your hands, palms outward, in blessing.

The hands can play a most potent part in transmitting spiritual energy, and one that is little understood. The "laying on of hands" is no idle phrase, nor is it confined solely to the operations of the episcopate of any faith. Gestures help to concentrate the mind, focus the attention and direct currents of energy. Physical movements help to give a sense of reality; but their value is chiefly symbolic and when it is not possible to make the movements, they can be performed in imagination, that is, visualized. They are effective in this way, owing to the creative power of imagination.

FIVE GESTURES FOR USE IN BLESSING

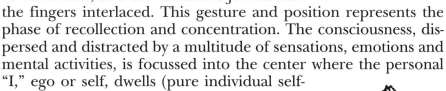

1. Recollection - Concentration

After the arms have been opened horizontally, they are folded in front of the chest, at heart level, and the hands are joined with the fingers interlaced. This gesture and position represents the phase of recollection and concentration. The consciousness, dispersed and distracted by a multitude of sensations, emotions and mental activities, is focussed into the center where the personal "I," ego or self, dwells (pure individual self-consciousness).

2. Elevation and Communion

The second gesture is performed by extending the arms upwards with the hands joined as they are usually held while praying. It symbolizes the raising of the personal cen-

247

ter of consciousness, propelled by aspiration, towards superconscious levels, the realm of Light, Joy, Love, and Power, where the Spiritual Self, the Soul, ever dwells. There, as "living, loving, willing Souls," we joyously realize our communion with other Souls (Group consciousness). "The Souls of men are one and I am one with them," in the One Soul (Unanimity).

3. Invocation-Evocation-Reception

The hands are opened with the wrists joined and the fingers forming a cup (the "Grail Cup"). In this position we invoke, with faith, joy, and gratitude, the blessing descent of the divine energies (**Light - Love - Power**) and remain in an inner attitude of reverent, silent receptivity.

4. Descent-Infusion

The arms and hands are lowered and brought back to the starting position, with the fingers interlaced in front of the chest. This movement and attitude represent the conscious bringing down of the Light, Love, and Power into the personality, which is thus being infused and pervaded by them.

5. Radiation-Blessing

The arms are extended horizontally with palms outspread forward. In this position we perform the actual **blessing**, made powerful by the preparation and recharging of the preceding phases. We radiate the divine energies telepathically in all directions, towards all living beings.

The Great Buddhist Blessing of the Four Divine States

1. LOVE TO ALL BEINGS
   North-South-East-West-Above-Below
   Love to all beings.

   (Silence)

2. COMPASSION TO ALL BEINGS
   North-South-East-West-Above-Below
   Compassion to all beings.

   (Silence)

3. JOY TO ALL BEINGS
   North-South-East-West-Above-Below
   Joy to all beings.

   (Silence)

4. SERENITY TO ALL BEINGS
   North-South-East-West-Above-Below
   Serenity to all beings.

   (Silence)

CHAPTER 11

BLESSINGS & DEDICATIONS

The Interfaith Minister will have occasion to officiate at many dedications of buildings, rooms, churches, items used for services (altars, organs, bells, etc.) and homes. This chapter includes prayers from various religions to cover these situations.

❧❧❧

NATIONAL SPIRITUALIST ASSOCIATION

Dedication of a Church Building

Organ Prelude

Congregational Hymn

Invocation:

Minister: We are met today upon a most solemn and joyful occasion. We meet that we, together, may dedicate this building to the service of humanity and to be witness to our belief and knowledge of the presence of Living Spirit Eternal, operating in this mundane expression of life. It is fitting that we dedicate our lives at this time to the work of telling the glad tidings of continuous individual life, both here and in the hereafter. The house of God has ever been a sacred house in all generations of man, in all countries and nations. It is not alone the house in which we pray. Within these walls we are taught true democratic ideals and values, and through the revelation of Spiritualism we are taught that the doorway of reformation is never closed against any human soul here or hereafter. Therefore, let us rejoice this day that we are permitted to meet in a building which is to be dedicated to the truth of continuous life and to the positive knowledge of spirit return.

The Minister addresses the Officers and Trustees: You have been selected by the membership of this Church to fill the responsible position of Officers and Trustees of this Church now being dedicated to the service of humanity and to the glory of the Living Spirit. You will, at all times, when you represent this Church, act in its behalf and for its welfare. The temple of Eternal Spirit is a sacred place. Nothing should enter this place to defile it. Protect it at all times. Preserve it for the service of God and Spiritualism. Enlarge its work as the occasion shall arise. To you is committed the task of keeping this temple a sacred place. From this time forward, because of your authority, you will hold this property sacred in the name of the Spirit. May the Living Spirit guide and inspire you in all the activities which fall within your authority as Officers and Trustees of this Temple.

Officers and Trustees Reply (Audibly and in Unison): We, the Officers and Trustees of this Church, do promise and covenant, before Eternal Spirit, before these witnesses both in and out of the body, that we will discharge our duties faithfully and that we will, at all times, seek to enlarge the work of Spiritualism. We promise to help make this Church a power for good in this community.

Minister: To the greater glory of Eternal Spirit, to the greater glory of the truth of Spiritualism, to the greater understanding of life hereafter, to the spreading of truth in this life.....

All: We dedicate this Temple.

Minister: For comfort to those who mourn, for the message of continuous life, for help to all people in distress; for the sacredness of home, for the teaching of truth, for the purity and guidance of childhood, for the promotion of brotherhood; for the teaching of true moral values, for the teaching of true patriotic ideals, for the eternal presence of Living Spirit....

All: We dedicate this Temple.

Prayer of Dedication

Address and ending blessing.

ᕲ

Dedication of Dining Room

Minister: God be merciful unto us and bless us and cause His face to shine upon us. That Thy way may be known upon the Earth, Thy saving health among all nations. Let the people praise Thee, O God. Let all the people praise Thee. Then shall the Earth yield her increase and God, even our God, shall bless us. (Psalm 57)

It is fitting that in the house of Living Spirit we should congregate to break bread, giving thanks for all the fruits of the Earth and by our presence here we show that we believe in the values of our Church in this community. It is fitting that we should eat in the house of God. It is fitting that we bring our friends here, that they, too, may enjoy the social life of our Church and be benefitted thereby. Whatever time we can properly use for our social welfare, it is most desirable that we spend part of that time in the Church recreational and dining room, that within these hallowed precincts we may be blessed in all our comings and goings.

We dedicate this dining room to the Living Spirit from whence all power comes and through Whom comes the genius of humanity, to cause the Earth to be more fruitful;

to the spiritual food which nourishes our souls; the food of friendship of spiritual love and fellowship, without which we are incomplete as representatives of Living 'Spirit....

All: We dedicate this dining room.

Minister: Religion is kept alive in the soul of humanity through friendship and example. God speaks to humans through humans, so will He judge the quality and worth of our religion. Those who would keep the name and values of Spirit alive in this world material must do so through the democratic ways of true religious under-standing. They must keep their lives pure and wholesome and, by caring for their physical bodies, show that they truly believe and understand that the body is the house of Spirit. They must present themselves before the world, as true living children of God. Human love and friendship display the light of Spirit through the windows of our soul. As we live with our fellow man, so shall the reality of Living Spirit be revealed. Through Spirit we are made more friendly, more forgiving, more gracious and merci-ful to each other.

All: Therefore, O God, we dedicate this dining room to ever Living Spirit, which Power and living Presence has been revealed through the positive return of individual spirit to us; who still express through our physical temples. In the glorious trinity of Spirit, soul, and body we will continue to grow in spiritual understanding forever. Amen.

Closing prayer.

Dedication of Church Organ

The organ which plays such an important part in the Church service should be recognized as the focal point in this service. It is desirable that music—organ, solo, anthem—should be the chief feature and that addresses should be confined to the actual dedication. **The Choir Master or Director of Music should be prepared to present as much of the above types of music as the occasion demands, always remembering that the too lengthy service can become boring. This is always undesirable.**

Service

Organ Prelude

Congregational Hymn

Invocation:

Minister: Infinite Spirit, may the understanding of the presence of beneficent angels fill us with joy today. May our souls be attuned to the harmonies of the Universe. Assure us that the songs and sweet music of our world are acceptable to Spirit and that through them we are expressing our divine heritage. We seek blessings upon our efforts today, and we pray that this Church may be further blessed, and that the message of Spiritualism will be enhanced and that it will be useful and acceptable to this community. We pray that the brotherhood of man and the assurance of the presence of Living Spirit will be a reality in our lives and in the lives of our fellowmen.

Anthem

Congregational Singing

Solo

Remarks by Church Leader, with a short history of the Church with a history of the new organ.

At this time there may be introduced a resume of the value of music in religion; the following may be found useful:

Music has played an important part in all religious groups and systems since the earliest times. It is certain that religion could not have succeeded without music. Music is the universal language, and it expresses the soul of a people. Nations are identified by their music, and the form and type of the prevailing religion can be identified by the music proceeding therefrom.

Orpheus is reputed to have been the world's first singer, and he is recognized as the mythological founder of religion. The ancient Greeks revered his name and his influence has persisted, even into the present day. He had a decided influence upon the early Christians and his likeness – playing upon his lyre, the forerunner of all types of stringed instruments – is to be found in the Roman Catacombs, where primitive Christians met in secret.

"Music is the mediator between spiritual and sensual life. Although the spirit be not master of that which it creates through music, yet it is blessed in the creation, which, like every creature of art, is mightier than the artist." (Beethoven)

"Music is the art of the prophets, the only art that can calm the agitation of the soul; it is one of the most magnificent presents God has given us." (Martin Luther)

"Music washes away from the soul the dust of everyday life. Music is the child of prayer, the companion of religion." (Auerbach)

"Music is well said to be the speech of angels." (Carlyle)

Anthem - Song - or Solo

Dedication (Congregation standing)

Minister: In a spirit of reverence, humility and happiness we would dedicate this Organ to the greater glory of Spirit and to the service of mankind. We are grateful that we are permitted to worship in this House dedicated to ever present Living Spirit. We are deeply conscious of the sacrifices of those who have erected this building and we shall be ever grateful to those who have made personal sacrifice that this Organ is here today to glorify Spirit and to delight man. We would dedicate this service to the men and women of past days who labored to make this day possible. May we continue to find inspiration for all future days. May the music which shall flow from this Organ be an inspiration to our arisen loved ones and a continuing glory to Infinite Intelligence.

All will repeat the following (it is desirable that the congregation be supplied with printed copies).

We dedicate this Organ to spiritual fellowship and to harmony among humankind. May the sweet music which shall flow from it serve as a key to better understanding among all peoples. We dedicate this Organ to the cause of Spiritualism and this Church. May the beautiful music bring comfort to the sorrowing and enhance the joy of happy hearts. Finally, we dedicate this Organ in loving memory and in grateful appreciation of all those who have preceded us into the land of perpetual Summer.

Solo - Anthem - or Organ Solo

Benediction

∽∽∽

THE LITURGY OF THE LIBERAL CATHOLIC CHURCH

The Blessing of Holy Water for Baptism

The priest takes holy water and says over it the following blessing:

O Lord Christ, Who in the mystery of Thy boundless love didst take upon Thyself the limitations of human form and in Thy gracious compassion didst gather little children into Thine arms; stretch forth, we pray Thee, the right hand of Thy power over this holy water and fill it with Thy heavenly + grace and + blessing, that those to be baptized therewith may receive the fullness of Thy love and ever remain in the number of Thy faithful children. Amen.

∽

The Consecration of Holy Oils

The celebrant is robed. The oils and balsam for consecration are brought in by a solemn procession. A hymn is sung then the following is said:

THE EXORCISM

In the name of God, I exorcise all influences of evil, that they may be cast out from this oil and balsam which we are about to dedicate to His service, in the power of the + Father and of the + Son and of the Holy + Ghost. Amen.

The vessels are now removed to another table, except that containing the oil for the sick.

THE CONSECRATION
OF THE OIL FOR THE SICK

In the name of our Lord Christ and invoking the assistance of the holy Archangel Raphael, I + consecrate and + hallow this oil for the healing of the sick; may the blessing of the Great Physician rest thereupon, that it may give refreshment and peace alike to soul and body. Amen.

The newly consecrated oil is carried in procession to the sacristy.

THE CONSECRATION
OF THE OIL OF CATECHUMENS

In the name of our Lord Christ, I + consecrate and + hallow this oil that it may serve for the cleansing and safeguarding of those who receive the holy rite of Baptism or consecration to the order of the priesthood. Amen.

The newly consecrated oil is carried in procession to the sacristy.

THE CONSECRATION OF THE HOLY CHRISM

In the name of our Lord Christ, I + consecrate and + hallow this oil, now set apart for the making of holy chrism, that it may bestow upon those who receive it of the fullness of spiritual strength. Amen.

The balsam and oil are now mixed, and the celebrant, extending both hands over the oil, continues:

Let us pray. O Lord Christ, the fountain of all goodness, Who dost pour down Thy gifts abundantly upon us for our strengthening, Who dost hallow and set apart these earthly things as a channel of Thy marvelous power, send forth, we pray Thee, Thy + blessing upon this holy chrism, that whatsoever persons or things shall be anointed therewith may receive the fullness of spiritual consecration. Let Thy heavenly blessing descend upon those who are signed by this chrism with the sign of Thy holy service that, guarding well their spiritual heritage, they may shed around them the fragrance of a godly life, O Thou great shepherd and ruler of the souls of men, to Whom be glory for evermore. Amen.

The celebrant now breathes three times in the form of a cross over the chrism. Each priest present also breathes over it in the form of a cross and it is then carried in procession to the sacristy.

The Blessing of a Church Bell

The bell to be blessed should be thoroughly cleansed beforehand, both within and without and should be suspended so that its lip may be three or four feet above the ground. Before the service is begun, four small crosses should be marked with chalk upon the upper part of the sides of the bell, denoting the north, east, south, and west points respectively. Also seven small crosses should be marked with chalk at equal distances upon the outside of

the lip of the bell, to indicate where the oil is to be applied. An acolyte or other assistant should precede the bishop or priest as he walks around the bell and should wipe off with a damp cloth each of the chalk crosses just before the bishop touches the spot with the holy oil.

The thymiama (which according to ancient custom is a mixture of ground myrrh, resin, and incense) should be prepared beforehand and a brazier with the glowing embers or charcoal. If the ingredients of the thymiama are not procurable, a plentiful supply of incense will suffice. Holy water having been made in the usual way, the bishop begins the service with:

THE INVOCATION

Bishop: In the name of the Father + and of the Son and of the Holy Ghost. Amen.

The bishop takes the aspergill and sprinkles the bell both outside and inside, saying:

In the name of God, I exorcise all influences of evil that they may be banished and driven forth from this bell which we are about to dedicate to His service. In the power of the + Father and of the + Son and of the Holy + Ghost. Amen.

The bishop takes upon his thumb some of the oil for the sick and therewith makes the sign of the cross four times upon the outside of the upper half of the bell, first upon the north side, then (passing by the east) upon the south, then on the west side and finally upon the east, saying:

In the name of the Most High, and invoking the aid of the holy Archangel Raphael, I anoint this bell for the healing of Christ's faithful followers, that whithersoever its sound may penetrate it may bear help and strength both to soul and body, through Christ the Lord of heaven and earth. Amen.

The bishop intones the following prayer, moving around the bell and making the sign of the cross upon it with the oil for the sick at the seven points indicated.

O Christ, Who art Thyself the great exemplar of all divine virtues, we pray Thee to pour down Thy blessing upon this bell, that its voice may arouse in the hearts of Thy loving children the discernment clearly to perceive and the will humbly to copy Thy + strength, Thy + wisdom, Thy + loving kindness, Thy + beauty, Thy + justice, Thy + devotion and Thy + guiding power, that so Thy servants, being of Thy grace made perfect in Thee, may finally attain the glory which Thou has ordained for them, Thou Who livest and reignest with the Father and the Holy Spirit, one God throughout the ages of ages. Amen.

The bishop then takes upon his thumb the sacred chrism and therewith anoints the inside of the lip of the bell at the four cardinal points, saying:

To the glory of + God Most High and of His servant + Mary, Queen of Heaven, Blessed + Michael the Archangel and the holy + Saint (here is inserted the name of the patron saint of the church, or of the saint to whom the bell is dedicated), I solemnly dedicate this bell. May its sound peal forth ever to the praise of God and the blessing of man.

Making five large crosses in the air over the whole bell, he continues:

May it be + hallowed and + consecrated to God's service for ever, in the name of the + Father and of the + Son and of the Holy + Ghost. Amen.

The thymiama is then cast upon the glowing charcoal in the brazier and the latter is placed upon a stool under the bell. The bishop intones:

As the sweet savor fills this bell and rises up before Thee, so pour Thou down, O Holy Spirit, the dew of Thine all-powerful blessing upon it and upon us Thy servants, Thou Who livest and reignest with the Father and Son, one God throughout the ages of ages. Amen.

A hymn may be sung while the bishop cleanses his hands. When it is ended he pronounces this blessing:

> Upon God's gracious love and protection I commit you. The Lord bless + you and keep you. The Lord make His face to shine upon you and give you His peace and blessing, now and for evermore. Amen.

The Blessing of Objects in General

THE EXORCISM

Priest: In the name of God, I exorcise all influences of evil that they may be banished and driven forth, from this (name the object being blessed) which we are about to dedicate to His service. In the power of the + Father and of the + Son and of the Holy + Ghost. Amen.

The object may now be sprinkled with holy water and censed.

THE BLESSING

Priest: Let us pray. O God, Who in the mystery of Thy boundless love didst breathe forth Thine own divine life into Thy universe and art Thyself the continual source of its existence, stretch forth, we pray Thee, the right hand of Thy power over this (name of object) which has in divers ways been purified, and fill this creature with heavenly + grace and + blessing. Grant that whosoever shall use this (name of object) may be enlightened in heart and mind and serve Thee in all good works, through Christ our Lord, Who liveth and reigneth with Thee in the unity of the Holy Spirit, God throughout all ages of ages. Amen.

The Blessing of A House

The priest, having vested, formally enters the house and says:

Peace be to this house and to all that dwell herein.

The priest draws a line with holy water at the entrance and says:

We pray Thee, O Lord, so to bless this doorway by Thy mighty power that those who enter here may leave behind them all unworthy thought and feeling and that Thy children who dwell in this place may ever serve Thee in peace and holiness of life; through Christ our Lord. Amen.

He then goes to all other entrances to the house and draws a line of holy water before each, repeating the same prayer. He next blesses the incense and, attended by one bearing the censer and another the aspergill, he sprinkles the various rooms with holy water. After which he says:

O God, Who in Thy providence hast appointed a wondrous ministry of angels, we pray Thee to send down Thy holy angel to + bless and to + hallow this house, that they who dwell herein may live in the power and love of Christ our Lord and Master and may continually serve before Thee in all good works, through the same Christ our Lord. Amen.

The Blessing & Laying of a Foundation Stone

A procession moves to the foundation stone and the following are said or sung:

Celebrant: Our help is in the name of the Lord.
Congregation: Who hath made heaven and Earth.

Celebrant: Trust ye in the Lord forever.
Congregation: For He is our Rock of Ages.

Celebrant: Let us bless the Lord.
Congregation: Henceforth and for evermore.

Celebrant: Glory be to the Father and to the Son and to the Holy   Ghost.

Congregation: As it was in the beginning, is now and ever shall be, world without end. Amen.

The celebrant takes the aspergill and sprinkles the stone with holy water, saying:

Let us pray. O Christ our Holy Lord, Son of the living God, Who art the one foundation and the chief corner-stone of Thy church, we pray Thee to + purify, + to accept and + to establish this stone to be placed in the foundations of Thine abiding place. We dedicate to Thee the work which here is to be accomplished, praying that the incense of true worship, joyous and unafraid, may ever rise within these walls. As we thus lay the foundation stone of this building to the honor and praise of Thy holy name, so may Thy love and Thy blessing make fruitful the lives of those who shall labor here, to the end that peace and happiness, joy and contentment may radiate from this center of spiritual life, O Thou great ruler of the hearts of humanity, to Whom be praise and adoration from humanity and from the angelic host. Amen.

The celebrant resigns the aspergill, takes in hand the trowel and spreads a layer of mortar where the stone is to be laid. The stone is lowered into its place. The celebrant asks of the assistant:

Is the stone plumb?

The assistant measures it with the plumb-line and replies:

The stone is plumb.

Celebrant: Is the stone level?
Assistant (after trying it with a level): The stone is level.

Celebrant (testing the stone with the square) says: I declare this stone to be well and truly laid. Let us pray. Almighty God and loving Father, without Whom nothing is strong, nothing is holy, look down in the might of Thy power upon this creature of stone, that it and this place, which we have dedicated to Thy service and consecrated to Thy work, may become radiant with the light of Thy undying fire.

During the prayer which follows, the celebrant anoints with chrism the cross carved on the face of the stone.

Wherefore do we + consecrate and + hallow this stone as the foundation of Thy church, to the glory of God, to the perfecting of humanity and in honor of His glorious martyr, the holy Saint (..name of the patron saint of the church..). In the Name of the + Father and of the + Son and of the Holy + Ghost. Amen.

The following canticle is said or sung:

Celebrant: Christ is our foundation.
Congregation: And our chief cornerstone.

Celebrant:

1. We are no more strangers and foreigners, but fellow citizens with the saints and of the household of God.

2. And are built upon the foundation of the apostles and prophets, Jesus Christ Himself being the chief cornerstone.

3. In Whom all the building fitly framed together, groweth unto a holy temple in the Lord.

4. In Whom ye are also builded together, for a habitation of God through the Spirit.

5. Except the Lord built the house, their labor is but lost that built it.

6. The foundation of God standeth sure, having this seal: let everyone that nameth the name of Christ depart from iniquity.

Glory be to the Father and to the Son and to the Holy Ghost.

Congregation: As it was in the beginning, is now and ever shall be, world without end. Amen.

Celebrant: Christ is our foundation.
Congregation: And our chief cornerstone.

Celebrant: Let us pray. O Lord Christ, in Whose presence all desire dies save the desire to be like Thee, we pray Thee to send down into our hearts and minds a ray of Thy loving kindness, that those who worship here may ever be gentle in speech, pure in thought, and kind in action, that they may be bearers of Thy love and a joy to all their brethren, O Thou Who art the master and friend of all that lives. Amen.

Turning to the people, the celebrant pronounces this benediction: The peace of God, which passeth all understanding, keep your hearts and minds in the knowledge and love of God and of His Son, Christ our Lord; and the blessing of God almighty, the + Father, the + Son and the Holy + Ghost, be amongst you and remain with you always. Amen.

CHRISTWARD MINISTRY
Dedication and Blessing
of a Home

This service is taken from the book "The Meaning and Value of the Sacraments" by Flower A. Newhouse which is available from The Christward Ministry, Route 5, Box 206, Escondido, CA 92025.

The type of service which is suggested here inaugurates the use of a place, a home (or business building) with which a family (or workers) will be involved. One who realizes the value of a permanent thought atmosphere and who can pray effectively and self-forgetfully is able to idealize and thereby create a permanent archetype which shall steadily influence the site as well as the building (or complex) that is being dedicated. This ritual is written especially for a home, but it can easily be adapted to the blessing of a monument, carillon bells, or of any place or building. Anyone who meditates or prays successfully can act as celebrant, though in this chapter a minister is envisioned as officiating.

Prior to the gathering of relatives and friends for the House Blessing, the home has been ideally and thoroughly cleansed. Flowers beautify at least one room (the living room) and soft music and incense are appropriate. A bowl of clear, fresh water should be on a table awaiting blessing.

THE HOUSE DEDICATION SERVICE

The Minister begins the ceremony by stating the inner value of such a service by saying:

Friends, we have gathered together to celebrate the dedication of this home. Each of us should add our thoughts of interest and goodwill to the general benediction of this home and grounds by envisioning the family as realizing this place as a home whose steadfast spirit always renews, heals, and uplifts everyone who steps over its threshold. Pray inwardly with me:

Eternal God Presence, in Christ's Powerful Name we ask for Thy permanent blessing to ray forth into every room in this home, and into every atom of the whole place. May Thy Light cleanse whatever currents of negativity might be in the atmosphere. Let Thy Ray of Benediction in permanent activity, bless, cleanse, renew, and protect every atom of the home and grounds on every plane of being. May Thy Light forever cheer and inspire everyone who enters its radius. So let it be; so is it now established in order and beauty. Amen.

The Minister goes to the bowl of water and blesses the water by lifting it and making the sign of the cross slowly and thoughtfully in this manner: with both hands the Minister raises the water to the level of the eyebrows in a straight line with the center of the body and prays:

Eternal Spirit, source of our lives, bless this water with cleansing, vitalizing and ever-active spiritual powers.

Then the bowl is lowered slowly to the naval area from which it is raised again in a straight line to the center of the chest in the region of the heart. From this position the left bar of the cross is drawn by extending the bowl toward the left side while saying:

Let Thy healing, regenerating and transforming forces permeate this water, O Christ Emmanuel.

The sign of the cross is now drawn to the right side as the celebrant concludes the blessing:

Holy Comforter, Spirit of Truth, quicken this water with Thy gifts of wisdom, guidance, and illumination. For the continual activities of these energies, we thank Thee, Holy and Everpresent Trinity. Amen.

The minister dips fingers into the blessed water and sprinkles the water in the directions of north, south, east, and west. The Minister then proceeds to enter every room and again sprinkles the water in the four directions. He (she) need not add any additional thought, as the water contains the spiritual properties with which the entire home and grounds are imbued. The Minister need not go outdoors, but should open the front and rear doors and sprinkle water outside. Returning to the group, the Minister may offer further explanation.

This custom originated with Jesus, Who said on His first visit to the home of a friend, "Peace be to this house." He taught His disciples the inner meaning of such a blessing and He encouraged them to use it. This particular ceremony has two main benefits. It causes a descent of power to enter the home from the Causal Level which radiates a charging of renewal. These energies help every occupant of the home. It also attracts an Angel to the dwelling who becomes known to the family as the Angel of the Home. Her work is to ensoul, protect, and harmonize the home and grounds. She is not present all the time, but this One interested Angel remains in constant telepathic communication with the family. When trees are planted on the grounds other intelligences, such as Tree Devas, will make their regular visitations.

The Minister concludes the service praying:

May the Spirit of Peace rest upon this home. May the Presence of Love dwell here steadily. May the inflow of happiness and laughter be here centered. May the beauty of friendship grace the home. May the impetus of progress be expressed in this family.

Dipping fingers again into the bowl, the celebrant invokes the name of the dwelling that the family has chosen, sprinkling the water at the same time in the direction of the fireplace, or toward the East if there is no hearth. The Minister now continues:

And now in awareness of the Presence Who observes us, we pray. In the names of the Divine Mother-Father Spirit; Lord Jesus, the Christ; and the Holy Comforter we christen this home (.... name ......). May Divine Powers faithfully hallow, purify, and sanctify the safety of this blessed place, bringing to everyone who crosses its threshold attunement to the Eternal Watcher Who is also our Divine Benefactor. Through the grace of the Lord Christ we ask this. Amen.

MY OWN FAVORITE HOUSE BLESSING

Here I have taken pieces of blessings from several religions and put in some of my own ideas.

Prepare a kit for yourself containing holy water (made from blessing pure water and adding exorcised salt, see pages 195-197 in Chapter 7), blessed oil, candleholders and candles, matches, incense and incense holder, a crucifix, and a tape of sacred music (I use Missa Benedictus). Check with the house-holder first to assure that they have a tape player. If not, take one with you.

If you have a minister's stole, wear it for the occasion.

Make an appointment for a time for the house blessing. Ask the householder to clean and air the house and have some flowers in the living room.

CEREMONY

Gather all present in the living room. Put on the music, light the candles and incense. If there are several people there, give one a candle to carry, one the holy water, and another the incense holder. Place at least 3 candles in a triangular shape in the living room.

Address those present:

Friends, we have gathered here today to celebrate the dedication of this home. Pray inwardly with me:

Eternal God Presence, in Christ's powerful Name we ask for Thy permanent blessing to ray forth into every room in this home, and into every atom of the whole place. May Thy Light cleanse whatever currents of nega-tivity might be in the atmosphere. Let Thy Ray of Bene-diction in permanent activity, bless, cleanse, renew, and protect every atom of the home and grounds on every plane of being. May Thy Light forever cheer and inspire everyone who enters here. So let it be forever.

Describe the inner meaning of the ceremony:

This custom originated with Jesus, Who said on His first visit to the home of a friend, 'Peace be to this house.' He taught His disciples the inner meaning of such a blessing and He encouraged them to use it.

This particular ceremony has two main benefits. It causes a descent of power to enter the home from the Causal Level which radiates a charging of renewal. These energies help every occupant of the home. It also attracts an Angel to the home who is known as the Angel of the

Home. Her work is to ensoul, protect and harmonize the home and grounds. She is not present all the time, but this One interested Angel remains in constant telepathic communication with the family. (If there are grounds sufficient to plant trees, continue with the following.) When trees are planted on the grounds other intelligences, such as Tree Devas, will make their regular visitations.

Ask all to say the Lord's Prayer. Then you say:

Father-Mother God, we ask your blessings and the help of your holy angels to guard and protect all who live here and all who enter here. Deliver this home from all negative energies. If there are any evil or lost spirits here, bring in your Angels of Light to take them to where they need to be for their own growth and salvation. God, Who came to bring peace, make this home a place of sanctuary and peace.

Now, starting in the living room, go to each corner of the room, accompanied by persons carrying the candle, holy water, and incense. Sprinkle holy water into the corner, then, holding a crucifix in your right hand, make the sign of the cross toward the corner while saying:

Father-Mother God, bless every atom of this room, removing any negative energies. We ask this in the name of the Father, the Son, and the Holy Spirit.

After repeating this in each corner of the living room, go through the house, blessing every corner including the bathroom and sprinkling holy water into closets. Finally go to the rear and front doors, open them, and sprinkle holy water over the thresholds.

Then return to the living room and say the following prayers:

Send, O Lord, your holy angels to watch and guard this place, to resist evil things and provide good things so that all disquiet and disaster may be banished from this home.

May the Lord bless and sanctify this tabernacle of His

servants and grant to them the riches of the kingdom of heaven.

May the Spirit of Peace rest upon this home. May the presence of love be here. May happiness and laughter be here and the beauty of friendship. Grant, O Lord, to those living here such earthly and heavenly blessings as are necessary for the maintenance of life and so control what they desire that they may be able to receive Thy mercy. Bless and hallow this home and let Angels of Light dwell within it to guard it and all its inhabitants.

Place your hands on the heads of the householders and say:

In the name of God most High may release from your pain be given you, and your health restored according to His holy will.

In the name of Jesus Christ, the Prince of life, may new life surge through your mortal body.

In the name of God the Holy Spirit may you receive inward health and the peace that passes understanding. And may God, Who gives us peace, make you completely His, and keep your whole being, spirit, mind, soul, and body, free from all fault at the coming of our Lord Jesus Christ. Amen.

Make the sign of the cross over all present and say:

The blessing of God Almighty, the Father, the Son, and the Holy Spirit be upon this home, all here present now and all who enter here, now and always. Amen.

This ends the ceremony. Blow out the candles, turn off the music, and extinguish the incense.

CHAPTER 12
PRAYERS FOR ALL OCCASIONS

MORNING PRAYERS

THE SIGN OF THE CROSS

"In the name of the Father, and of the Son, and of the Holy Ghost. Amen."

MORNING BLESSING

May all things and all beings
with whom I am, or shall come in contact today,
be blessed, now and forever.

Blessed be this day
towards the perfect consummation of the Divine Plan.

EFFECTIVE PRAYER

1. I release all of my past, present, future, negatives, all human relationships, all human desires, sex, money, judgement, communication and identity to the Light.

2. I am a Light Being or I am a Child of God.

3. I radiate the Light from my Light Center (solar plexus) throughout my whole being, body, mind and spirit.

4. I radiate the Light from my Light Center to everyone.

5. I radiate the Light from my Light Center to everything.

6. I am in a bubble of Light, only Light can come to me and only Light can be here. Nothing can ever harm me.

7. Thank God for everything, for everyone, and for me, but most of all, thank You, God, for Thee.

MORNING CALL

I call on the I AM Presence and the CHRIST SELF to thank you for a good night's sleep and for taking me to the retreats to study with the Masters. May the knowledge that I received be brought into my outer consciousness as it is needed. I call to the Beloved Ascended Master Saint Germain, Chohan for the Seventh Ray, to radiate into my consciousness His Divine Plan for my part in the transformation into the Golden Age. And I make the call to the Beloved Ascended Lady Master, Mother Mary, to hold in consciousness, the Immaculate Conception for this Great Plan.

MORNING PRAYER OF THE EARLY CHRISTIANS

O God, Who are faithful and true, Who has mercy on thousands and ten thousands of them that love Thee, the Lover of the humble, and the Protector of the needy, of Whom all things stand in need, for all things are subject to Thee; look down upon this Thy people, who bow their heads to Thee, and bless them with spiritual blessing. Keep them as the apple of Thine eye. Preserve them in piety and righteousness, and vouchsafe them eternal life in Christ Jesus, Thy beloved Son, with Whom glory, honor, and worship be to Thee and to the Holy Spirit, now and always, and forever and ever. Amen.

⤚

FOR A PERFECT DAY (MOZARABIC LITURGY)

Let this prayer come unto Thee, O Lord, in the morning. Thou didst take to Thyself our frail and suffering nature. Grant unto us that we may pass this day in peace and joy, that we fall not into sin. So reaching the evening free from sin, may we be able to offer Thee our praise.

⤚

A DEDICATION TO GOD (GELASIAN SACRAMENTARY)

Into Thy hands, O God, we commend ourselves this day, and all those who are dear to us. Let the gift of Thy wonderful Presence be with us even to the end of the day. Grant that we never lose sight of Thee all the day long, but rather praise and beseech Thee, that our thanks may come to Thee again at its close.

⤚

FOR GUIDANCE (ROMAN BREVIARY)

O Lord God almighty, Who has brought us to the beginning of this day, defend us in the same by Thy power; that we may not fall into any sin, but that all our thoughts, words, and works may be directed to the fulfillment of Thy will. Through our Lord Jesus Christ, Thy Son, Who liveth and reigneth with Thee in the unity of the Holy Ghost, God, world without end. Amen.

⤚

THE PRESENCE OF GOD

Most holy and adorable Trinity, one God in three Persons, I believe that Thou art here present; I adore Thee with the deepest humility, and render to Thee with

275

my whole heart the homage which is due to Thy sovereign Majesty.

❧

THANKSGIVING AND OFFERING

My God, I most humbly thank Thee for all the favors Thou has bestowed upon me up to the present moment. I give Thee thanks that Thou hast created me, that Thou hast redeemed me by the Precious Blood of Thy dear Son, and that Thou has preserved me, and brought me safe to the beginning of another day. I offer to Thee, O Lord, my whole being, and in particular all my thoughts, words, actions, joys and sufferings, of this day. I consecrate them all to the glory of Thy name, asking Thee, that through the infinite merits of Jesus Christ, my Savior, they may find acceptance in Thy sight. May Thy divine love animate them, and may they all tend to Thy greater glory. Amen.

❧

PRAYER OF RESOLUTION

Adorable Jesus, my Savior and Master, model of all perfection, I resolve and will try this day to imitate Thy example, to be like Thee, mild, humble, chaste, zealous, charitable, and resigned. I will redouble my efforts to see Thy image in all those I meet and deal with this day, and to be as helpful to them as I would be to Thee. I resolve to avoid this day all those sins which I have committed heretofore, and which I now sincerely desire to give up forever. Amen.

❧

MORNING OFFERING

O Jesus! Through the Immaculate Heart of Mary, I offer Thee my prayers, works, and sufferings of this day for all the intentions of Thy Sacred Heart, in union with the holy Sacrifice of the Mass throughout the world, in reparation for my sins, for the intentions of all our associates, and in particular, for the intentions of our Holy Father, the Pope.

PETITION FOR GRACE

O my God, Thou knowest my weakness and failings, and that without Thy help I can accomplish nothing for the good of souls, my own or others. Grant me, therefore, the help of Thy grace. Grant it according to my particular needs this day. Enable me to see the task Thou wilt set before me in the daily routine of my life, and help me to work hard at my appointed tasks. Teach me to bear patiently all the trials of suffering or failure that may come to me today. Amen.

TO MY GUARDIAN ANGEL

O Angel of God, my guardian dear,
To whom God's love commits me here,
Ever this day be at my side,
To light and guard, to rule and guide.

PRAYERS TO MARY

HAIL MARY

Hail Mary, full of grace, the Lord is with thee, blessed art thou amongst women and blessed is the fruit of thy womb, Jesus. Holy Mary, Mother of God, pray for us now and at the hour of our death. Amen.

CONSECRATION TO MARY

My Queen! my Mother! I give thee all myself, and to show my devotion to thee, I consecrate to thee my eyes, my ears, my mouth, my heart, my entire self. Wherefore, O loving Mother, as I am thine own, keep me, defend me, as thy property and possession.

THE MEMORARE

Remember, O most gracious Virgin Mary, that no one ever fled to thy protection, implored thy help, or sought thy intercession, without obtaining relief. Confiding, therefore, in thy goodness and mercy, I fly unto thee, my mother, and cast my self at thy most sacred feet. Hear my prayers, O Mother of the Word Incarnate, and grant my petitions. Amen.

EVENING PRAYERS

AN EXAMINATION OF CONSCIENCE

To overcome our failings we must know them. A daily checking of our service of God and neighbor will show us what we must watch, in order to root out of our lives imperfect or sinful habits. The following questions are a useful form of examination.

Have I tried to live this day mindful of the presence of God? Have I tried in all things to do His will? Have I murmured or been impatient with the reverses or the difficulties I have met?

Have I been guilty of any act or word contrary to truth, honesty, or purity?

Have I given way to pride, envy or hatred? Have I spoken of the faults of others? Have I hurt anyone's feelings by my words or actions? Have I encouraged those who were speaking of the faults of others?

Have I been seriously trying today to lead a holy life by avoiding sin, loving God, and by being concerned for all with whom I come in contact? Do I live selfishly, as though the people with whom I come in contact did not matter to me?

Am I concerned over the salvation of the souls of those around me? Am I willing to inconvenience myself to help others? Am I kind only to my friends, or do I help also my enemies?

Another form of examination of one's day is Retrogression.

After saying your evening prayers and laying down to sleep, review your day backwards from now to the time you awakened that day. It is like rewinding your tape. If anything in the day is not as you would have liked it to be, redo the situation, making it as you would have liked to have done it. This helps us learn from our mistakes and imprints better habits of action on our minds. It also clears our minds so our dream time can be used for learning and guidance.

BEFORE RETIRING (SAINT ALPHONSUS LIGUORI)

Jesus Christ my God, I adore Thee and thank Thee for all the graces Thou hast given me this day. I offer Thee my sleep and all the moments of this night, and I beseech Thee to keep me without sin. Wherefore I put myself within Thy sacred side and under the mantle of our Lady, my Mother. Let Thy holy angels stand about me and keep me in peace; and let Thy blessing be upon me.

FOR PROTECTION (SIXTH CENTURY COLLECT)

Be present, O Lord, and protect us through the silent hours of this night, that we who are wearied with the work and changes of this fleeting world, may rest upon Thy eternal changelessness.

↬

FOR A QUIET SLEEP (LEONINE SACRAMENTARY)

O Lord God, wearied as we are with the labor of the day, do Thou with quiet sleep refresh us, that receiving this help to our weakness, we may serve Thee in body and mind.

↬

PRAYER OF A LAY APOSTLE

Thanks, my God, for the day that is ending, thanks for the coming night. Bring sleep to the weary, bring repose to those I love, and give me rest until tomorrow.

All was not fine, perfect, and beautiful today. Give me the strength to do better tomorrow.

In this day that is ending I have not been what I should have been. Make me better, my God, less harsh towards others, more gentle, more patient. Make me, too, more determined, more demanding of myself, more truthful in speaking, more faithful in my promises, more active in my work, more obedient, and more submissive. Let me be cheerful, too, and may tomorrow be a finer, fuller day than this.

Thanks, my God, for the day that is ending, thanks for the coming night. Bring sleep to the weary, bring repose to those I love, and give me rest until tomorrow.

↬

THANKSGIVING AT NIGHT
(PRAYER OF THE EARLY CHRISTIANS)

O God, Who art without beginning, without end, the Maker of the whole world by Christ, and the Provider for it, but before all, His God and Father, and Sender forth of the Spirit, and the King of intelligible and sensible beings; Who has made the day for the works of light, and the night for the refreshment of our infirmity, – for "the day is thine, the night also is thine; Thou has prepared the light and the sun," – do Thou now, O Lord, Thou lover of mankind, and fountain of all good, mercifully accept this, our evening thanksgiving. Thou Who has brought us through the length of the day, and hast brought us to the beginnings of the night, preserve us by Thy Christ, afford us a peaceable evening, and a night free from sin, and vouchsafe us everlasting life by Thy Christ, through Whom glory, honor, and worship be to Thee in the Holy Spirit for ever. Amen.

PRAYER FOR REST

Bless, O Lord, our rest this night, that we may renew our bodily strength and awake refreshed, able to serve Thee better. O all you angels and saints, and thou especially, O Mother of God, intercede for us, not only during this night, but for the rest or our life, and particularly at the hour of our death. Amen.

Jesus, Mary, and Joseph, I give you my heart and soul.

Jesus, Mary, and Joseph, assist me in my last agony.

Jesus, Mary, and Joseph, let me breathe forth my spirit in peace with you.

PRAYERS FOR HEALTH

FOR THE RECOVERY OF HEALTH

O Father of mercies, and God of all comfort, our only help in time of need: We lift our hearts unto Thee on behalf of this Thy servant. Look graciously upon him (her) we beseech Thee, and strengthen him (her) with Thy grace. We know, O Lord, that all things are possible with Thee. In keeping with Thy will, restore him (her) to health and strength; and to Thy name shall be the praise forever. Amen.

(Universal Spiritualist)

FOR ONE ABOUT TO UNDERGO AN OPERATION

Almighty God, our heavenly Father: We pray Thee graciously to comfort Thy servant (.......name........) in his (her) suffering, and to bless the means made use of for his (her) cure. Fill his (her) heart with confidence, that, though he (she) be sometimes afraid, yet may his (her) trust be ever firmly in Thee. Amen.

(Universal Spiritualist)

FOR ONE CONVALESCING

Eternal God, our Father, Thou Who art with us when we are restless, Thou Who dost visit us when we are lonely, quiet Thou our impatience. In the long hours of our waiting may we remind ourselves of Thine eternal presence. In the hurried hours of the morning may we rest our minds in Thee; in the long hours of day may we meditate upon Thy purpose for us; in the still hours of the night may we rest ourselves in Thee; knowing that morning, noon, and night Thou art renewing us in strength and health and faith. Thou dost heal us when we are quiet. Thou dost make us whole when we are trustful. We give Thee thanks for health, and pray that we may use it to Thy satisfaction. Amen.

(Universal Spiritualist)

FOR ONE ABOUT TO DIE

I am the resurrection and the life, saith the Lord. He that believeth in Me shall never die but shall have everlasting life. Amen.

O Father of mercies, and God of all comfort, our only help in the time of need; we lift our hearts unto Thee. We pray in behalf of this Thy servant, here lying in great weakness of body. Send Thy ministering angels unto him (her) to be near in his (her) time of need. As birds seek their nests and children the shelter of home at eventide, so we come unto Thee and are comforted, knowing that underneath are Thine everlasting arms. Amen.

Be not afraid, saith the Lord, for lo, I am with thee always. Amen.

(Universal Spiritualist)

FOR HELP IN SICKNESS

Lord Jesus, Incarnate Son of God, Who for our salvation didst will to be born in a stable, to endure poverty, suffering, and sorrow throughout Thy life and finally to die the bitter death of the Cross, I implore Thee, in the hour of my death to say to Thy divine Father: O Father, forgive him (her)! Say to Thy beloved mother: Behold thy son, thy child! Say to my soul: This day shalt thou be with Me in paradise! O my God, my God! forsake me not at that moment! I thirst! O my God, truly my soul is athirst for

Thee, the fountain of living water. My life has passed away like smoke; yet a little, and all is consummated. Therefore also, adorable Savior, into Thy hands I commend my spirit for all eternity. Lord Jesus, receive my soul. Amen.

(The Prayer Book, The Catholic Press)

∾

FOR ONE PASSED ON

Almighty God, Who hast dominion over life and over death, and dost hold all Thy creation in the everlasting arms of Thy love, we pray Thee for the peace and progression of Thy servant (..name...) that he (she) being dead unto the physical, yet ever living unto Thee, may find in Thy continued and unceasing service the perfect consummation of happiness and peace. Amen.

(Universal Spiritualist)

∾

AFTER A DEATH IN A FAMILY

Almighty God, Who art ever near to uphold and bless, hear now our prayer for Thy servants bowed down with grief. May they find strength and peace in Thee, and be able to say, "Thy will be done." Visit them with Thy comfort, and be Thou Thyself the companion of their spirits. Let them not be unmindful of the many good things which still remain to them to make life worth while. Unite the hearts of those who are left in a closer bond of love and sympathy, and give them strength to carry on with hope and courage. May they feel that Thou art their refuge, and that underneath are the everlasting arms. Amen.

(Universal Spiritualist)

∾∾∾

OCCASIONAL PRAYERS

SALUTATION TO THE ARCHANGELS

1.   Hail Archangel **RAPHAEL**, Son of God, Son of Righteousness, Archangel of the East,

(Repeat above, insert ....)

    GABRIEL, Son of God, ... (**SOUTH**)

    URIEL, Son of God, ... (**WEST**)

    MICHAEL, Son of God, ... (**NORTH**)

    Thank you for all that you are doing for the Cosmos, the Universe, the Galaxy, the Solar System, me, my body, and world of affairs.
THANK YOU, THANK YOU, THANK YOU.

2.   In the NAME, and by the POWER and AUTHORITY of the God within me, I call forth from THE ONE SOURCE A RICH BLESSING FOR YOU.

    I ask you to send a Blessing to the Earth and all life evolving here.

3.   With reverence and love, I bow to the God within you.

    I send you my LOVE, JOY and GRATITUDE.

PRAYERS FOR DAYS OF THE WEEK

These prayers are taken from "The Prayer Book" from The Catholic Press, Chicago, Illinois. The early Christians were forced to accept the established names for the days of the week, which honored pagan deities. The names remain unchanged, but in the course of time the days have rededicated to God, Christ, Mary, Saint Joseph, and the Angels.

SUNDAY - THE HOLY TRINITY

Most Holy Trinity, Godhead indivisible, Father, Son, and Holy Spirit, our first beginning and our last end, since Thou hast made us after Thine own image and likeness, grant that all the thoughts of our minds, all the words of our tongues, all the affections of our hearts, and all our actions may be always conformed to Thy most holy will, to the end that after having seen Thee here below in appearances and in a dark manner by means of faith, we may come at last to contemplate Thee face-to-face in the perfect possession of Thee for ever in paradise. Amen.

MONDAY - THE HOLY GHOST

Come, Holy Ghost, Sanctifier all powerful, God of love, Thou Who didst fill the Virgin Mary with grace, Thou Who didst wonderfully transform the hearts of the Apostles, Thou Who didst endow all Thy martyrs with a miraculous heroism, come and sanctify us. Illumine our minds, strengthen our wills, purify our consciences, rectify our judgments, set our hearts on fire, and preserve us from the misfortune of resisting Thine inspirations. Amen.

TUESDAY - THE HOLY ANGELS

O glorious servants of God, surrounding the throne of the Most High, I praise you for that splendor with which God has adorned you so bountifully. To you He granted the grace to remain faithful when Lucifer and his followers rebelled. Implore for me also the grace to persevere in His holy service.

Glorious lights of heaven, resplendent hosts of the celestial court, protect the Church and lead her to victory over all her enemies.

O angelic ministers at the throne of the Most High, conquer all evil and lead the good to victory. Amen.

WEDNESDAY - SAINT JOSEPH

Great Saint Joseph, most chaste spouse of the Queen of Virgins, foster-father of the Word made flesh, I choose thee today as my special protector against the enemies of my salvation. I pledge myself to remain faithful to thee till death, and to advance thy honor as far as may be in my power. In return, O great Saint, deign to admit me into the number of thy clients, enlighten me in my doubts, strengthen me in my weakness, comfort me in my sorrows, protect me in my last hour, and help to bring me safe to heaven, there to praise with thee for ever the most holy and adorable Trinity. Amen.

THURSDAY - THE HOLY EUCHARIST

My Jesus, I believe that Thou art present in the Blessed Sacrament. I love Thee above all things and I desire Thee in my soul. Since I cannot now receive Thee sacramentally, come at least spiritually into my heart. As though Thou wert already there, I embrace Thee and unite myself wholly to Thee; permit not that I should ever be separated from Thee.

(St. Alphonsus Liguori)

FRIDAY - THE SACRED PASSION

O Jesus, Who by reason of Thy burning love for us had willed to be crucified and to shed Thy most Precious Blood for the redemption and salvation of our souls, look down upon us here gathered in remembrance of Thy most sorrowful Passion and Death, fully trusting in Thy mercy; cleanse us from sin by Thy grace, sanctify our toil, give unto us and unto all those who are dear to us our daily bread, sweeten our sufferings, bless our families, and to the nations so sorely afflicted, grant Thy peace, which is the only true peace, so that by obeying Thy commandments we may come at last to the glory of heaven. Amen.

SATURDAY - THE BLESSED VIRGIN MARY

O glorious Virgin, Mother of God, blessed among all nations, worthy of praise and the greatest of praise, intercede for me with Thy beloved Son. O honored Lady, Mother of the King of angels and archangels, assist me and deliver me from every difficulty and danger.

O blossom of the patriarchs, the virgins and the angels, hope of glory, beauty of virgins, admiration of the angels and archangels, remember me, and forsake me not, I beseech thee, at the terrible hour of my death. O star of the sea, gate of heaven, temple of God, palace of Jesus Christ, harbor of safety, flower of all nations, pearl of all sweetness, hope of the faithful; O Queen who shelters the guilty, who surpasses in radiance the virgins and the angels, thy presence gives joy to all the hosts of heaven.

Therefore, O Mother of mercy, I place in the protection of thy holy hands my going out, my coming in, my sleeping, my waking, the sight of my eyes, the touch of my hands, the speech from my lips, the hearing from my ears; so that in everything I may be pleasing to thine own beloved Son. Amen.

A UNIVERSAL PRAYER

Pope Saint Clement, the third successor of Saint Peter, intervened in the affairs of the Church at Corinth, which had been led by a few men into sedition against its rulers. The intervention was in the form of a letter, written about 96 A.D., which contains a prayer, of which the following is a part. This is the oldest non-scriptural prayer and it enables us to pray in the

words of a first century saint.

May the Artisan of the Universe preserve inviolate upon the earth the number of His elect, through His well-beloved Child, Jesus Christ.

Through Him He has called us from the darkness to light, from ignorance to knowledge of the glory of His name.

We place our trust in Thee, Principle of all creation. Thou hast opened the eyes of our hearts, that they may know Thee.

Thou Who alone art Most High in the heavens. The Holy One Who dwellest with the saints.

Thou humblest the proud in their insolence,
Thou bringest to naught the plans of nations,
    Thou does exalt the lowly and put down the mighty;
Thou enrichest and Thou dost impoverish,
    Thou takest and Thou givest life.
Sole benefactor of the spirit and God of all flesh;
    Thou scannest the depths,
Thou watchest over the works of men;
    Refuge in danger, Savior of those in despair!
Creator and Guardian of every spirit!
    Thou dost multiply the peoples of the earth,
Amongst all these, Thou hast chosen those who love Thee,
    Through Jesus Christ, Thy well-beloved Child,
Thou dost teach, sanctify, and ennoble them.
    We pray Thee, Almighty One be our refuge and our
        defender.
    Save the oppressed, take pity on the humble.
Raise those who have fallen, manifest Thyself to those in need.
    Heal the sick, bring back those who have strayed from Thy people, give food to those who are hungry.
    Give freedom to our prisoners; strengthen the weak.
Comfort the timid; and let all nations acknowledge that

Thou alone art God, that Jesus Christ is Thy Child, that we are Thy people, the lambs of Thy fold.

⤳

FOR TRAVELERS

Along the ways of peace and prosperity may the almighty and merciful Lord lead us, and may the Angel Raphael accompany us on the journey. So may we in peace, health, and joy return unto our own.

⤳

FOR A SPECIAL NEED

Saint Francis of Sales (1567-1622), preacher, reformer, author, and later bishop of Geneva, had a childlike devotion to the Blessed Virgin. Following is his prayer to her.

Say not, merciful Virgin, that you cannot help me; for your beloved Son has given you all power in heaven and on earth. Say not that you ought not to assist me, for you are the mother of all the poor children of Adam, and mine in particular. Since then, merciful Virgin, you are my mother and you are all-powerful, what excuse can you offer if you do not lend your assistance? See, my mother, see, you are obliged to grant me what I ask, and to yield to my entreaties.

⤳

OUR FATHER - STANDARD VERSION

Our Father, Who art in heaven, hallowed be Thy name; Thy Kingdom come; Thy will be done on earth as it is in heaven. Give us this day our daily bread; and forgive us our trespasses as we forgive those who trespass against us; and lead us not into temptation, but deliver us from evil. Amen.

⤳

OUR FATHER - THE ARAMAIC VERSION

The following is a translation of the Our Father from the aramaic language (ancient eastern manuscripts) by George Lamsa (Philadelphia: A.J. Holman Co.).

> Our Father, Who is throughout the Universe,
> Let Your Name be set apart.
> Come Your Kingdom,
> Let Your delight be in Earth
> As it is throughout the Universe.
>
> Give us bread for our necessities today,
> And forgive us our offenses as we have forgiven
> our offenders.
> And do not let us enter into materialism
> But set us free from error
> Because yours is the Kingdom and the Power
> And the Song from age to age sealed in
> faithfulness and truth. Amen.

GRACE BEFORE MEALS

Bless, O Father, Thy gifts to our use and us to Thy service. Amen.

> Give us grateful hearts, our Father, for all Thy bounty and all Thy mercies, and make us mindful of the needs of others.   Amen.

> We thank Thee, O Lord, for all Thy goodness and for all Thy bounty. Bless this food to our service and us to Thine. Amen.

(Universal Spiritualist)

Bless us, O Lord, and these Thy gifts which we are about to receive from Thy bounty through Christ, our Lord. Amen.

(Roman Catholic)

PRAYERS FOR HEBREW FEASTS
ROSH HASHANAH

THE SHEMA

Hearken, O Israel; the Lord is our God, the Lord is One. Blessed be His Name, whose glorious kingdom is for ever and ever. Amen.

And thou shalt love the Lord thy God with all thine heart, and with all thy soul, and with all thy might. And these words, which I command thee this day, shall be upon thine heart; and thou shalt teach them diligently unto thy children, and shalt talk of them when thou sittest in thine house, and when thou walkest by the way, and when thou liest down, and when thou riseth up. And thou shalt bind them for a sign upon thine hand, and they shall be for frontlets between thine eyes. And thou shalt write them upon the door-posts of thy house, and upon thy gates.

SUPPLICATION

Father of mercy and forgiveness, open the gates of heaven unto our prayers on this Sacred Festival (this Festival sacred to Thy Jewish children), and pardon our transgressions. Create in us a pure heart; and make us worthy to walk in the way of righteousness before Thee, loyal to Thy Torah and clinging to good deeds. Keep far from us all manner of shame, grief, and care; and send healing for all our sorrows. Remember us unto life, O King Who delightest in life; and inscribe us in the Book of Life, for Thine own sake, O Living God. Amen.

YOM KIPPUR (THE DAY OF ATONEMENT)

THE SHEMA
(as above)

Atonement Supplication

O God and God of our fathers, pardon our iniquities on this Day of Atonement; blot out our transgressions and our sins, and make them pass away from before Thine eyes. As it is said, I, even I, am He that blotteth out thy transgressions for Mine own sake, and I will not remember thy sins. And it is said, I have blotted out, as a cloud, thy transgressions, and as a mist, thy sins. Return unto Me, for I have redeemed thee. And it is said, For on this day shall atonement be made for you, to cleanse you; from all your sins shall ye be made clean before the Lord. Sanctify us by Thy commandments, and grant our portion in Thy Torah; satisfy us with Thy goodness and gladden us with Thy salvation. Blessed art Thou, O Lord, Thou King Who pardonest and forgivest our iniquities and the iniquities of Thy people, the house of Israel, who makest our transgressions to pass away year by year, King over all the Earth, Who hallowest Israel and the Day of Atonement. Amen.

Native American Prayers
AN INDIAN PRAYER

O GREAT SPIRIT, Whose voice I hear in the winds,

And Whose breath gives life to all the world, hear me!

I am small and weak. I need Your strength and wisdom.

LET ME WALK IN BEAUTY, and make my eyes ever behold the red and purple sunset.

MAKE MY HANDS respect the things You have made and my ears sharp to hear Your voice.

MAKE ME WISE so that I may understand the things you have taught my people.

LET ME LEARN the lessons you have hidden in every leaf and rock.

I SEEK STRENGTH, not to be greater than my brother, but to fight my greatest enemy--myself.

MAKE ME ALWAYS READY to come to You with clean hands and straight eyes.

SO WHEN LIFE FADES, as the fading sunset, my spirit may come to you without shame.

KIOWA 23rd PSALM

The Great Father above a Shepherd Chief is.
    I am His and with Him I want not.
He throws out to me a rope, and the name of the rope is love.

    He draws me to where the grass is green, the water is not dangerous, and I eat and lie down and I am satisfied.

Sometimes my heart is very weak and falls down, but He lifts me up again and draws me into a good road.
    His name is Wonderful.
Sometime, it may be very soon, it may be a long, long time, He will draw me into a valley.

    It is dark there, but I'll be afraid not, for it is in between those mountains that the Shepherd Chief will meet me.
And the hunger I have in my heart all through life will
    be satisfied.

Sometimes He makes the love rope into a whip, but afterwards He gives me a staff to lean upon.
    He spreads a table before me with all kinds of foods.
He puts His hand upon my head and all the tired is gone.
    My cup He fills 'til it runs over.

What I tell is true – I lie not.
    These roads that are a way ahead will stay with me through this life and after. And afterwards I will go to live in a big teepee and sit down with the Shepherd Chief forever.

             Princess Pale Moon
      American Indian Heritage Foundation

Prayers of Saints

PRAYERS BY SAINT FRANCIS OF ASSISI

Lord, make me an instrument of your peace,
Where there is hatred, let me sow love;
Where there is injury, pardon;
Where there is doubt, faith;
Where there is despair, hope;
Where there is darkness, light; and
Where there is sadness, joy.

O Divine Master, grant that I may not so much
seek to be consoled as to console,
To be understood as to understand,
To be loved as to love.
For it is in giving that we receive.
It is in pardoning that we are pardoned.
And it is in dying that we are born to eternal life.

Be praised, my Lord, through
all your creatures!
Brother Sun.....
Sister Moon....
Brother Wind.....
Sister Water ....
Be praised, my Lord,
For Sister Earth!

A PRAYER TO SAINT ANTHONY

O Blessed Saint Anthony! The grace of God has made you a powerful advocate in all necessities, and the patron for the restoration of things lost or stolen. To you I turn today with child-like love and heartfelt confidence. Oh, how many thousands have you miraculously aided in the recovery of lost goods! You were the counsellor of the erring, the comforter of the afflicted, the healer of the sick, the raiser of the dead, the deliverer of the captive, the refuge of the afflicted. To you do I hasten, O Blessed Saint Anthony. Help me in my present affliction. I recommend what I have lost to your care, in the secure hope that you will restore it to me, if it be to the greater glory of God, and to the spiritual benefit of my soul, that I may praise and thank you, in time and eternity, for your glorious intercession in my behalf. Amen.

CHILD'S PRAYER TO SAINT ANTHONY

Dear Saint Anthony, please come round.
Something is lost and cannot be found.

I AM THE LIGHT PRAYER

I AM the Light.
The Light is within me;
The Light moves throughout me;
The Light surrounds me;
The Light protects me;
I AM the Light.

Consuelo Newton

Author Dressed as Samaritan woman in Samaria, Israel.

About the Author

Angela Plum was baptized Roman Catholic and attended 12 years of parochial school. In 1950 she had a "death experience" which awakened her to the spiritual world and so began her study of the major religions. After reading the holy books of the various religions, Angela made a commitment to God to be of service. She entered the seminary of the Spiritual Science Fellowship in Montreal, Quebec and was ordained as an interfaith minister in May 1990. Then, to complete her studies, Rev. Plum entered The International College of Spiritual and Psychic Sciences. This book is her doctoral thesis.

❧❧❧